A Decent Place to Live

A Decent Place to Live

FROM COLUMBIA POINT TO HARBOR POINT

A Community History

JANE ROESSNER

CALF PASTURE PRESS • BOSTON • SECOND EDITION

With a new Foreword by Lawrence J. Vale, Ford Professor of Urban Design and Planning, Massachusetts Institute of Technology

Calf Pasture Press
Copyright 2000 by Jane Roessner and The American City Coalition

ISBN-13:
978-0998954400 (Calf Pasture Press)

ISBN-10:
0998954403

Library of Congress Cataloging in Publications Data

Roessner, Jane.
    A decent place to live : from Columbia Point to Harbor Point—a community history / Jane Roessner.
    Includes bibliographical references and index.

SECOND EDITION
Cover designed by Michael Grinley

A Decent Place to Live was originally published by Northeastern University Press in 2000.
This edition, with a new foreword, was published by Calf Pasture Press in 2017.

To my mother,
Dorothy Hector Roessner

Contents

Part 3. Columbia Point, 1978–1987

Part 4. Harbor Point, 1988–2000

Foreword

As a native Chicagoan who moved to Boston in 1985, I never witnessed Columbia Point when it was synonymous with New England's largest and most troubled public housing project. Yet I very quickly found out about its proposed alternative.

While a graduate student at the Harvard Graduate School of Design, I had won a small grant from the Graham Foundation to study public housing redevelopment in Boston and Cambridge. By coincidence, in April and May of 1986, Harvard offered a professional development course on "The Revitalization of Public Housing," jointly taught by housing consultants Jim Stockard and Gayle Epp, together with Marty Jones from the firm of Corcoran, Mullins, and Jennison.

Much of the seminar focused on more conventional efforts to rehabilitate low-rise public housing, but Marty's presentation presented the more radical possibility then underway to transform the three-quarters-vacant Columbia Point project into the mixed-income, mixed-race alternative of Harbor Point. This class proved far more pressing and engaging than anything else I had found at Harvard, and I was hooked. More than thirty years later, I am still writing about public housing transformation and the subject matter is more urgent than ever.

Studies by the National Low Income Housing Coalition (NLIHC) show that there are only 35 affordable and available rental housing units for every 100 households with extremely low incomes. This shortage creates significant dilemmas for the most economically vulnerable households, since three-quarters pay more than half of their income for housing and utilities. This excessive spending on housing means too little income is left to cover other expenses, such as healthy food, necessary medicine, and higher education—critical for all Americans if the nation is to grow and prosper.

NLIHC studies also make clear that the nationwide shortage of affordable housing hurts even those with full-time work. A renter earning the federal minimum wage of $7.25 per hour would need to work 90 hours per week to afford a one-bedroom rental home at what HUD considers a fair market rent, 112 hours per week to afford a two-bedroom place.

Unlike Social Security or food stamps, housing subsidies in the United States have never been considered entitlements so most of the lowest-income Americans receive no subsidized housing assistance. Meanwhile, the federal government annually offers tens of billions of dollars in mortgage-interest tax deductions that subsidize home ownership for countless, better-off Americans, but neglects to call these "subsidies." And, as the gap in the provision of affordable housing continues to widen, HUD has authorized the demolition of hundreds of thousands of public housing units. The overall stock is down more than 20 percent since 1994, when it peaked at 1.4 million apartments.

Much of the most recent loss of public housing can be directly linked to the federal HOPE VI program, which ran from 1993 to 2010 and invested more than $6 billion into converting hundreds of "severely distressed" public housing developments into mixed-income communities. Soon after launching HOPE VI, HUD convened a meeting of grant recipients at Harvard and took attendees, including me, on a field trip to show what was possible. The tour skipped the Boston Housing Authority's own celebrated revitalization of Commonwealth Development, which had remained 100 percent public housing, and instead headed right for Harbor Point. Clearly, HOPE VI proponents viewed this privately developed mixed-income alternative as the preferred national model.

The national influence of Harbor Point is enough in itself to warrant reading Jane Roessner's compelling account. But this book is emblematic in other important ways. Much previous writing about public housing followed a familiar "decline and fall" plot, in which high hopes get quickly dashed by the compounding failures of bad design, shoddy maintenance, poor management, inadequate funding, and ill-behaving tenants. By contrast, this is a narrative of rise, fall, and rebirth—told with enough verve and detail to make this a kind of photo-enriched collective community memoir, not just a community history.

A Decent Place to Live is part of a broader trend in public housing scholarship that has properly put resident voices back at the center, has documented the early successes of subsequently vilified places, and has revealed the social, cultural, political, and financial complexity of what it takes to return such places to being desirable living environments.

In 1995, Ellen Pader and Myrna Breitbart pioneered this kind of thinking in an article about the role of black women's leadership in the Harbor Point transformation and, fortunately, work about other places quickly followed. The collective result has been a series of community-centered articles and books that have delved into the complex dynamics of neighborhood transformation, not simply real estate development, management reform, design innovation, and social programs.

This newer scholarship on public housing has highlighted the power of residents to take action on their own behalf, to forge coalitions, and to do all they can to make sure that the more problematic portions of their community—and in the neighborhoods beyond it—are not permitted to stop progressive change. Such struggles have not always yielded wholly satisfactory outcomes, but they make clear that public housing communities, however impoverished and marginalized, can sometimes be effective advocates for their own future.

For all of Harbor Point's impact on subsequent HOPE VI housing redevelopment, it is actually an influential outlier. Because just 400 of its 1,283 apartments have been reserved for deeply subsidized households, Harbor Point rightly, or wrongly, conveyed the message that public housing could (or even should) be reconfigured as a form of mixed-income housing in which extremely low-income residents constitute a minority of the total in the new community. Harbor Point's development team initially hoped to have a middle tier of affordable housing between the two extremes of market-rate and public housing, but could not get the financing for it.

Subsequently, however, 1986 Tax Reform legislation launched the idea of Low Income Housing Tax Credits (LIHTC), and HOPE VI grantees used these to diversify their mix just as Harbor Point's proponents would have preferred. Across the country, many people started talking about one-third/one-third/one-third mixes and some cities—notably Chicago and Atlanta—directly adopted this view of income mixing. These new projects became the country's largest public housing redevelopment ventures as well as the subject of the most attention from scholars and the press.

Yet most of the 260 examples of public housing carried out under HOPE VI "revitalization" grants left public housing residents as the majority in the new communities. In other words, most of the attention has gone to the places that followed the Harbor Point "one-third' public housing" model, but most of the actual practice has not. At the same time, many HOPE VI processes proved to be highly contentious and sometimes heavily litigated. Harbor Point did not happen easily but, importantly, it did happen through a genuinely respectful partnership between developers and residents. Unfortunately that too has been hardly typical of national practice.

This combination of mix and process points to another way that Harbor Point has been unusual. This redevelopment saga commenced in earnest only after occupancy had dropped from 1,502 to 350 households, whereas many of the HOPE VI efforts that attempted to remake public housing developments as no more than one-third public housing did not start with such a diminished occupancy. In these other places—such as Techwood/Clark Howell in Atlanta and Cabrini-Green in Chicago—the process of redeveloping the housing had to exclude a large proportion of the existing community. The resulting displacement proved highly controversial. In short, all too many places adopted *parts* of the Harbor Point model—the ideas that private development companies should be involved, that resident organizations should be heavily engaged, and that public housing residents should share revitalized developments with a majority from higher income groups—but did not deal equitably with the issue of mass displacement from well-located properties.

Harbor Point is also an outlier in its own city. The Boston Housing Authority received five HOPE VI grants, but when creating new mixed income communities it reserved, on average, 70 percent of units for public housing residents—pretty much the opposite of what happened at Harbor Point. Today, Harbor Point stands as one important approach to mixed-income housing, but it is hardly the only way to go.

The Obama administration deployed a successor program to HOPE VI, Choice Neighborhoods. This new mixed-income housing initiative fixed many of its predecessor's shortcomings and ambitiously targeted far more than public housing, aiming at comprehensive neighborhood transformations of schools, services, and vacant properties. At this writing, however, prospects for further investment in public housing from HUD seem particularly dim. Under a Trump administration with little interest in expanding the affordability of housing, HUD is under siege and starving.

Harbor Point salvaged one notoriously failed project in Boston and inspired progress elsewhere, but the larger task of tackling the enormous shortfall of affordable housing supply will need a dramatic infusion of funding. Fortunately, the National Housing Trust Fund (HTF), which released its first $174 million in 2016, is designed to provide just such a dedicated revenue stream to assist communities with building, preserving, and rehabilitating rental housing to serve those with the lowest incomes.

Because the HTF is funded annually out of proceeds from the Federal National Mortgage Association (Fannie Mae) and the Federal Home Loan Mortgage Corporation (Freddie Mac), it represents an important start in shifting housing subsidies to those who need them most. In the meantime, the ongoing search for "a decent place to live" will take many forms, and the need to respond to it is more urgent than ever.

Lawrence J. Vale
Ford Professor of Urban Design and Planning
Massachusetts Institute of Technology
May 2017

Acknowledgments

This book is built on the stories of people who lived in and were associated with Columbia Point and Harbor Point. I thank all those who gave me their time, opening their doors or picking up their phones, to tell me their stories. No one person's version of Columbia Point or Harbor Point is the "right" one, or the complete one, and there are hundreds more where these came from. Put together, they begin to tell the true story of a remarkable community.

Thank you, Ruby Jaundoo, Esther Santos, Betty Quarles, Roger Taylor, Etta Johnson; Patricia McCluskey, Kevin McCluskey, Erline Shearer, Deborah Shearer, Anna McDonald, Jim Duffy, Chris Aylward, John Aylward, Father Larry Wetterholm, Dave Hanifin, April Young; Eleanor Wessell; Jack Geiger, Jan Wampler, F. Lee Bailey; Stephan Ross, Don Strong, Peggy McLeod, Nina McCain; Gary Jennison, Joe Mullins, Marty Jones, Dave Connelly, April Mercedes Hernandez, Joan Goody, Antonio DiMambro, Miles Byrne, Dan Murray, Wendell Yee; Harry Spence, Paul Garrity, Arthur Winn, Sy Mintz, Bob Kuehn, John Stainton; Ted Kennedy, Henry Cisneros, Kevin White, Michael Dukakis, Ed Logue, Bob Ryan, Ed Martin, Bob Quinn, Bob Wood; Langley Keyes, Bob Whittlesey, Dick Garver, Jim Haley, Hubie Jones, Julia O'Brien; Eleanor White, Elaine Werby, Jean McHallam, Rachel Garshick Kleit, and Rachel Bratt.

Special thanks to Marie Kennedy of the College of Public and Community Service at the University of Massachusetts, Boston, for the interviews she and her colleagues Charlotte Ryan, Jeanne Winner, Janice Gadson, and Mary Puopolo conducted in 1985–86 as part of the Columbia Point Oral History Project. Marie generously opened her files to me and shared transcripts of wonderful interviews with Marie Heath, Angie Hines, Carole Katz, Joshua Powell, Joe Slavet, Charlie Titus, and Sandy Young.

Thanks to the American City Coalition, a nonprofit organization dedicated to revitalizing distressed urban neighborhoods and spurring the growth of racially and economically integrated communities, for underwriting the research and development of this book.

Thanks to the *Boston Globe* for generously donating the use of photographs from its library for this book and thanks also to the newspaper's library staff, especially Lisa Tuite, Kathleen Hennrikus, and Wanda Joseph-Rollins, for graciously responding to our requests.

Thanks to Julie Michaels, who provided ideas and edited an early draft; Suzanne Corcoran, Sue Connelly, and Ryan Bettez, who shared their special knowledge of Harbor Point and its history; Tara Wood, researcher; Annie Atherton, photo researcher and photo editor; Paul Rudolph, photo researcher; and Elliott Wade and Christopher Mills, computer support.

Thanks above all to Otile McManus, director of the book project, for her editorial contributions and for her unfailing and invaluable support. Always insightful, encouraging, cheerful, and dedicated, she is truly the mother of this project, and I couldn't have done it without her.

Thanks to Northeastern University Press, director William Frohlich, editor John Weingartner, and production director Ann Twombly for their commitment to Boston's history.

Finally, thanks to Joe Corcoran, for giving hundreds of people a decent place to live, giving thousands more an example to believe in, and giving me free rein to write this story.

Prologue

"Are you Ruby?"

"Sometimes. Not today."

"Will you be on Monday at 10 A.M.?"

"I don't know."

"I guess I'll just have to take my chances."

Ruby Jaundoo is a cool customer. She wasn't eager to talk with the writer who was telling the story of the transformation of Boston's notorious Columbia Point housing project into Harbor Point, a model of mixed-income housing.

After years of being ignored—years of being shunned—the residents of Harbor Point, and formerly of Columbia Point, are suddenly finding themselves sought after. Academics are writing articles and dissertations, journalists are writing multi-part stories, government officials are visiting and having their pictures taken. Columbia Point has a new name and, thanks to millions of dollars, a new look; it is being held up to the rest of the country as a sorely needed solution to the nation's housing crisis.

Ruby Jaundoo has watched it all come and go—and come again. Through all of the changes—from the darkest years when fire engines and ambulances refused to enter Columbia Point without a police escort, when the only people who wanted to do business at Columbia Point were the drug dealers, to the bright, new days of polite but firm security guards at Harbor Point's entrance gate and tennis players on the carefully landscaped mall that leads to a breathtaking view of the harbor—Ruby Jaundoo has been the same person, living in the same place, wanting the same thing: a decent place to live.

This is the story of how she got it.

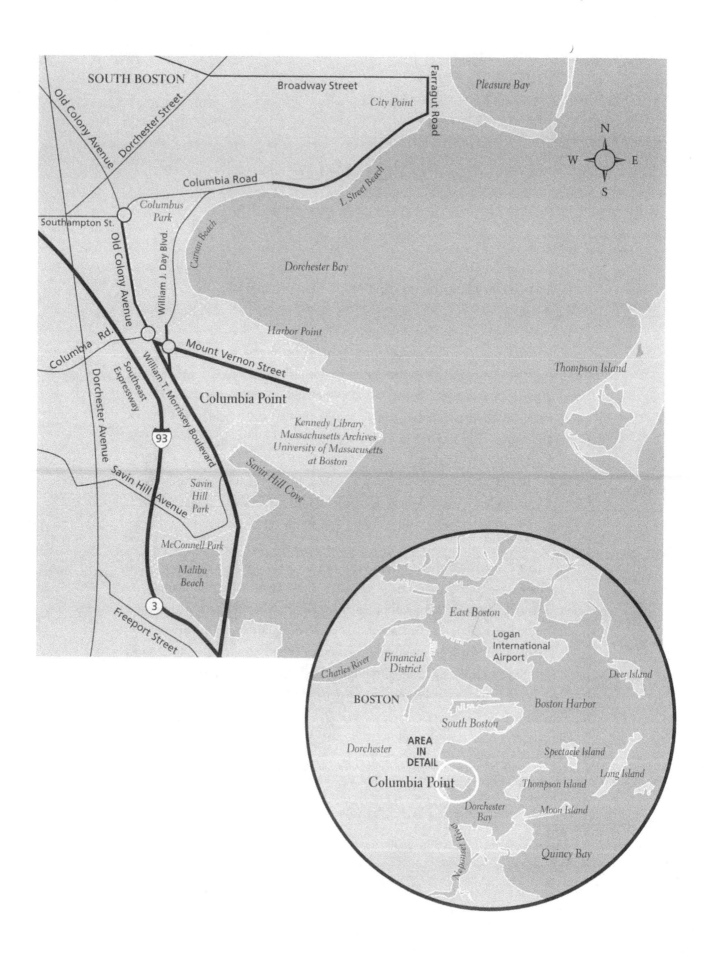

Columbia Point stood out starkly on the Boston landscape. It was not necessarily the worst of Boston's housing projects, but it was certainly the most visible. For thousands of commuters driving up and down the Southeast Expressway in the late 1970s and early 1980s, it was a haunting sight: a forbidding mass of flat-topped yellow brick buildings, their windows covered with red plywood, isolated out at the edge of the bay. From afar there were no signs of life, and most people had no reason to get any closer. Stories in the newspapers told of drug dealers, prostitution, shootings. Columbia Point was a symbol of failure—the failure of public housing, the failure of racial integration, the failure of the war on poverty—that many people would just as soon forget.

It had not always been so. Columbia Point had a very different past, and it would have a very different future.

Part 1
Columbia Point, 1951–1962

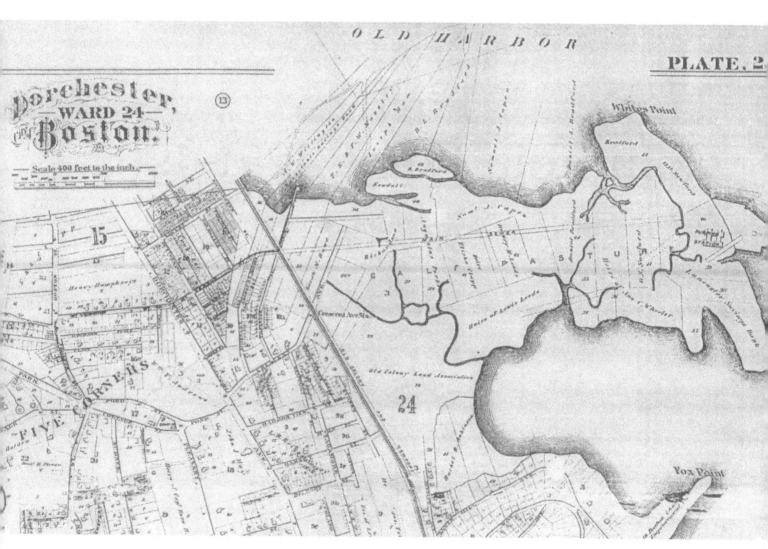

Columbia Point as it appeared in a nineteenth-century map. *Hopkins, 1882. Vista Environmental Information.*

1 Breaking Ground at the Calf Pasture

On Thursday, July 12, 1951, at 1:30 in the afternoon, the Honorable John B. Hynes, mayor of Boston, presided over a short ceremony on the deserted mud flats out on the edge of Dorchester Bay. An offshore breeze fanned the handful of politicians standing dutifully before him. A mile to the north, across from the long arc of Carson Beach, lay South Boston, the working-class Irish Catholic enclave, and beyond it, downtown Boston. A mile to the west lay the established three-decker neighborhoods of Dorchester. But here, for acres all around them, was nothing but marsh.

Mayor Hynes had come to herald the construction of a $20 million low-income public housing development, the largest in New England. After a short speech he climbed aboard a huge steam shovel, and with the push of a lever the machine took an easy bite into the soft earth of the area known as the Calf Pasture. Thus, ground was broken for the Columbia Point housing project, the future home of six thousand people.

Even though technically part of Dorchester, the Calf Pasture was really a no-man's-land. One hundred and twenty-five acres of tidal marsh on a peninsula jutting into Dorchester Bay, it had

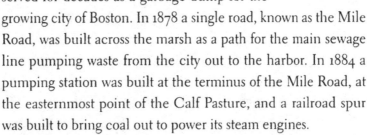

served for decades as a garbage dump for the growing city of Boston. In 1878 a single road, known as the Mile Road, was built across the marsh as a path for the main sewage line pumping waste from the city out to the harbor. In 1884 a pumping station was built at the terminus of the Mile Road, at the easternmost point of the Calf Pasture, and a railroad spur was built to bring coal out to power its steam engines.

People came from all over the world to admire Boston's sewage system, a wonder of modern engineering. Sewage from the main line coming down from Boston was pumped into huge holding tanks built out on the mud flats. Two steam pumping engines raised the sewage to a level of thirty-five feet. At the turn of the tide, the gates of the holding tanks were opened and the sewage was discharged directly into the harbor, washed out with the help of gravity and the outgoing tide.

Decades of dumping on the mud flats had brought about an unnatural expan-

Origins

Columbia Point was the landing place in Dorchester for Puritan settlers. Native Americans called the site "Mattaponnock." Between 1630 and 1869, the marshlands of the peninsula were used as a cow or "calf pasture." Its land mass originally totaled only 14 acres; however, numerous landfills from the mid-19th through the mid-20th centuries have increased the acreage to its present size.

> —U.S. Department of the Interior, National Park Service, "Calf Pasture Pumping Station, Boston, Massachusetts," *National Register of Historic Places*

Boston's Marvelous Sewage System

The sewage pumping station, built in 1884, handles today the sewage of somewhat less than half of Boston's resident population but nearly all of the transient population, since it is part of the system that drains the central areas of the City.

> —Boston City Planning Board, *Proposed Plan for Future Development of the Calf Pasture Area in the Dorchester District,* September 22, 1953

The two great steam pumping engines were designed by Erasmus D. Leavitt of Cambridgeport, Massachusetts. . . . The Leavitt Pumps were the world's largest at the time, their fly wheels each weighing 72.5 tons and measuring 50 feet in diameter.

> —U.S. Department of the Interior, National Park Service, "Calf Pasture Pumping Station, Boston, Massachusetts," *National Register of Historic Places*

Leavitt pumping engine steam turbine. *Boston Water and Sewer Commission.*

Calf Pasture pumping
station, built in 1884.
*Boston Water and Sewer
Commission.*

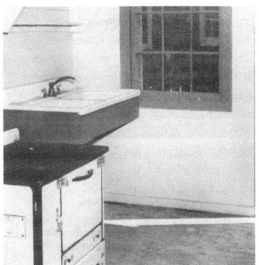

Left: Columbia Village
veterans' housing project,
281 units (the former
Camp McKay army
barracks), 1946. *Courtesy
of the* Boston Globe.

Above: A kitchen, with oil-
burning stove, at Colum-
bia Village housing
project, 1946. *Courtesy of
the* Boston Globe.

sion of the land mass of the peninsula. Over the years, the accumulating garbage had raised the surface level as much as thirty feet.
Three hundred and fifty acres that had once been harbor were now
land. The dump was home to a huge, thriving, and firmly entrenched rat population.

At the time of the groundbreaking for the housing project, the
only other human habitation on the peninsula was a former U.S.
Army barracks called Camp McKay. A complex of one-story
wooden barracks built in 1942 on the north side of the peninsula,
Camp McKay was used to house Italian prisoners of war during
World War II. In 1946, when the prisoners of war moved out, public
housing tenants moved in, and Camp McKay became known as the
Columbia Village housing project.

Squatters' shacks occasionally appeared and then disappeared on
the peninsula. The shacks were the temporary homes of hoboes,

Back to the Future: Public Housing Problems at the Calf Pasture

The first problems with public housing on the peninsula were reported months before ground was broken for Columbia Point. On February 1, 1951, the *Boston Globe* reported trouble at the Columbia Village housing project, converted from a prisoner of war camp to "temporary" public housing some five years earlier. The caption beneath a photo of three ruddy-cheeked children with a blanket pulled up to their chins reads: "Lack of heat in the Columbia Village project forced many children to stay in bed the whole day yesterday. Here Lester Kramer, 4, and his sister, Linda, and 3-months-old Nancy huddle to get warm. The residents of the project are up in arms about the situation."

The article, entitled "Columbia Tenants Protest," reports that the project was completely without heat on one of the coldest days of the year:

> Complaints from residents flooded the offices of the Boston Housing Authority, who have maintained the converted barracks as a temporary housing project for the past five years.
>
> Albert Kramer, army veteran and postal employee of 43 Strandview, who has three children, the youngest of whom is but three months old, said that the whole village is called a "pest-hole" by its residents and that there was no heat in his house during a 20-hour stretch from Tuesday night.
>
> "The houses all shake when you walk around them," said Kramer. "We have been furnished storm doors, but the joker to that deal is that there is no glass in them, just a wooden frame," he said.

known locally as "bayzos" because of their penchant for drinking bay rum. Over the years, a few scattered heavy industries also found a home there—the Boston Consolidated Gas Company, the American Radiator Company, a warehouse for the Firestone Company—in the words of the City Planning Board, "industrial uses of the more offensive type."

For kids growing up in Dorchester and Southie in the 1930s and 1940s, the peninsula was a place of adventure and mystery. Robert H. Quinn, the former Massachusetts attorney general who during the late 1950s and early 1960s was the state representative for the district that included Columbia Point, remembers roaming the peninsula as a boy. On cold winter nights large pockets of water at the dump would freeze, and overnight the place would be transformed into the perfect skating pond. If it was lucky enough to be a Saturday, Quinn and his buddies would head out to the dump and have the place to themselves, alone with their fantasies of playing hockey in a rink or even in Boston Garden—with acres and acres of garbage all around and beneath them.

Sometimes the kids would forage through the dump, looking for potatoes dumped by the potato chip factory in nearby Uphams Corner. They'd light a fire, put the potatoes on a stick, and play hoboes. One of them kept a lookout for the custodian who guarded the dump. He never bothered them, as long as they didn't bother him. The Mile Road dump before 1951 was a desolate place, but through the eyes of a kid from Dorchester, it was fertile ground for the imagination.

Camp McKay was a particular source of fascination, fear, and excitement to the kids from Dorchester and Southie. On weekends they would go over and peer through the high wire fence surrounding the barracks, trying to get a closer look at the enemy. Girls from the North End and East Boston would go out to Camp McKay, too—looking for Italian cousins or boyfriends, pushing food through the wire fence to the prisoners. In fact, many of the prisoners ended up staying in the United States after they were released—finding jobs, marrying American girls, starting families.

In 1950 an unusual and respectable neighbor moved out to the peninsula. Boston College High School, a private high school run by the Jesuits, relocated there from its campus in Boston's South End. The high school's administrators, having concluded that the school was outgrowing its increasingly seedy downtown location, chose the mud flats of the Calf Pasture because of its price—some seventy acres at six cents a square foot—and easy access to public

This photograph (circa
1908) shows children
foraging at Columbia
Point. It was taken by
Lewis Hine, in his famous
series of photographs
documenting children's
working conditions.
Library of Congress.

transportation for students from the middle-
and lower-middle-class towns located on the
transit lines. Dorchester residents preferred
the Jesuits to various potential buyers who
had shown interest in other uses for the
property, including a midget automobile
race track, a marina, and a drive-in movie
theater. One of the owners of record of one
of the Calf Pasture parcels was Mary E. Day,
the mother of Louise Day Hicks, the South
Boston politician who would be a major figure in the inflammatory battles over court-
ordered busing that would rip apart Southie
and Columbia Point in the 1970s.

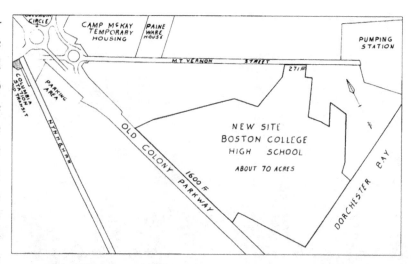

If the land the Jesuits purchased was inexpensive, building on it was not. Construct-
ing buildings on land that consisted of a
dump and marshy tidal flats was a challenge
faced by B.C. High that would come back to
haunt the construction of Columbia Point.
The landfill that had accumulated over
decades wasn't well compacted and was full
of junked automobiles and empty steel
drums. The solution developed for B.C.

High was to sink more than one hundred caissons—hollow steel
barrels filled with concrete—some twenty-five feet, pour a ten-foot-
deep mat of concrete over the caissons, and build on the mat. It was
an expensive proposition.

The Boston Housing Authority had had its eye on Columbia
Point since 1946, when it had proposed to create additional land,
more than three hundred acres, on the peninsula by filling the bay
from Carson Beach to the end of the Mile Road, and from there to
a point near Patton's Cove at the Old Colony Yacht Club. That proposal failed, but in 1951, the year after the construction of B.C. High
was completed, the housing authority successfully petitioned to
have the zoning on part of the peninsula changed from "unre-
stricted" to "residential," clearing the way for the construction of
housing there. The housing authority, in the midst of a major building campaign to meet the need for low-cost housing in the aftermath of World War II, had big plans for the barren stretch of land:
not just the fifteen-hundred-unit public housing project, but also a

Above: Site plan of the
new Boston College High
School, 1949. Old Colony
Parkway was later renamed
Morrissey Boulevard.
Courtesy of the Boston
Globe.

Below: Architect's drawing
of the new Boston College
High School, 1949.
Courtesy of the Boston
Globe.

separate state-funded veterans' housing development of six hundred units on a sixteen-acre site on the other side of the Mile Road. Although the veterans' housing was not built, the Calf Pasture, never before deemed fit for human habitation, was entering a new phase.

After his groundbreaking performance on the steam shovel, the mayor climbed down, and the politicians got in their cars to drive back downtown, kicking up dirt on the Mile Road. The unlikely site they left behind—with not a store in sight, no supermarket, no school, no church, no trees, no houses for three miles in any direction—would soon become the largest housing project in New England.

Photograph of Mayor John B. Hynes from the *Report of the Activities and Accomplishments of the Boston Housing Authority* (January 1, 1950, to December 31, 1952), BHA Annual Reports (CD6, 1440x). *Courtesy of the Massachusetts Archives.*

Photograph of the Boston Housing Authority Board (left to right: Owen A. Gallagher, Cornelius T. Kiley, James J. Mahar, Joseph J. Benkert, John Carroll) as it appeared in the *Report of the Activities and Accomplishments of the Boston Housing Authority* (January 1, 1950, to December 31, 1952), BHA Annual Reports (CD6, 1440x). *Courtesy of the Massachusetts Archives.*

Christa McAuliffe on the Columbia Point Peninsula

The most notable resident of the Columbia Village housing project, located on the site of a former U.S. Army barracks called Camp McKay, was Christa McAuliffe. The schoolteacher, who was to be the first civilian in space before the 1986 *Challenger* disaster, moved there in 1949 as a one-year-old child with her parents, Grace and Ed Corrigan. After World War II her father enrolled at Boston College. But housing in Boston was tight. In her 1993 memoir, *A Journal for Christa*, McAuliffe's mother writes about the difficulties of finding an apartment:

> [A friend] had a friend working in Mayor Curley's home. She suggested that it might help if I could tell the mayor our story and have Christa with me when I did. It was worth a try.
>
> Early one morning, [the friend] drove us to the mayor's red brick Georgian house on the Jamaicaway. His friend let us in and had us wait in the hall at the foot of the stairs. When Mayor Curley came down for his breakfast, there we were. I explained the problem. He patted Christa on the head and told me to leave my name and address. . . .
>
> Well, something worked. About a week later, a telegram was sent to Ed. . . . "This Authority is happy to advise that you appear eligible for occupancy of its veterans' housing development [Columbia Village, formerly Camp McKay]. Please be at the management office, 220 Mount Vernon Street near Columbia Station, Dorchester . . . prepared to make the deposit of $5.00. . . ."
>
> We found the manager's office and showed him the telegram. He took us over to apartment 24 at 47 Strandview Road and opened the door. We entered into a decent-sized room. Off to the back was a large kitchen with an icebox and a big black oil stove. The floor slanted, so later we discovered that the water from the pan under the icebox would run down the floor and out the back door if one forgot to empty it. There was a small bedroom and a bathroom, including a shower stall. We were thrilled. . . . The manager was amazed. "Gee," he said, "usually they look at these places and say, 'What a dump.'" We signed on the dotted line.

2 The Promise of Public Housing

The groundbreaking ceremony for the Columbia Point housing project—the tableau at the Calf Pasture on a hot day in 1951—took place against the complex backdrop of national and local housing policy that prevailed in post–World War II America. In fact, only against that backdrop does the incongruity of building a large public housing project on a dump in the middle of nowhere begin to make sense.

By the time ground was broken for Columbia Point, public housing in the United States had evolved considerably from its original purpose. The federal public housing program was created in 1933 by the Public Works Administration (PWA), the federal agency charged with creating jobs to pull America out of the Great Depression. Surprisingly, the primary objective of the public housing program was not to provide housing for the poor; rather, in keeping with the mission of the PWA, it was to create jobs. At the time, America was still mired in the depression, with some 15 million people out of work. The government estimated that one-third of these unemployed had skills in the building trades. The PWA, frustrated in its efforts to motivate private developers to generate jobs, created a separate housing division as a way of putting people with building skills to work.

The mission of this new division of the PWA, in addition to creating jobs, was to clear slums. Providing public housing was secondary to the objective of eliminating areas that were believed to breed a host of ills, both biological and social. A careful reading of the 1937 United States Housing Act, the establishing legislation of the federal public housing program, makes the program's priorities clear: "An Act to provide financial assistance to the States and political subdivisions thereof for the elimination of unsafe and unsanitary housing conditions, for the eradication of slums, for the provision of decent, safe, and sanitary dwellings for families of low income, and for the reduction of unemployment and the stimulation of business activity."

Certainly, the hard-core poor were never the target market for public housing.

Posters created to promote public housing after the Housing Act of 1937 was passed. *Corbis.*

PWA staff deliberately selected as public housing residents not the unemployed but working people, families with modest incomes. Public housing was meant to provide interim shelter for those temporarily down on their luck, a helping hand until they could get back on their feet financially. Housing authorities screened applicants carefully, often visiting families to make sure they were qualified candidates who took pride in keeping a good home.

The federal government stipulated that to be eligible for public housing, a tenant had to demonstrate income at least 20 percent below the income needed to afford the cheapest available private rental housing. Tenant families could be forced to move out if their income rose above a certain limit. At the same time, in order to be selected, families could not be destitute; they had to demonstrate their ability to pay the minimum rent needed to cover operating expenses.

In 1937 the United States Housing Act defined the housing program as a cooperative effort between the federal and local levels. The act created a network of local housing authorities that, unlike the fed-

eral government, had the right of eminent domain—that is, the
power to purchase and clear property. The federal government,
through the U.S. Housing Authority, would provide local authorities
with the capital funds to build public housing by making low-cost,
sixty-year loans. For their part, the local authorities were expected to
raise enough revenue through rent to maintain the property. If the
local authorities couldn't make ends meet, the federal government
would help municipalities repay their sixty-year mortgages and would
make annual grants to local authorities to make up the difference between each year's actual rental income and operating costs.

From the very beginning, opinion on public housing was sharply
divided. Those in favor of a public housing program considered decent housing to be a basic right of the American people and felt that
the government should be responsible for providing it. In 1937 the
U.S. Senate Committee on Education and Labor clearly articulated
this position: "There is no immediate aim of the American people
. . . more widely supported and more insistently voiced than the de-
sire to attack the social evils of the slums and to provide decent living quarters for . . . the underprivileged." Those opposed to public
housing felt that, although poor housing conditions were indeed a
pressing problem, it was not the government's responsibility to remedy that problem. That position was forcefully argued in a suit
brought—and ultimately lost—against the Boston Housing Authority for taking a South Boston property by eminent domain:

> No doubt bad housing conditions are an evil, and so is an insufficiency
> of food and clothing. All result from the ever present curse of poverty.
> But it does not follow that it is the function of government to attempt
> to remedy these evils by the expenditure of public money raised from
> the people by taxation and by the taking of private property. The doc-
> trine is a dangerous one that everyone is entitled to be well fed, well
> clothed and well housed, and if one by reason of misfortune, incompe-
> tence or sloth cannot achieve that end by his own efforts the public
> will pay the bill. No permanent improvement to mankind can result
> from the attempt by government to remove the necessity of the strug-
> gle for existence. (Excerpt from legal brief in *Stockus v Boston Housing
> Authority*, 1939)

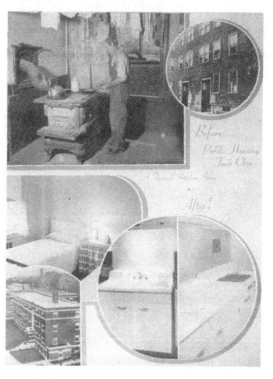

Before and after "public
housing took over," 1951.
Boston Housing Authority.

Although the language in which it is expressed has changed in sixty
years, the basic underlying argument has remained remarkably consistent. At the heart of the matter are two linked questions: Who is
responsible for the "evils" of "the ever present curse of poverty"?
And who is responsible for remedying those evils?

The argument against public housing assumes that "the struggle for existence" is not only necessary but even salutary—classic social Darwinism. We all struggle, the argument suggests, and if some are more successful in the struggle than others, that's only natural. The social world, like the natural world, is and indeed should be governed by the principle of survival of the fittest. The implication, of course, is that if the poor were not "incompetent" or "slothful," they wouldn't be poor. Those of us who are not poor are so because we are more fortunate, more competent, and more industrious. Having made and paid our own way, why should we pay for anyone else?

Opponents of public housing saw it as the slippery slope to socialism. Instead of establishing a federal housing program funded by taxpayers, they argued, the government should provide subsidies to banks and builders to stimulate home building and keep the prices of homes down, or subsidize individuals directly to help them buy their own houses in the private market. Private builders, anxious to ensure that they would have no competition from public housing, argued that publicly funded projects should be demonstrably inferior to private housing.

For example, because approximately one-third of the housing units in the country in the late 1930s had no indoor plumbing, many argued that public housing units certainly shouldn't have indoor plumbing. Public housing was to be low-cost construction; hence, limits were imposed on spending per room or per unit. Gradually, notions of "social engineering" crept into the design of public housing. Closets were built without doors, to encourage neatness; and master bedrooms were intentionally small, so parents wouldn't share their bedroom with small children.

In 1949 the Taft-Ellender-Wagner Act signaled a new direction for public housing. Just as the 1937 housing act reflected the needs of depression-era America, the 1949 housing act reflected the agenda of postwar America. In the aftermath of World War II, the economy was shifting from war to peace, and thousands of returning veterans were ready for jobs, homes, and families. The focus of the bill was to encourage and subsidize "urban renewal" through private development. By that time some private real estate interests were lobbying for a more direct role in federally funded redevelopment. Title I of the housing act of 1949 responded by stipulating that builders and developers undertaking redevelopment of any area in which 20 percent of the housing could be classified as "blighted" would be reimbursed by the federal government for two-thirds of the cost of the entire project. The act ushered in an era of big downtown redevel-

---

"Are You Eligible? Look Inside—"

New Public Housing Apartments
Locally Built • Locally Owned • Locally Operated
Are You Eligible? Look Inside—
How will a family qualify?
To qualify a family must—

a. Be 2 or more *related* persons living together.
b. Be that of a citizen except in case of a family of a veteran or serviceman.
c. Be a resident of the City of Boston.
d. Be living under unsafe, unsanitary, overcrowded or other substandard conditions.
e. Be low-income, with yearly income not more than the following amounts for most families. (Amounts may vary slightly with the number of adults and children. If your income is several hundred dollars more do not hesitate to apply because future changes may make you eligible.)

2 Persons	$2600	6 Persons	$3500
3 Persons	$2900	7 Persons	$3800
4 Persons	$3000	8 Persons	$3900
5 Persons	$3400	9 Persons	$4000
	10 Persons	$4100	

Expenses in connection with employment such as pension or Social Security payments, union dues, etc., are deductible in determining the income of your family for admission; as are veterans' disability or death payments received from the U.S. Government.

What about rents?
Rents are based on ability to pay, vary with the number of minors, and have no relation to apartment size. Since rents are subsidized, they are low. For example, a family of four, with two minors and an income of $40 a week would pay about $34 a month; the same size family with $50 a week income would pay about $43.

—Boston Housing Authority flyer

The Tower in the Park

In 1932 the Museum of Modern Art in New York City launched an exhibit entitled "Modern Architecture: International Exhibition," featuring the work of modern architects including Le Corbusier, Mies van der Rohe, and Frank Lloyd Wright.

High-rise towers had a certain appeal for the designers of public housing because they could help achieve their goal of improving the lives of "slum dwellers." Built of concrete, they provided protection from fire. With plenty of cross ventilation, they also provided protection from tuberculosis.

The strange marriage of modern architecture's utterly unadorned towers and public housing's need for low-cost, high-density housing produced a generation of monolithic, high-rise housing complexes across the country. Over the next five decades, these would-be "towers in the park" would become notorious as "vertical slums."

opment, with the familiar mixture of luxury apartments, convention centers, sports arenas, and office buildings that now defines the downtowns of large cities across America.

Federal housing policy played out on the local stage in characteristically Bostonian fashion. Boston was a city of old neighborhoods and faded tenements. James Michael Curley, mayor of Boston for a total of four terms between 1914 and 1947, was a great supporter of public housing, partly because it served the patronage machine so well, with its steady stream of contracts for jobs and services. In the Curley era the Boston Housing Authority was, by all accounts, a case study in political patronage. Monsignor Thomas R. Reynolds, who served as a member of the BHA board from 1935 to 1946, reportedly examined the list of applicants selected for public housing and approved or disapproved each assignment. In fact, tenant selection and assignment—not only who would be accepted for public housing, but also to which particular housing project they would be assigned—was one of the primary functions of the BHA board members. What public housing tenants long suspected—that you had to have someone moving your application for you; that you had to know someone if you wanted to get into one of the "good" projects like South Boston's Old Colony—was in fact how things worked.

To meet the surge in demand for low-cost housing after World War II, the Boston Housing Authority, under the direction of Mayor John Hynes, built several projects in rapid succession: Fidelis Way in Brighton in 1950; Cathedral in the South End in 1951; an extension of the Mission Hill project in 1952; and in 1954 Bromley Heath in Jamaica Plain, Franklin Field in Dorchester, and finally Columbia Point. After the completion of Columbia Point, Mayor Hynes shifted his attention and energy from building public housing to developing downtown Boston.

Eager to use the 1949 housing act as a tool to bring about urban renewal, Mayor Hynes, followed by John Collins (1960–68) and Kevin White (1968–82), all strong proponents of "the new Boston," oversaw the construction of large projects that changed the face of the city. For example, the West End, a densely populated, ethnically diverse downtown neighborhood, was razed to make way for the homogenized, high-rent Charles River Park. Neighboring Scollay Square was cleared to make way for Government Center. In fact, much of the refuse hauled to the dump right next to Columbia

"Tower in the park" design at Le Corbusier's La Cité Radieuse, Marseille. *Art Resource.*

Point in the late 1950s was trucked directly from the West End demolition—the refuse of "urban renewal" dumped right next to Boston's last public housing project.

With the new emphasis on downtown renewal beginning in 1949, public housing was no longer built in neighborhoods where slum clearance had taken place. The city and private developers could reap far more profit building office buildings or luxury apartments on these sites. Instead, public development was largely limited to vacant sites that private developers would not be interested in. Given this context, the choice of the Calf Pasture made perfect sense as the site of Boston's last—and New England's biggest—public housing project. The city was looking for land that was cheap and preferably vacant. In both respects, the Calf Pasture fit the bill perfectly.

If the shift in public housing policy in 1949 helps explain the choice of the Calf Pasture as the site of Columbia Point, the concomitant

"Tower in the park" design
at Chicago's Cabrini-
Green housing project.
UPI/Corbis-Bettmann.

shift in the architecture of public housing helps explain the design of the project. Why design a cluster of twenty-seven monolithic brick buildings, fifteen of them seven stories high, massed together at the edge of Dorchester Bay? In the early 1950s the trend in public housing architecture in U.S. cities was toward large projects that housed tenants in imposing blocks of buildings. One reason was high land values; another, believe it or not, was aesthetics. As Elizabeth Wood, head of the Chicago Housing Authority, explained in 1945, public housing "must be bold and comprehensive—or it is useless and wasted. If it is not bold, the result will be a series of small projects, islands in a wilderness of slums."

The embodiment of such "bold" design was the high-rise tower—the hallmark of public housing architecture of the 1950s. It is difficult to understand why high-rise elevator buildings massed together were ever anyone's idea of successful housing, especially with nearly fifty years' hindsight of the colossal failure of such high-rise structures. The answer is straightforward: housing authorities across the country saw high-rise buildings as the essence of economic efficiency, a way to house the greatest number of people on the smallest amount of land at the lowest cost.

Modern architecture had been extolling the virtues of high-rise, unadorned towers since the 1930s. The French architect Le Corbusier called them "towers in the park." No matter that his were luxury towers; public housing borrowed the concept, and in the 1950s low-cost "towers in the park," albeit many without the "park," began to spring up across the country. Their names—the *Titanics* of public housing—might have been proud at one time, but now only evoke colossal failure: St. Louis's Pruitt-Igoe, Chicago's Cabrini-Green, Detroit's Renaissance Park, and Boston's Columbia Point.

3 Ignoring the Warnings

T he site and the design of the Columbia Point housing project may have been politically and financially expedient in the short term. In the long term, however, both would prove to be a protracted political and financial — not to mention human — nightmare.

None of the problems that would plague and in the end destroy Columbia Point were surprises. In 1950 the Boston Housing Authority hired the firm of Glaser and Gray, architects and city planners with offices in Boston and Washington, D.C., to study and evaluate the feasibility of building public housing on

the Calf Pasture site. The firm's two reports cautioned strongly that "the development is not a housing project but a neighborhood." Therefore, the report argues, the BHA's plans for building public housing at the Calf Pasture must take place within a larger context of coordinated city, state, and federal efforts to create a complete neighborhood there. "The many groups and agencies who will have a hand in the neighborhood should be approached first of all," the Glaser and Gray report advises.

The community would require "further public areas for grade schools, playgrounds, parks, and community facilities of approximately 45 acres, and a commercial development of not less than 20 acres."

The Boston Housing Authority ignored the loud and clear warning of the Glaser and Gray report. Passing over the firm altogether, the Housing Authority chose as architects the M. A. Dyer Company, a local firm that was a longtime favorite of the agency. Dyer's plan was to build housing only, functional and unimaginative: a $20 million project, housing 1,504 families in 15 seven-story buildings and 12 three-story buildings.

Three years later, two years into construction of the housing project, the city planning board conducted its own assessment of the suitability of the Calf Pasture site for public housing. The planning board's report to the Boston City Council on "the future development of the Calf Pasture area" came to conclusions that were very much in line with those of Glaser and Gray. The planning board report clearly spelled out the problems that were

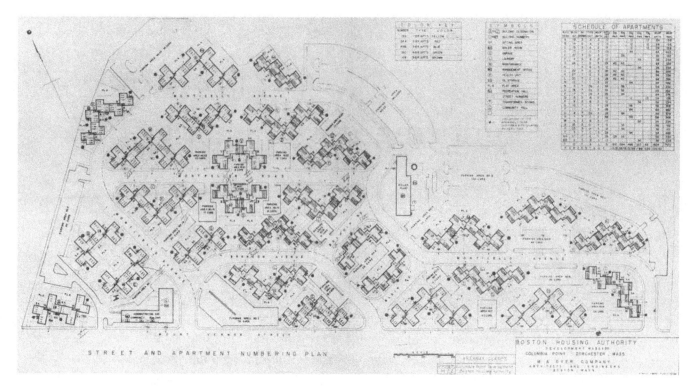

STREET AND APARTMENT NUMBERING PLAN

Site plan for Columbia
Point, M. A. Dyer
Company. *Boston Housing
Authority.*

inherent in the project from the start and issued a clear warning to
the city of the consequences of not providing for the needs of the
new community:

> Within the next few years, 9,000 people, more or less, will take up resi-
> dence at Calf Pasture under public auspices. Boston has a serious re-
> sponsibility toward these people to assure that they will have not only
> "decent, safe, and sanitary" dwellings, but a decent, safe, and sanitary
> environment as well, as far as possible. It must be remembered that
> these people will reside on a peninsula with water on three sides and a
> heavily traveled arterial highway on the fourth. Moreover, their isola-
> tion will be further accentuated by the fact that for a considerable dis-
> tance the opposite side of that highway is unpopulated. Thus, many of
> the facilities and amenities essential to good community living must be
> provided within Calf Pasture itself, or not at all.

The planning board's conclusion was as prescient as it is obvious.
You can't just build the buildings, move thousands of people in, and
expect to have a viable community. If the city was going to build a
housing project from scratch, on a completely isolated site, the planning board argued, it must provide the basic infrastructure that any
community needs—schools, shops, recreational facilities, transportation. Moreover, it must eliminate what any community would
find harmful—in particular, a rat-breeding, soot-belching dump.

Columbia Point under
construction, in a series of
1953 photographs. *Boston
Housing Authority*.

Aerial view of the
Columbia Point housing
project (looking south,
Dorchester Bay at left,
Mount Vernon Street, also
known as the Mile Road,
at right, terminating at the
pumping station), 1957.
Courtesy of the Boston
Globe.

Columbia Point's
administration building
(Mile Road in foreground,
with railroad tracks leading
to pumping station), 1954.
Boston Herald.

In 1953 two dumps were in full operation at the Calf Pasture: the
Coleman or Mile Road Dump, sixty-two acres of landfill operated
by Dooley Brothers, Incorporated, on the south side of the Mile
Road, and a thirty-five-acre dump on the north side operated by the
city of Boston, where ash was dumped from the city incinerator. The
city planning board's report zeroed in on the hazard posed to the
coming community by these dumps, "half land, half water—a vacant tract currently leased to the City of Boston and used by a disposal contractor for dumping of truck-borne waste matters, mostly
commercial waste from Boston's hotels, restaurants, and market district. Even though reduction of this waste is a fairly constant process
through open incineration at the site, the area is unsightly and obviously a breeding ground for vermin and a generator of obnoxious
odors." The planning board's recommendation was clear: Close the
dumps, now. The board pressed its case with considerable urgency:
"Rubbish disposal in its present form *must* be discontinued *immediately* and the present dump area must be cleaned up *before* the new
housing is occupied. And if dumping *must* continue, adequate fencing of the area, a new route for trucks, and the sanitary land-fill
method of disposal must be adopted."

The warnings were straightforward. In order to have a viable community in an isolated location, the city must plan and build not just

a housing project, but a neighborhood. Yet the BHA proceeded to do exactly what it had been warned not to do. Construction of the twenty-seven buildings proceeded with no reconsideration, and by January 27, 1954, the *Boston Globe* was optimistically anticipating the opening of Columbia Point:

> Nine three-story buildings in the largest single housing development in New England—the one at Columbia Point, Dorchester—have been completed and formally accepted by the Boston Housing Authority, and ready for occupancy by spring. . . .
> He [Owen Gallagher, chairman of the BHA] revealed that when the low-rent project on the sea-breeze swept peninsula is completed and ready for occupancy, Mount Vernon Street will be an 80-foot wide, double-barreled roadway, with safety traffic devices and cross-walks.

The journalist's description of the "sea-breeze swept peninsula" nicely recasts the site's isolation into an image of romance. But the "double-barreled roadway" sounds ominous—not the kind of street anyone would want running through an area filled with children, even "with safety traffic devices."

On April 29, 1954, Mayor Hynes again presided over a ceremony at the Calf Pasture, this time the grand opening of "New England's largest housing project," attended by a large audience, including the members of the state legislature, the City Council, and local civic organizations. According to the *Boston Globe*'s account, local officials waxed eloquent at the dedication ceremony. Archbishop Richard J. Cushing declared, "Those of us who were born and played near here never foresaw the day that buildings of this type would ever occupy the area. No other area in the country can compare with the housing project of our city." Mayor Hynes announced proudly, "This project represents one of our last housing projects in the city. We have met the housing shortage and will now pause to digest our accomplishments."

Despite the mayor's self-congratulatory tone, the city had left crucial work undone. The warnings of the consultants and the planning board had fallen on deaf ears. The city had built not a neighborhood but a housing project. While the mayor was pausing to digest the city's accomplishments, both dumps were still in operation twenty-four hours a day, right next door to Columbia Point. There was no public transportation, no school, no grocery store, no church.

Rezoning the Calf Pasture

The rezoning of the Calf Pasture was debated before the Boston City Council in June and July 1951; it was the subject of some disagreement between the two city councillors in the two districts that abutted the proposed public housing project. Councillor John J. McColgan, representing Ward 7 and South Boston, believed that the entire peninsula should be taken by eminent domain and zoned residential to protect the housing from industrial encroachment. Councillor Thomas Hannon, representing Ward 13 and the Savin Hill section of Dorchester, favored taking additional land on the peninsula piece by piece and instituting spot zoning that would allow existing businesses, including the Coleman dump, to continue operating.

At a City Council meeting on June 4, 1951, McColgan chastised those who opposed eminent domain and residential zoning for the entire Columbia Point peninsula:

> We had a group of individuals who were selfish-minded. We had the Boston Consolidated Gas Company. We had the Tomasello Company. We had Mary E. Day and Samuel Kramer and Francis Doyle, Salada Tea Company and many others, including Coleman Disposal Company and Ellis Coleman.
>
> It seems the Coleman Disposal Company had some kind of secret agreement between themselves and the Boston Housing Authority, they wouldn't tell what it was, but, in fact, admitted later that the business zone would not suffice, they had to have an industrial zone. Later on they admitted they had to have railroad tracks in there.
>
> What kind of housing project will we have? We will have . . . land on one side with 1,500 houses, and on the other side we will have 600 more, but down in the middle . . . we will have a railroad going through. . . .
>
> I never saw such a selfish group in my life. They were all trying to get their slice. Either the Boston Housing Authority is very stupid or somebody is making money on it, and looking over the members of the Housing Authority, I don't see any stupid members.

—Meeting minutes, City of Boston Archives and Record Center

Above: Columbia Point's boiler room, touted as "the largest low-pressure boiler layout in the East," 1954. Boston Herald.

Below: Tot lot at Columbia Point, 1954. Boston Herald.

At the opening ceremony, the mayor went on to announce that a major shopping center, chapel, school, playgrounds, and a beach would be constructed in or near the project to make it "the most self-sufficient section of the city." No such plans materialized. As it turns out, Mayor Hynes's public proclamations about Columbia Point were at odds with his private confessions. As James W. Haley, Boston's commissioner of public works from 1960 to 1965, confides, the mayor was well aware that selling the project as "self-sufficient" was just a euphemism for its isolation:

On the 17th of March I sat next to Mayor Hynes at the annual St. Patrick's Day lunch—this was just a couple of years after the project opened. In chatting, he made a very humble, Harry Truman–type con-

SUMMARY OF WALL LEAKS AT COLUMBIA POINT, MASS-2-20

Apartments With Leaks	516
Apartments Without Leaks	855
Tenants Not At Home	109
Vacant Apartments	24
Total	1504

APARTMENTS SHOWING LEAKS IN FOLLOWING NUMBER OF ROOMS

1 Room	2 Rooms	3 Rooms	4 Rooms	5 Rooms	6 Rooms	7 Rooms
197	147	98	47	19	5	3

TOTAL LEAKS BY ROOM TYPE

Living Rooms	Bedrooms	Kitchens	Bath Rooms	Total Rooms With Leaks
253	556	239	71	1119

In addition to the above, tenants at the following addresses report that water comes down from top stairhall on days when the rain is heavy. Apparently this water is coming in under the roof flashing and comes inside down tile wall at top floor landing.

2 Brandon Avenue   76 Monticello Avenue
6 Brandon Avenue   80 Monticello Avenue
19 Brandon Avenue   84 Monticello
                       15 Montpelier Road

It is further reported that rain is apparent coming in under glass block at the following addresses:

23 Montpelier Road - 6th floor
23 Montpelier Road - 4th floor
115 Monticello Ave. - 6th floor

Window Drip Sills are missing at the following addresses:

Apt. 1075 - 33 Montpelier Road
Apt. 705   - 10 Blair Road

Jeremiah F. Sullivan
Supervisor of Management

Leaking roofs and walls were a problem at Columbia Point from the start, according to a 1954 report of the project's supervisor to the Boston Housing Authority. *Courtesy of the Massachusetts Archives.*

Index of Board Meetings, Boston Housing Authority, 1953–56

Entries in the "Index of BHA Board Meetings" offer interesting clues about issues arising at Columbia Point in the early years, ranging from faulty foundations and leaking roofs to inadequate transportation and the various hazards of the dumps, including rats, fly ash, and methane gas accumulating in the basements of buildings.

Discussion alleged errors in foundation walls. Existing foundations not accepted. 2/4/53

Sample face brick, Alliance Clay Products Co. 3/4/53

Discussion removal of fly ash. 3/4/53

Discussion on problems of gas generation, vermine [sic], etc. 3/26/53

PHA [Public Housing Authority] disapproves installation of showers. 7/22/53

Lengthy discussion on foundation correction problems. 6/24/53

1504 electric refrigerators, $103.40 each. 10/21/53

Matter of roof leaks referred to General Counsel for conference with Architect as to his decision under terms of his contract. Also matter of leaks in exterior walls. 3/12/56

Meeting on gas conditions in basements. 12/20/54

Authority to cooperate with group to procure land to erect Jewish synagogue. 12/22/54

MTA [Massachusetts Transit Authority] to be notified inadequate night and week-end service. 1/26/55

Comm'r of Health to be advised of difficulties connected with deposit of fly ash. 11/7/56

—Courtesy of the Massachusetts Archives

fession to me. He said that the biggest mistake he ever made as mayor of Boston was putting Columbia Point out there, and he had done it at the request of [Boston College High School administrator] Father Gilday. Father Gilday wanted to move B.C. High out there, and he persuaded the mayor that a housing project would be a nice thing to put out there, too.

Little did the mayor know at the time how costly a "mistake" it would turn out to be. It would be four years before a school was built for Columbia Point's children. It would be twelve years before a shopping center opened at Columbia Point. And it would be nine years later that a tragedy, the death of a six-year-old girl, would finally put the problems at Columbia Point in the spotlight and force the city to make good on its often-broken promise to close the dumps.

Sign on the Mile Road,
Columbia Point, 1962.
Boston Herald.

4 Moving In: A Tale of Two Families

t the time of the mayor's dedication ceremony in April 1954, sixteen families had already moved into Columbia Point. Over the next several months, hundreds more would follow. Each of them has a story—where they had come from, why they moved to Columbia Point, how they felt about their new home—and each story is different. The McCluskeys and the Shearers are just two among fifteen hundred of those stories.

THE McCLUSKEYS

In July 1954 Patricia McCluskey, seven months pregnant, moved into the Columbia Point housing project with her husband and two young boys. The family was rapidly outgrowing its shared-bath apartment at 139 Bowdoin Street in Dor-

chester. The McCluskeys considered it "a step up" to move into an apartment at Columbia Point. Large families had a hard time finding housing anywhere, and the McCluskeys were glad to get good, clean housing with a private bath and lots of hot water. John McCluskey's earnings as a cab driver put the family within the income limit for public housing tenants. And the man from the housing authority who visited the family at their Bowdoin Street apartment was satisfied that they were "fulfilling their housekeeping requirements."

Pat McCluskey, tall and thin as a beanpole, with auburn hair and large metal-rimmed glasses, was born and bred in South Boston. From Columbia Point she could just make out her former home at City Point at the far end of the long, arcing line of Carson Beach. As she sums it up, "I always say I went from City Point to Columbia Point."

The McCluskeys were the first family to move into apartment 816, on the sixth floor of the seven-story high-rise at 18 Brandon Avenue, where everything was brand-new. With their third son born in October and a daughter fourteen months later, the McCluskeys soon qualified for a larger apartment. In 1957 they moved into a four-bedroom apartment at 400 Mount Vernon Street, at the far end of the project. They lived there, raising

Easter at 400 Mount Vernon Street, 1960. Left to right: A neighbor, Johnny, Stephen, Kevin, and Noreen McCluskey. *Courtesy of Patricia McCluskey.*

their family, which would eventually number seven children, for the next eleven years.

One of Pat McCluskey's favorite stories is about her large family: "Once I went for a job interview with a doctor," she explains. "And he said, 'Do you have a family?' and I said, 'Yes, I have seven children.' 'Oh,' he said, 'a conscientious Catholic.' I said, 'Well, how do you know I wasn't a passionate Protestant?' And he laughed. I got the job, too."

Pat McCluskey has vivid memories of what it was like living at Columbia Point in the late 1950s. The McCluskeys' neighbors were working-class people like themselves. "Mr. Cronin was a carpenter," Pat recalls. "Mrs. McDonald's husband was disabled during the war, so he didn't have a regular job. Mr. Malloy worked for the post office for a while, and later on he went on to the MBTA [Massachusetts Bay Transit Authority], as my husband did. And Mr. Duffy was a postal worker."

Although the community opened without the basic facilities any community requires—playgrounds, grocery stores, schools—she remembers these as inconveniences, not hardships: "The children played around the building. We were at 18 Brandon and those were elevator buildings. When my older son, John Jr., became old enough and he knew the other children were going out to play, he would say, 'Mama, can I go play?' And I had the other little one, so I'd take him out to the elevator and put him on the elevator, and he'd go down. Then I'd look out the window to make sure he was downstairs. You put your trust a lot hoping that things would be all right."

The lack of recreational facilities may have turned grassy areas into dirt, but the children used their imaginations to improvise all the games they wanted. Getting groceries was a major production, but the daily trip to the grocery store became part of the rhythm of Pat McCluskey's day:

They used to have a bus that would come in there where you could go buy your groceries. They would park the bus over in an open area where the ball field was. But they would charge you all outdoors for the simplest things. And so every day I would just take the little ones, after the older ones went to school. And I would walk from 400 Mount Vernon, the whole length of the project, and cut through a big empty field, which is all filled in now. I crossed a pedestrian bridge over Morrissey Boulevard to the First National Store, which is now Channel 56. So it was like a little outing for me too, you know? In those early years, most residents had to walk to the First National or walk to Uphams Corner to the Elm Market, and then walk back.

We didn't have that much money to spend. Every morning when my husband came home—he worked the night shift driving a cab—he'd give me his tip money, and I'd spend that money on groceries. But the children, even as they're grown up now, they said they never remember being hungry. So I guess I did the right thing.

When we first moved, there wasn't any local school either. The children were bused to South Boston. I think even then that there wasn't any kindergarten. We used to take them up to the administration building, and they had some teachers there. When the Paul A. Dever School opened up, John Jr. went to kindergarten, and it was quite nice that all seven of my children had the same teacher.

Columbia Point Pride

The March 1955 edition of *Your Home Bulletin,* a Boston Housing Authority publication, extolled Columbia Point's virtues:

We take great pride in publishing the facts relative to our Columbia Point Development in Dorchester, the largest Public Housing structure in New England, and the third largest in the Country. It cost twenty million dollars to build.

Its geographical location is unique, in that it sets on a neck of land surrounded on two sides by the waters of Bostons' inner harbor. Its South West boundry is in proximity to the William T. Morrissey Boulevard and to the MTA Rapid Transit Columbia Station. The Columbia Park playground is about a stones throw from the development as are the beaches of L Street and Carson Beach. Its massive buildings add impressiveness to Bostons' sky line, and is, indeed, a town within a town. [All spellings as in original.]

Christmas at 400 Mount Vernon Street, #346, 1959. Clockwise from lower left: Noreen, 4, Kevin, 5, Johnny, 7, Stephen, 6, and Brian McCluskey, 2. *Courtesy of Patricia McCluskey.*

Above: Pat McCluskey with Brian, 1960.

Above, center: Noreen McCluskey.

Above, right: Dinner at the McCluskeys'.

Second row, left: Brian McCluskey's first birthday.

Second row, right: A day at the beach.

Photos courtesy of Patricia McCluskey.

In the early days, Pat McCluskey was busy not just raising her family but also working to build a strong community—not just putting food on the table and keeping the apartment clean, but also giving special recognition to an excellent teacher or doing something extra to spruce up her building. She and her husband were active in various community groups; Pat was president of the Improvement Association, and John started a credit union at the housing project. Although she looks back on these years fondly, Pat McCluskey is clear-eyed and still rueful about the obstacles she occasionally encountered:

At 400 Mount Vernon, there were four families on each floor. So there were twelve families in one building using the one stairwell. [There are] rules that they have when you live in a project, and because there were twelve families that meant that each month of the year it was a different family's turn to clean that hallway. And I'll never forget one time I cleaned the hallway. And right next to our apartment door was a window looking out on the back courtyard. So I thought I'd brighten it up a little bit, and I put a curtain on that window. Someone took a match, and burned the curtain right off the window.

I mean, it was just as if you were fighting—I don't know how to explain it—some people looked at housing just as housing. We were looking at it as a place to live, and something that we could improve while we were there.

Despite occasional hints of trouble foreshadowing the future, Columbia Point, as the McCluskeys saw it, was a good place to raise a growing family. The community nurtured them in important ways, and they in turn worked hard to give back to the community.

THE SHEARERS

In January 1956 Erline Shearer moved into Columbia Point with her five children. They had been living in her mother's house in Roxbury, but when her mother became seriously ill and the house was put up for sale, Shearer decided to try public housing. She was offered apartments in several projects, but the one at Columbia Point was the first one she looked at, and she decided to take it on the spot—apartment 607 at 164 Monticello, on the second floor of a seven-story building. As she recalls, she "just liked it":

When I moved there, the building was not completely occupied. But we were the first blacks in that building. When I first went out there it was very strange. I had never been out to that part of the city before. I had been out to Carson Beach, but I hadn't been beyond that. In fact I didn't know anything *was* beyond that. And I don't think there was until they built the Point. We always knew it as that's where they did a lot of dumping.

But I loved the apartment. I loved the location because my kitchen window—let's see, a bedroom, and the kitchen, and the living room—looked out on the ocean. Oh, and I could look right straight through to Castle Island and beyond.

Alert to the subtle cues that might indicate how she and her children, one of the few black families in the project, would be treated by their white neighbors, Erline Shearer saw in a neighbor's greeting a reassuring sign that Columbia Point would be a good place for her family to live: "I met one neighbor in the hallway coming in. I guess they knew that I was coming to look at an apartment. But she was

Linda and Debby Shearer in their Easter outfits, on their way to the Pilgrim Congregational Church at Uphams Corner. *Courtesy of Erline Shearer*

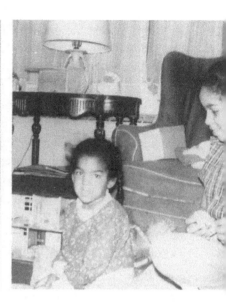

Left: Boy Scouts at
Columbia Point, 1958.

Center: Chuck Shearer
(right) with a friend, 1958.

Right: Christmas morning
at the Shearers', 1959.

*Photos courtesy of Erline
Shearer.*

very friendly. She said, 'Good morning.' And I took that as a good
sign. The only thing that bothered me a little was I did feel some isolation because I didn't see any transportation or anything. I didn't
see any buses or anything. But I figured I wasn't going anywhere."

Pat McCluskey and Erline Shearer would soon become friends,
brought together by their shared commitment to building a strong
community. In the years to come, they would walk the picket line
together demanding that the city close the dump. They would
watch their children grow from infants to far-ranging teenagers. As it
turned out, all seven of the McCluskey children grew up to attend
and graduate from Boston's "exam schools"—two of the boys went
to Boston Tech, two to Boston Latin, and the three girls to Boston
Academy. Kevin, the third oldest, went on to attend Harvard University and serve as a member of the Boston School Committee.
Four of the five Shearer children went on to college: one boy went
to Brown and another to Boston University; one of the girls went to
Brandeis and another to Northeastern. Over the years, Pat Mc-
Cluskey and Erline Shearer would respect each other's privacy as
each dealt with her own difficult times. They would become friends
for life.

Getting Out the Vote

Columbia Point was in Ward 13, which was my ward, Savin Hill. I was first elected as a state rep in 1956. The first time Columbia Point voted in such an election was 1954, but it voted then I think as part of another precinct. The first time it voted as a precinct itself was 1956. So I did a lot of campaigning out there, figuring it was virgin territory. We went in against incumbents. There were half a dozen of them. . . .

I used to go out there with an automobile with a big sound truck and as soon as the kids saw you, they went scrambling after you. Well, you didn't want the kids. You wanted to be able to talk to the parents. Somewhere along the line I realized that every one of these kids had two parents. If I could make friends with them, I may get two votes. . . . I think I won Columbia Point precinct by about seven or eight votes. . . . When you win by eighteen votes altogether, every vote counts. My first education was of the importance of all the votes. Eight of my plurality came from Columbia Point.

—Robert H. Quinn, former Massachusetts attorney general, Speaker of the House, and state representative from Savin Hill

Above: Erline Shearer's
lease, June 1, 1956.
Courtesy of Erline Shearer.

Left: Erline Shearer at a
friend's apartment at
Columbia Point. *Courtesy*
of Erline Shearer.

5 Building a New Community

Unless you were lucky enough to have a car or a get a ride, the way most people arrived at Columbia Point was by what was then known as the MTA train. The only way to the project from there was on foot. You'd get off the T at Columbia Station and walk a mile or so across fields and empty lots out to the project—an imposing wall of tall, drab yellow brick buildings clustered out at the edge of Dorchester Bay. The Mile Road, also known as Mount Vernon Street, cut across the peninsula from west to east, running along the front of the project out to the pumping station and the Mile Road Dump. But the most direct route from the T station was across the fields. It wasn't long after the project opened before the fields were marked with well-worn paths.

Crossing the fields brought you to Mount Vernon; across the street was Columbia Point. A left on Brandon just after the administration building took you into the project. It had three main streets, running parallel to Mount Vernon Street between it and the bay. Ironically, the major streets in the project had been named after the grand homes of the American presidents: Washington's Mount Vernon, Jefferson's Monticello, Madison's

Montpelier. Brandon was nearest to the front; off it ran Belvoir and Blair. The next street back was Montpelier, lined with seven-story high-rises. Forming a ring around the back of the project was Monticello, swinging along the bay, then past the big brick smokestack to the sunny buildings at the far end where the senior citizens lived. The large families lived in the three-story buildings, where the three-, four-, and five-bedroom apartments were located. These buildings had four families on each floor, for a total of twelve families. The seven-story buildings typically housed smaller families, with twenty-eight units per building.

Some of the buildings were arranged in groups of four, with a courtyard in the center. Each building had a "clothes yard," an area enclosed by a Cyclone fence where people hung their clothes out to dry. In the beginning, each floor of a building was assigned a certain day to hang out the laundry.

Columbia MTA station, 1927. *Courtesy of the Boston Globe.*

The administration building, known to Columbia Point residents as "the mini." *Courtesy of Father Larry Wetterholm.*

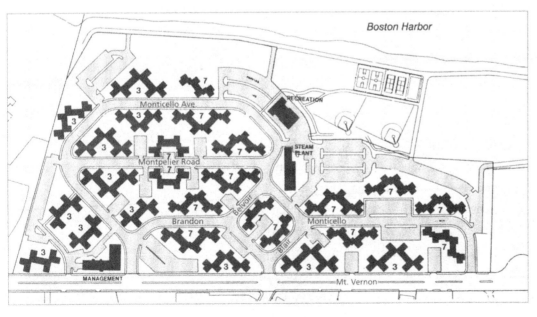

Site plan for Columbia Point. *Boston Housing Authority.*

Columbia Point Senior
Citizens Club, 1957.
*Courtesy of Father Larry
Wetterholm.*

When families began moving in during the spring and summer of
1954, the finishing touches were still being put on the project.
Grounds were newly landscaped, with little areas marked by green
iron fences in the front of each building with new grass and planted
trees. Some of the streets were still dirt, and the sidewalks hadn't yet
been paved. As hundreds of children moved in, the grassy areas didn't
last long. Although a large playground was built in the back of the
project near the bay, most children played near their own buildings.

Within a matter of months, fifteen hundred young and rapidly
growing families moved into Columbia Point. People remember the
windows with open views of the harbor, trees, flowers, lovely new
apartments that they could fix up the way they always wanted. One
early tenant recalls of his waterfront apartment, "There was nothing
between myself and the water. You could see the sun coming up in
the morning from my bedroom." Another remembers "green grass,
rose bushes, intact benches, clean hallways, sparkling clean windows, curtains, flowers. It was a very, very nice community."

The first residents of Columbia Point felt extremely fortunate to
be able to live there. "It's funny if you think of it now," one early tenant recalls, "but when we first moved into Columbia Point, public
housing was something that people wanted. It was a good thing that
happened to you." Public housing did not yet carry the stigma it
would in later years, and the brand-new Columbia Point housing
project in particular was full of promise. "The recollection I have of
people talking was that Columbia Point was the best place to go," re-

calls another. "It was new and there were rave reviews about what it was going to turn out to be."

Many residents had been living in cold-water flats, heated with coal or wood stoves, with ice boxes and ice delivered by the ice man. For them, a brand-new apartment with unlimited heat and hot water, a refrigerator with a freezer, and a private bathroom complete with bathtub was a dream come true. One resident recalls, "When we were first told that we had gotten the apartment in Columbia Point, that very next evening my husband got paid, and we went to the store and we bought so much meat, because now we were going to have a refrigerator with a freezer." She continues, "In the South End, we did not have a bathtub, and I used to have to fill up a tin tub in order to bathe the kids. So the bathroom was a luxury. You should have seen us fighting the first night to get into the bathtub." The new tenants also liked the fact that everything was covered in one monthly rent—$41.75 per month for a one- or two-bedroom apartment, and $49.75 per month for a three-, four-, or five-bedroom apartment.

This sense of new beginning seemed to spread through each building and throughout the community. Feeling fortunate to be able to live in this brand-new community, the tenants were determined to keep it neat and in good repair. Their determination was more than matched by the first manager of Columbia Point, John N. Steele. "Mr. Steele" was something of a legend at Columbia Point. Some residents thought he was strict, even mean, but all respected him for taking his job seriously and doing it well. John Steele was the manager of Columbia Point from the time the very first families moved in, in the spring of 1954, until his sudden death of a heart attack in 1960, while traveling on the T after work one night from Columbia Point to his home in Belmont.

John Steele personally screened applicants for Columbia Point, very careful to oversee who got in and who didn't. Maintenance was excellent; if something broke, it was fixed the next day. If you were late with your rent, one tenant recalls, "Mr. Steele would take over on you quick." People sometimes remember Mr. Steele as an imposing keeper of the rules, but they unanimously applaud his doggedness in keeping the place well maintained. "The man would be out there, sometimes eleven or twelve at night, seeing that you did what you were supposed to do. . . . He kept after the place," one resident recalls. "People knew he was looking."

The children who grew up at Columbia Point remember the

Spray pool at Columbia
Point, 1960. *Courtesy of
the* Boston Globe.

stern glare of Mr. Steele to this day; you didn't throw a candy wrap-
per in the hallway for fear of his wrath. If a child was involved in
fighting or caught damaging anything, his or her name would be
turned into the office, Mr. Steele would send the family a "calling
letter," and the child and parents had to visit the office to receive a
warning and discuss the problem. If the problem was not corrected
and the vandalism or fighting persisted, the family would face eviction proceedings. Everyone knew the manager had that authority
and would not hesitate to use it—and most families appreciated it.

John Steele had two assistant managers and two maintenance su-
pervisors, who oversaw a maintenance crew of eight to fourteen
men. They were highly visible and accessible in the community.
"When I first moved there," one resident recalls, "the maintenance
men were always on the ball. You'd see them out there in the morning, sweeping in the summer, shoveling in the winter, making sure
that the incinerators worked right, the elevators were working, the

glass in the front doors was kept clean." The tenants were on friendly terms with the maintenance men, inviting them in for a cup of coffee.

The fact that standards were strict, and strictly enforced, was key to the strength of the community. "Before I could move in," one tenant recalls, "somebody came to my apartment in the South End to check my housekeeping. You had to swear an allegiance. And when I did move in, you had a gentleman by the name of Mr. Steele . . . and if there was so much as a piece of paper on the floor he knocked at your door and told you to pick it up or get out. And we loved it. You know why? Because it helped to keep the place clean and it helped to keep people together. Everybody took part in keeping the building clean — black folks, white folks, all kinds of folks."

Apartments were small, with notoriously thin walls, but families made the best of them. One resident remembers moving in in 1956, when she was five years old, one of twelve children. The family moved into a five-bedroom apartment at 50 Monticello, one of the three-story buildings that housed most of the large families. Although the apartment was crowded, with fourteen people sharing a single bathroom, she remembers it fondly. "If it was a real hardship," she recalls, "my parents didn't let on. Because we didn't live hard. The apartment was always nice; it was never really cluttered. Even though there was a lot of people in there, there was order to it. We may have fought for the bathroom, but no one died because they didn't use the bathroom at a certain time. My mother was one of those survivors. I guess she could live anywhere. She brought order, some semblance of order, to a very small apartment."

Not only did each family "bring order" and individuality to each apartment; families in many buildings also worked together to make their buildings homes. In the early days, buildings used to have competitions, putting curtains in the halls, waxing the hallway floors. Some buildings even held competitions for the cleanest floor in the building, or for the cleanest building in a group of buildings. These "competitions" had nothing to do with the housing authority; they were organized by the residents themselves and had no official judges. The reward, as one tenant explains, "was just a feeling inside, when someone would come into the building and they would really admire it."

Even though the early Columbia Point tenants didn't own their apartments, they were proud of them. They kept their apartments clean and demanded the same of their neighbors. The housing authority required the tenants to take turns cleaning the hallways—a task the tenants don't seem to have found onerous. In fact, many took to it with zeal. "When we first went there," one tenant recalls, "my wife used to go out and wax the floors in the hallway and wax the walls—they were tile. And she wasn't alone doing that. A lot of people went way beyond."

The tenants' care for the physical details of the community is a reflection of deeply held and shared values. "I never thought that it was too hard to take care of where you lived," one mother explains. "I considered that my home. Though I was one of twenty-eight apartments in the building, that was still our home. I'd say to the kids, 'Do you want somebody to come and say, "How can you live in a place like this? Why can't you get out there and sweep?"' If you said, 'It's not my week,' or 'That's not my job,' that wasn't acceptable. You live here, you clean it. And most people felt that way." Even though she shared the building with other families, the entire building was her home. And even though hers was only one of twenty-seven buildings, the entire community was her home.

In the same spirit, neighbors looked out for one another's children. People could count on the other people in their building to look after their kids if they were coming home late, or if a child was sick. "In your individual building of twelve families, you became very, very friendly," one tenant recalls. "Like even if we were sick, my parents could come pick me up [at a neighbor's apartment] . . . and vice versa. We all exchanged."

Likewise, children knew that anybody in the building would tell their parents if they were caught stepping out of line. "If they knew you and they'd seen your kid doing something that he shouldn't be doing," one resident recalls, "they'd jump in and help you in correcting that kid." There was a clear sense of extended family, not only in each building but throughout the project. Charles Titus grew up at Columbia Point and is now director of athletics at UMass Boston, a stone's throw from his childhood home. He recalls that it was reassuring, if a bit oppressive, as a child to know that he had "mothers" all over the project. "I remember people like Mrs. Winn, I remember people like Thelma Peters, I remember people like Drena Young and Ellen Jones," he says. "These were all friends of my mother, but they were almost like your mother, because if they caught you doing something you were going to catch hell from them, and then they were going to call your mother and she was going to be waiting for you when you got home."

Not only did Columbia Point residents value looking out for one another, but they also valued minding their own business. Living in such close quarters, tenants recognized the importance of respecting one another's privacy and one another's differences. Perhaps the strongest example of this respect is the level of racial integration in the early days. Mirroring the population of the city at large, the housing project was 93 percent white and 7 percent black shortly after it opened. There were virtually no racial conflicts among the adults at Columbia Point. When there were problems among younger people that couldn't be resolved within the building, they would be referred to the Community Development Council. As a former council member explains, "We would bring the kids together. Ninety-nine percent of the time it was because you had people who had lived in South Boston, who had never lived next door to a black, let alone walked down the street with them, who were suddenly living together in the same building. . . . You had to find out that you are in this building, you are in this community, and you are going to have to learn to live with people. Now, we are not expecting you to love each other, but you *will* respect one another for who you are."

"Housewives' Delights. A compact kitchen work area which will save some housewife millions of steps." Columbia Point, 1954. Boston Herald.

Even though Columbia Point had problems—most of them related to the extreme isolation of the project—the community came together with energy and enthusiasm to solve them. As one resident put it, "Even though we were isolated, we were more like an isolated group of people out on a desert island. We didn't have any disputes. Everybody seemed to help one another. Which was like it should be." The racial or social class prejudices that may have seemed important to hold on to back on the "mainland" were suddenly irrelevant, rendered moot by the much more important shared goal of building a good community.

6 The Mothers Club

The new community's needs were obvious and urgent, most of them related to its utter isolation. Columbia Point had opened with no grocery store, no shops, no bank, no school, no churches, no health care, no buses. If you had a sick child, day or night, you had to make your way to City Hospital, miles away, as best you could. In the 1950s many residents did not have a telephone, and only a few had cars. In an emergency—a child with a severe asthma attack, a deep cut, or a broken arm—you had to run out to the single pay phone and then wait for an ambulance.

In addition to buying groceries from the bus that parked near the ball field at the back of the project, a resident could make the longer trek across the field and over

Morrissey Boulevard to the First National—and back with a load of groceries. A succession of vendors, reputable and otherwise, filled the shopping vacuum, bringing their wares into the community. Residents recall the bleach man, the crab man, the candy truck, the ice cream truck, the Cushman's bakery man, the egg man, Bert the fruit and vegetable man, the Hood milkman, the butter man, the dry cleaning man. "I remember a man named Mr. Bliss who sold furniture to people in the Point," one resident recalls. "He would come in with his catalogues and books and people would pick out the furniture they wanted and he would deliver the furniture, and then he would come once a month, just like the insurance man, and make his collection." Shortly after the project opened, a small group of stores was built across Mount Vernon Street from the project: the Beehive coffee shop, a drug store, and the superette. Mothers often sent their kids to the superette on errands—a loaf of bread, a bottle of milk, baseball cards, candy.

There was no school on the peninsula when Columbia Point opened. Kindergartners attended a half-day program at the administration building, and school children were bused to the William E. Russell School in Dorchester or the Thomas N. Hart School in South Boston. In 1957, three years after Columbia Point opened, the Paul A. Dever School was built directly across Mount Vernon Street from the project, serving some nine

The Mothers Club pays a visit to Mayor John Collins in the early 1960s to press for more programs at Columbia Point. Pat McCluskey is standing third from left. *Courtesy of Erline Shearer.*

Shops across Mount Vernon Street from Columbia Point. *Courtesy of Father Larry Wetterholm.*

Columbia Point, 1962. Boston Herald.

Above: First day of school at the Paul A. Dever School, Mount Vernon Street, 1963. *Courtesy of the* Boston Globe.

Below: Left to right: Rev. Lawrence E. Wetterholm, Rev. Francis Moseley, Rev. James Rogers, St. Christopher's Church. *Courtesy of Father Larry Wetterholm.*

hundred children from kindergarten through the third grade. The Dever School—named after the governor who was an early supporter of the housing project—was an important asset to the community. Not only was it more convenient to have young children go to school right across the street, but the same sense of expectations and accountability that pertained to building a strong community extended to its school. Children were expected to work hard and learn. "If you had a child that wasn't doing his work," one resident recalls, "his teacher or the principal would make sure they got in touch and would sit down and talk about it."

Before St. Christopher's Church was built on the peninsula in 1956, Catholics from Columbia Point attended St. Margaret's Church in Dorchester or St. Monica's Church near the Old Colony housing project in South Boston. The relatively affluent St. Margaret's parish made it clear that Catholics from Columbia Point were not welcome. In fact, the parish had meetings before the opening of Columbia Point to discuss how to keep the church separate from "the project people," who they feared would be a drain on their resources.

Similarly, some Columbia Point residents felt their children were not welcome in the Dorchester schools, particularly the William E. Russell elementary school. Dorchester politicians felt that the project would attract a "different element": people who were poor and people who were "more diverse"—in other words, not white like most of the citizens of Dorchester and South Boston. They already had two projects—Old Colony and Old Harbor, both in South Boston—and they didn't want a third nearby.

Indeed, in the 1950s the Dorchester community was already

stressed, as the Southeast Expressway plowed its way through to downtown Boston. John Aylward recalls watching streets of triple-decker houses make way for the new highway: "When we used to walk home from school at the Russell, we'd watch them jacking up three-family houses and pulling trucks underneath them and driving the houses off to a new location. I can remember watching them for hours, just pulling houses out and driving them away—driving a whole three-family house right down the street."

Fires burning at the dump, 1958. *Courtesy of the* Boston Globe.

Father Francis Moseley, who officiated at St. Monica's, began saying mass for Columbia Point churchgoers in the gymnasium at B.C. High. When St. Christopher's was built, he and Father James Rogers moved there permanently once the rectory was completed. St. Christopher's received special permission from Cardinal Richard J. Cushing to say mass at midnight, and the service proved so popular that the church added two more, at 1:30 and 2:30 A.M. These masses were standing room only, filled not only with people from the project but also with workers from the nearby *Boston Globe* and Catholics from South Boston and Dorchester eager to meet their Sunday obligations early.

Black families went to the Pilgrim Congregational Church in Uphams Corner. A regular bus took kids from the Point to Sunday school in the morning, then brought them home, and back to the church for services later in the day.

Besides problems related to the isolation of Columbia Point, its other major problem was its nearest neighbor—the dump. Children from the project played at the dump and people scavenged there. One resident even recalls making her children skating outfits out of a bolt of material scavenged from the dump. But the dump was toxic to the community in many ways. Rats were a constant presence and a constant menace. Dump trucks roared up and down the Mile Road making hundreds of trips every day. And the dumps burned refuse all night, turning the sky red and black, and pouring acrid smoke into the project.

What the housing project lacked, its residents—particularly the mothers—were determined to get. The mothers at Columbia Point were, for the most part, young, energetic, and resourceful. The community was extraordinarily focused, with many of the mothers com-

ing together in a common space each morning. After they walked
their kids to school, the mothers would pack up their babies and
head over to the administration building, known as "the mini," for
coffee and visiting. They rarely met in one another's apartments. As
one mother explains, "We were all friends to a certain degree, but
we never sat in each other's house, because we didn't believe in it.
We weren't raised like that."

The "Mothers Club," as they called themselves, formed as a natural support group—mothers getting together for company, talking
about their kids, finding they weren't alone in their problems. They
quickly formed strong bonds. "As parents, we kind of understood
each other," one mother recalls. "When it was time to shed tears,
somebody was always there that you could shed your tears with, because basically we all were experiencing the same kinds of problems. You know, working husbands, limited incomes, desires—looking to really grow."

Together, over coffee, it was only natural for the Mothers Club to
begin thinking of ways to make their brand-new community better—
to develop the tools they needed to grow. "We wanted the same
things for our kids that everybody else wanted," one of the mothers
explains. "Regardless of whether you live in Columbia Point, Welles-
ley Hills, or wherever, we all had the same kinds of wants and desires
and values." Women who may have come to the project with prejudices soon set them aside because they discovered common goals.
"There were white families from South Boston who did not associate
with you because you were black, in the beginning," one mother recalls. "But when they realized that, in order to become involved we
all had to come together, you kind of set those racial attitudes aside
because we all were experiencing the same thing."

One of the projects the Mothers Club took on was getting bus
service out to the project. The mothers formed a committee and
handed out assignments, talking to Mr. Steele and going into town
to talk to the mayor. They were successful in getting limited bus
service. Under more pressure from the Mothers Club, the city also
provided a shopping bus that took residents from Columbia Point
into South Boston. The bus ran to the shopping area on Broadway
every hour on the half hour, free of charge, as long as you got a pass
from one of the stores. Families from the Point, black and white,
would take the bus into South Boston on March 17, Evacuation
Day, for the St. Patrick's Day parade. "You wore green," one black
resident recalls of St. Patrick's Days in Southie when she was a
young girl. "You didn't have to, but I'd always put on a little green,

THIS TICKET GOOD FOR
1 BUS RIDE
To Columbia Point Housing Project
Good Only
FRIDAY   SATURDAY
Children under 15 not allowed on bus without parent

Ticket for a free bus ride
from Columbia Point to
South Boston. *Courtesy of
Erline Shearer.*

just to blend in. And we never had any problems for that reason."

Early on, the Mothers Club realized that, to get the city to pay attention to their needs, they couldn't wait for City Hall to come to them—they had to go to City Hall. They would put on their hats and gloves, dress up in their suits and carry their pocketbooks, and ride the T to City Hall to take their concerns directly to the mayor. They recognized that it was important to have a say in designing programs for the community—the after-school program, for example. They believed their input was important, not only because they knew firsthand what was needed, but also because if new programs imposed by the city failed, they could be blamed.

The Mothers Club sponsored a dizzying array of activities for the community. They held spaghetti suppers, fried chicken suppers, and special suppers during Lent. They held fashion shows, modeling clothes from Lerner's, a downtown clothing store that gave the women the opportunity to purchase the clothing afterward. They had "blitz" parties—playing a bingo-like game—dancing classes, and cooking demonstrations. The events were not just social occasions for the community members; they were opportunities to raise money for a variety of projects.

They formed Cub Scout and Brownie troops, with the mothers as den mothers. One mother organized a group of teenage girls called "the Debs," who would have dinners and dances. The group sponsored teas for the senior citizens. Once a month, the mothers would take a group of children on a trip to the Fernald School, a residential treatment facility for the mentally disabled, bringing gifts and company. In 1955 and 1956 the mothers formed their own softball team, playing in several tournaments against neighboring teams, even challenging the maintenance men.

When basic things they needed—simple things, like a haircut—

Above: Outside 350 Mount Vernon Street, Columbia Point, 1962. *Courtesy of the Boston Globe.*

Below: Columbia Point Brownie Troop, behind the "wishing well." *Courtesy of Erline Shearer.*

Single Mothers and Women Activists at Columbia Point

The activists [at Columbia Point] were mostly women. Some had husbands in the service or working. "The women pushed for changes out here," one now elderly father of thirteen explained, "while the men had to feed those babies." In addition, from its earliest day, there were a considerable number of single mothers. Female-headed households tend to be under-represented in official BHA statistics because BHA tenant policies in the early 1950s required a husband to sign the lease; women who were separated or divorced had to ask former partners to help them hide their single status.

The first problem the women tackled was the lack of public transportation to the Point. With 1,400 units of low-income housing on a peninsula, the Authority seemed to assume all would have cars. The women . . . assigned each other different tasks; they hounded the BHA offices and they lobbied city councillors and the Metropolitan Transit Authority. For their efforts, they gained a fairly inadequate bus route—Mondays through Fridays from early morning until six in the evening. For those who worked later, or shopped on Saturdays, there was still no transportation.

For some, [demanding bus service] was their first experience of organizing, of pushing for a common goal. For some, it was their first experience working in an interracial group as well.

—Marie Kennedy, Charlotte Ryan, and Jeanne Winner, "The Best Laid Plans . . . The Early History of Boston's Columbia Point Public Housing," for the Columbia Point Oral History Project, Center for Community Planning, College of Public and Community Service, University of Massachusetts at Boston, 1987

weren't provided, the residents devised ways to get them. One teenager organized an innovative haircut program: once a month, he would take a group of kids to the barber school in the South End. Every kid set out with fifty cents; they would walk to Columbia station, take the T into town, get the haircut, and have enough time and money left over for a trip to the store that sold comic books, three for a dime if the covers had been removed.

Every Saturday afternoon, the Mothers Club showed movies at the "mini" building, and the place was always packed. One of the older boys drove to Melrose to pick up the movie reel, the Boy Scouts would set up the chairs, someone would buy candy wholesale, and someone else would pop popcorn at home and rebag it. The first feature movie was *Song of the South*, the Disney classic featuring Uncle Remus. The charge for admission was minimal—ten cents per kid, twenty-five cents for a family admission. The revenues, admission plus the sales of candy and popcorn, might amount to as much as twenty dollars, all of which was plowed into more activities.

The Mothers Club also organized countless field trips. One year a group of parents and children went to the New York World's Fair, eleven dollars round trip for the day. Another group traveled to the Montreal Expo, leaving at three in the morning and returning late that night. Walter Brown, owner of the Boston Garden, would provide free tickets to basketball games, the circus, and the Ice Capades. Arthur Fiedler, conductor of the Boston Pops, provided free tickets to concerts at Symphony Hall.

One of the most active members of the Mothers Club recalls that her youngest son once participated in a program in which children from the project spent two weeks living with suburban families. "The family called me one evening and said, 'I thought these kids that were coming to visit with us were poor kids who didn't get to go places. Everywhere that we plan to take your son, he's been two, three times,' she said. 'He's been to places that my children haven't been to.' 'Well,' I told her, 'those are the kind of things our kids do.'"

The Mothers Club may seem quaint and anachronistic, with its fashion shows and spaghetti suppers. But what these mothers were doing was creating a community where there was none, giving their children everything any mother—"project mother" or suburbanite—strives to give her children. Soon enough, the Mothers Club would prove a formidable political force, one the city would have to reckon with, when a longtime threat to the community, one that they had worked for years to stop, proved fatal to one of its own children.

7 Children of the Point: I

We had a very privileged childhood. The world was at our doorstep,
and everybody I know just opened the door and said, "Let's go!"
—Deborah Shearer

Columbia Point in the early days was a community of children. In the late 1950s some four thousand children lived in the project, concentrated in twenty-seven buildings on seventy acres. For children, it was a bonanza: more than a hundred kids in your own building, and hundreds more just outside your door.

The boys and girls who grew up at Columbia Point in the 1950s and 1960s are now men and women—"adult children" of the Point, as it were. Across the years, they remember the project as a place they loved, a place full of fun. They are protective of the project, sensitive to the stigma that later became associated with it. The place they knew and loved, the place where

they grew up, was very different from the place described in the newspaper and magazines, or

the place outsiders imagined. "It's very dear to my heart," Chris Aylward, typical of many, emphasizes, "and I don't want to hear people talk negatively about it." The media always paid plenty of attention to negative stories about Columbia Point, they argue, but ignored the positive stories—the children of the Point who went on to college, to graduate school, to productive jobs.

The youngest of five brothers in a family of nine children, Aylward lived at Columbia Point for twenty-three years, attending Northeastern University on a football scholarship and earning a place in the university's athletic hall of fame. His work as a juvenile probation officer sometimes brings him back to the old neighborhood. "When I was growing up there," he recalls, "it was a place of real community spirit. Families were real close to each other. I can remember, back then, that you never locked your doors."

People who grew up there remember the project as a place to roam and play, a labyrinth not of danger but of endless games. "The high-rise buildings were good for us with baseball, because everybody tried to hit it over the seven-story roof,"

Columbia Point, 1962.
Boston Herald.

Butchie Arroya and Chuck
Shearer at the baseball
field in back of the project,
1961. *Courtesy of Erline
Shearer*

Joshua Powell recalls. "The way the streets went was nice for kids, too—the streets were like a maze. You could go down Mount Vernon, turn in on Monticello, then turn around here at Montpelier and come back on Monticello and come all the way around on Mount Vernon. We used the whole project to play games."

Some games, though, had inherent dangers. Chris Aylward's older brother John recalls that kids used to ride on the tops of the elevators; for bigger thrills, they would ride the weight on the cable above the elevator. In 1956 John's friend Tommy Gaskell was killed riding the weight.

Kids and policemen knew one another on a first-name basis—or rather, police called kids by their first names, and kids knew the police as "Officer Kinneally," "Officer Olbrys," and so on. Kids had the sense that the police knew them well enough that, if they ever stepped out of line, a patrolman would soon be knocking at their door.

When Columbia Point first opened in 1954, school-age children were bused into South Boston. Each morning, twelve buses would pick up children in front of the administration building on Mount Vernon Street. The boys were bused to the Thomas N. Hart School on Eighth Street in South Boston, and the girls to the Gaston School. The busing was uneventful, nothing like the traumatic era of court-ordered busing in the 1970s. "We had busing before 'busing,'" Chris Aylward recalls. "You just got on the bus and you did what you had to do, and whether it was a black student sitting next to you, or Irish Catholic, or Chinese, or Spanish, it didn't matter. You had to get along, and you had to try and work things out."

For Joshua Powell, the only black in his classroom at the Thomas N. Hart School, the experience was not wholly trouble-free. "Some kids were okay and some weren't," he recalls. The few racial incidents he remembers are characterized by the usual mixture of cruelty and banality. "In sixth grade, this kid named Thomas Courtney—some of these names I just don't forget—was sitting in front of me. He just turned around and said, 'You're black, I'm white,' and there was a Chinese kid and he said, 'He's yellow.' And it was just that." In another incident around Halloween, Powell recalls, "This one kid said, 'You don't need a mask 'cause you already got one.' I never even put the connection together until years later." It was casual racism—but no less hurtful, or less memorable, for being offhand. For the most part, tensions ran more along Southie versus Columbia Point than racial lines, and didn't amount to much.

For Kevin McCluskey, one of the seven children of John and Pat McCluskey, life at Columbia Point revolved around sports. Of a

Swimming at the Point

Columbia Point was virtually surrounded by water. While adults recall the joys of living right on the water—watching the sun rise, seeing the tall ships entering the harbor in 1976, enjoying the cool breezes on the Point on summer evenings—the kids recall the joys of playing in it. Different groups and ages swam in different areas. The teenagers swam at "the rocks," near where the prisoner of war camp used to be. The younger kids usually swam at "the cove," down at the end of the project, near the buildings that housed the elderly. When the tide came in at the rocks, the older kids would dive into the deeper water. "I had three or four sons who'd go over to the beach and swim off the rocks," Jim Duffy recalls. "My son and a group of his buddies cleared out all the rocks, and they had a little rug, and they went over and they weighted the rug down with heavy boulders, and they used that as their walkway into the water."

typical afternoon in his youth, Kevin recalls, "You'd come home and get out of your 'good clothes' and into your 'play clothes,' and then you'd go out and start playing whatever sport was in season. You had everyone else spilling out of their buildings, too. With a core group of anywhere from a dozen to twenty guys, I used to just take my basketball and go up to the hoops outside St. Christopher's and play ball for three hours." Although there were big fields "in the back" of the project, toward the water, the kids preferred the asphalt to the grass. "The parking lots had the perfect configuration for a football field," Kevin explains. "You'd just roll right out of your door. You learned how to run in between the cars."

In the first few years, according to John Aylward, white kids played sports with whites, and black kids with blacks—just as they had in their former neighborhoods. After a couple of years, though, the racial lines broke down and everybody played together. As Aylward says, "It came down to who could play." From then on, athletic teams were racially integrated—not by conscious decision, but because race was a non-issue. Hundreds of children at the project played sports together without incident. "It was all mixed," Kevin explains. "We didn't really know there was a racial issue. This is who lived in the projects. All different kinds of people. In our building, we had twelve families, and for the bulk of my time there it was evenly divided between black and white. If there was a fight, it wasn't viewed as a racial thing; it was just a fight."

The one group that held itself apart from the rest of the community were the West Enders, mostly Italians, who were relocated to Columbia Point in the late 1950s when the West End was being demolished as part of Boston's urban renewal. John Aylward recalls that West Enders were protective of their own group:

Chuck Shearer at his job in South Boston. *Courtesy of Erline Shearer.*

> When they came to Columbia Point, they were traumatized by the forced taking of their community—not only their house but their whole community. By then, most of the groups at the project were pretty well established. . . . We were thinking, "Why doesn't he want to come and hang out? Why doesn't he want to come out and shoot baskets?" I was too young to realize what the impact of their having been thrown out of their community was to them.

Many children who lived at Columbia Point were familiar with other parts of the city. Once you walked across the field to the T sta-

St. Christopher's Briga-
diers, 1964. *Courtesy of
Father Larry Wetterholm.*

tion, you could get anywhere you wanted for a dime. Kevin Mc-
Cluskey remembers the excitement of getting a job in town. "For a
couple of years," he recalls,

> my brother and I would go downtown after school and sell newspapers
> at the corner of Summer and Washington, right there at Filene's Base-
> ment. That was a great education. You were eleven years old, you were
> in town, and you were with your brother—it's a different day. You'd
> just travel freely around the city. You don't have the issues you have to-
> day. Your parents would tell you, "If you run into any wise guys, just
> walk the other way." Not like today. . . . I loved it: you made some
> money and you got to see what was going on in town.

Other kids found jobs right at the project. "I remember working
as far back almost as I can remember," Charlie Titus recalls,

> but I think that my first job was on the milk truck at Columbia Point.
> In those days, Hood's used to deliver the milk right to the doors, and
> they had milk crates that you could carry maybe eight bottles of milk
> in. I would meet the milkman in the morning at six o'clock, and if it
> was a school day, I would work until it was time to go to school. On
> Saturdays we would get started at five o'clock in the morning and work
> to two or three o'clock in the afternoon, lugging milk cases. I remem-
> ber doing that all day until I was ten.

For children, Columbia Point was a great place to grow up, a self-
contained community with, as Kevin McCluskey puts it,

all the traditional markers of a strong community—a strong adult presence, the sense of an extended family, the strong role of the church and all the community institutions. There was a feeling of safety, a sense of knowing the local police. We knew who all the cops were—it was community policing before it was part of the jargon. Eddie was our maintenance man, and you didn't throw anything on the ground or make a mess because Eddie might hit you with his broom.

St. Christopher's Church, directly across the street from the housing project, was the center of athletic activities for boys and girls living at Columbia Point. Father Francis Moseley, head of the newly established parish, was joined in 1961 by Father Larry Wetterholm, a charismatic young priest who would be a major influence in the lives of hundreds of children at Columbia Point. "Because of Father Wetterholm," Kevin McCluskey recalls, "I always wanted to be a priest. Then I hit puberty." Father Wetterholm ran an extensive sports program through the church. He had himself once been headed for pro baseball, signing with the Philadelphia Phillies upon his graduation from Brockton High School and playing on their farm teams from 1946 to 1948—a matter of no small wonder to the Little Leaguers from Columbia Point.

From the start, St. Christopher's centered attention on the children of the project. The church's athletic program included basketball, baseball, and football for the boys, and basketball and softball for the girls. Although technically CYO—the Catholic Youth Organization—teams, St. Christopher's paid no attention to whether the players were Catholic or not.

The Little League team began by building itself a ballpark behind the church, on an empty field that had once been a huge hole filled with hundreds and hundreds of junked cars. Father Wetterholm was adept at mustering the resources needed to construct the ballpark without a budget. "The Boston Housing Authority helped me with

Above: St. Christopher's CYO basketball team, 1966. Front row, left to right: Peter Barbuto, Dennis Marchant, Larry Joyce, Dennis Gambon. Standing, left to right: Kevin McCluskey, Stephen McCluskey, Fran Cronin, Jay Cronin, John Quirk (coach). *Courtesy of Kevin McCluskey.*

Below: St. Christopher's CYO baseball team, 1964. Father Larry Wetterholm standing, center. John McCluskey standing at far left, John Quirk standing at far right. *Courtesy of Kevin McCluskey.*

the equipment and with their professionals. We needed welders to put up a backstop and to help in erecting bleachers and benches for the players," he explains. "Also, to fill in that area properly and level it off, I was able to get loads and loads of loam from the city. I don't know where they got it, but they dumped it off at my place."

Father Wetterholm had a ready and ample supply of labor in the Little Leaguers themselves. "We had to mow the grass and rake it all up," recalls Chris Aylward, who was eleven years old at the time. "Then we had to bring in the loam, spread it, throw the grass seed, and try to get it to look as nice as it could be. . . . It was a labor of love, I suppose." That spring, some three hundred youngsters played Little League on their brand-new, homemade field.

Father Wetterholm's right-hand man in the athletic programs was John Quirk, described by one of his players as "a crusty old character with a heart of gold," who coached the CYO teams for fourteen years. Through their connections, John Quirk and Father Wetterholm managed to get uniforms and equipment for the CYO teams from local colleges—Tufts, Boston College, Northeastern, Harvard.

Father Wetterholm saw sports not just as a way to occupy kids' time but also as an important way for kids to learn and grow as people. "I have always said that the great equalizer in racial relationships is athletics," he explains, "and particularly among the youngsters. When you have Little League, you have blacks and Puerto Ricans and Chinese and whites—no one asks what you are. You're just one of the ball players."

The children who grew up at Columbia Point seem to have been remarkably unaware of racial differences, let alone racial prejudice. "People laugh at me," Deb Shearer recalls, "but I never knew that I was black until I got out of Columbia Point. Until I went to high school. The only difference between me and my friends was that they were Catholic and I was Protestant. That was it." In fact, Deb got her firsthand education about racial prejudice in the suburbs. "I never heard the 'n-word' until I went to Metco," she recalls, citing the program that bused black, inner-city children to suburban schools. "That's where I first heard it, when I went to Lexington High."

Angie Hines moved into Columbia Point in 1956, at age five, and lived there until she

St. Christopher's girls' basketball team, 1969. *Courtesy of Father Larry Wetterholm.*

Children of the Point.
Courtesy of Pat
McCluskey.

was eighteen. She remembers being the recipient of racial slurs—
and, for that matter, dishing them out. But for her, it was "personal,"
not "general." And to her, that made all the difference:

> If someone called me a nigger, I wouldn't think that they meant every-
> body who was black was a nigger. I'd think that they were calling me
> that name, only. Because they were angry at me or they didn't like *me*.
> I just never thought it was any larger than that—because I was also
> quick to call somebody "honky" or something, and I didn't mean the
> whole world. I was talking about that individual person, so I always
> thought that's what the extent of all our problems was, was individual
> issues.

In fact, the racial conflict Angie remembers most vividly, and
with the most shame, wasn't between blacks and whites. It grew out
of differences between northern urban blacks and southern rural
blacks in her own building. "There was a black family that moved in
who were from the South, but at the time I thought they were from
Africa," she recalls.

> I'd never seen anybody like them before. The mother was wearing
> dresses that were kind of long. Her hair wasn't straightened. They
> didn't have much; they were on the poor side. Now, I didn't think folks
> from Columbia Point were poor; in fact, they weren't poor. They were
> middle-class working people, it seemed to me. So this family was differ-
> ent. They ate different kinds of foods and everything. . . .
> I went up and asked them, "Are you from Africa?" And they looked at
> me like I was crazy and I'd insulted them. Plus I couldn't understand
> what they were saying half the time. They'd ask me something and I
> didn't know what in the world they were saying. Me and some other
> folks—black and white—decided to make them the end of any point of

our frustrations. We did some horrible things to these people. We didn't like them, and we just made sure that everybody else didn't like them, too. They were so different. And not until maybe three years later did I ever pay attention to them and treat them like human beings.

Angie Hines's memories of how she and her girlfriends, black and white, treated a southern black family are a perfect example, almost a parable, of how racism starts and runs its course. What bothered her was that "they were so different," nothing more, nothing less. And their sheer difference—different hair, different clothing, different food, different accent—was enough justification for Angie and her friends to set about making the family's life miserable. It wasn't enough for Angie and her friends to "not like" them; they had to make sure that everybody else joined in ostracizing the family as well.

In the end, the stories people tell of growing up at the Point are the most eloquent testimony to the values of the community. For Chris Aylward, a worn-out baseball was something to be cared for and mended and preserved as long as possible—because you had to have it to play. It is a small metaphor for how kids grew up in the world of Columbia Point. He recalls: "We'd all go down there to play baseball. When the cover got torn off the ball, someone would bring a roll of tape, and we'd tape the ball up. We'd hit until the tape came off, and then we'd tape it up again. That was our existence. We didn't have money to keep buying baseball after baseball, so we'd try to preserve it as long as it would go."

"You learned to survive and you learned to appreciate what you had," Chris reflects. "I wouldn't trade growing up at Columbia Point for anything. It gave me an understanding of what I am, and who I should be."

For another child of Columbia Point, the acres of asphalt surrounding the housing project provided an immense drawing board. Almost magically, chalk was offered up from the ocean, and the whole board was periodically washed clean by the rain:

We had so much black asphalt, blacktop, around there. In the summer, there was a lot of chalk available, I guess from the rocks or something. We always had chalk, and we would draw games on the asphalt to play, you know, like hopscotch. We had some very elaborate games; they were amazing. And if it didn't rain for a couple of weeks, the asphalt would be covered. We wouldn't be able to find a spot to draw a game. And this is acres of blacktop covered with chalk, with drawing and games and names. And then it would rain, and it would be like a clean slate, and you could start all over.

Transportation and Recreation

Chris Aylward's father worked in a foundry in Hingham, several miles south of Boston. The family didn't have a car, so his father hitched a ride with a fellow worker who lived north of Boston, in Medford, and who drove through Boston on his way to work. Each morning, Chris's father would walk a mile or so up to the Southeast Expressway and wait for his co-worker to pick him up.

Every Saturday morning, Chris's father would take his kids to the Lucky Strike bowling alley in Dorchester. The deal was, whoever among the nine kids got up early Saturday morning and was ready on time went. Most of the time, all of the kids took their father up on the offer. They would walk up to Columbia Station, pay the nickel fare to take the train to Fields Corner, and walk to the bowling alley.

8 Columbia Point in the Spotlight

I n the years immediately following its opening, Columbia Point was rarely mentioned in the Boston press. On October 21, 1956, the *Boston Globe* reported that a six-year-old boy nearly drowned at Columbia Point when he fell into an excavation ditch filled with ten feet of rainwater. Arthur Hanley and two young friends were playing when Arthur fell into a "ten-foot puddle." One of the boys ran to get his mother for help, and a dramatic rescue ensued:

> Mrs. Foley ran forward, lost her footing and fell headlong in the mud and water. The Hanley boy was about five feet away and only the back of his head and an arm showed above the surface. [A passerby] leaped out to where the boy was, and immediately sank. He touched one foot to the side near the bottom when he went down, and pushed himself up. On the way up, he caught the boy in his arms and managed to grip the earth at the side of the pool.

The boy was given artificial respiration and rushed to the hospital. The article concludes with the ironic comment, "The excavation, residents said, is part of a new playground development."

Columbia Point was quiet and uneventful, at least in the press, until April 25, 1962,

when another accident involving a child, this one tragic, finally forced the greater Boston audience to pay attention to the problems at the project. Mount Vernon Street, also known as the Mile Road, was not just the only road to the housing project; it was the only access to two dumps, one owned by the city and one private, just beyond the project. In spite of the city planning board's warning, almost ten years earlier, that dumping must be discontinued and the dumping area cleaned up before any residents moved into Columbia Point, in 1962 some five thousand people were living in the housing project and both dumps were still in full operation.

During the day, dump trucks were still barreling up and down Mount Vernon Street, making some 250 to 300 trips a day. Pat McCluskey's building was at the "far end" of the project, right next to the dump. "It was the most amazing thing," she recalls. "They would dump all during the day, and then at night they'd light it up where you would think that you were in the bowels of hell really. That

whole skyline was lit up. And you can imagine the fumes that came
off of there. I mean, you'd hang a wash out during the day—we
didn't have washers and dryers; we had to put our wash out in the
back courtyard—and it was almost worthless to put it out because it
would be covered with soot."

The dump trucks were not just a nuisance; they were also dan-
gerous. Sometimes the mothers took matters into their own hands.
"Right across the street was what they call a coffee shop," Pat Mc-
Cluskey explains.

Well, the truck drivers would come down, go into the dump, dump
what they had, turn around and come back, and park in front of our
building. One of the things they were told was not to park there anymore. But they would park in front of the building and leave the motor
running on these big trucks. Now imagine how awful that is.

One day I was sitting outside with the baby carriage and a couple of
the children. It was a little place that the mothers used to come and
meet and talk. And there's one of the trucks sitting out in front of our
building with the motor running. I was just teed off. So I had one of
the women watch the kids, and I said, "Look what I'm going to do."
And I went over, and I got up on the truck, and I leaned on the horn. I
put my elbow right on it. And it's blasting all over the place. The truck
driver came out of the coffee shop. "What's the problem?" he says. And
I said, "Get it out of here!"

However gutsy their ad hoc protests, and however earnest their
years of entreaties to City Hall, the residents of Columbia Point
were unable to bring about an end to the dumping. That would be
up to a six-year-old girl named Laura Ann Ewing.

Pat McCluskey remembers the morning of April 25, 1962, as clearly as if it were yesterday:

I always used to make sure that my oldest boys were going to some kind of summer camp. And this particular day I was on the bus with Steven and Kevin—Johnny couldn't go because he was asthmatic. And I was taking them on the bus into town to enroll them in Morgan Memorial Camp. We were on the bus, and the bus was going up the street. I saw this little girl on the other side of the street. It looked like she was going to try to cross. And I said to myself, "Oh, I hope she makes it across." Because all these big trucks were going down the length of the street. I turned to look. And as I turned to look, she darted out in front of a truck, and it ran right over her. And I just let out a yell. I saw the truck driver get out of the truck, and put his hands up in the air like he was in shock, you know? And the bus just kept going.

Laura Ann Ewing, one of seven children of Mrs. Ruth Ewing, who lived at 260 Mount Vernon Street, was killed by a city dump truck, the *Boston Globe* reported, "as she skipped across Mount Vernon Street on an errand for her mother Monday noon." One of the saddest and most infuriating things about the little girl's death was that it took no one by surprise. A group of Columbia Point mothers, Pat McCluskey among them, had been pleading with City Hall for years to get the dump closed. "The year before that we had gone in to the State House and begged them to please close that dump, because someone was going to get killed," Pat remembers. "If not one of the children, someone was going to get killed crossing that street because those trucks, they just come barreling down. They wouldn't care who was there. And of course they refused us because at that time all the urban renewal was going on in Boston. The West End was being torn down. And of course they would lose a lot of money if they had no place to dump all this stuff that they were bringing in. So almost a year to the day this little girl was killed."

The Columbia Point residents' reaction to the tragedy was swift and public. The mothers set up a picket line across Mount Vernon Street, bringing the dump trucks to a halt. And the following day, Columbia Point was in the news. A banner headline in the *Boston Globe* the day after the death of Laura Ewing reads, "Mothers Bully 10-Ton Trucks." The tag line reads, "Will March 'Until Doomsday.'" The "mothers," who up to this point had been loosely organized in a social way, were suddenly galvanized into public protest. What the Columbia Point mothers had endeavored to draw attention to through years of entreaties to City Hall was suddenly a media event. The same geography that had caused the accident—only one road

"Mrs. Ruth Ewing being escorted from a Cambridge funeral home following services for her daughter, Laura Ann, killed outside Columbia Point housing project by a city dump truck." 1962. *Courtesy of the* Boston Globe.

Mrs. Ruth Ewing (left) and Columbia Point mothers (above) picketing in front of the State House to have the two dumps adjacent to the project closed, 1962. Boston Herald.

Right: Pat McCluskey's notes, with names and phone numbers of newspapers and radio stations, from a meeting of Columbia Point residents to close the dumps, 1962. *Courtesy of Pat McCluskey.*

Above: Columbia Point mothers and attorney F. Lee Bailey pleading their case to close the dumps, 1962. Boston Herald.

Below: Meeting of the Columbia Point Improvement Association (CPIA) to continue efforts to close the dumps, 1962. Left to right: Joanne Ross, Keesler Montgomery (attorney for the CPIA), Anna McDonald, Ruth Morrison, Janet Burnham, Mildred Dickey, Joseph Deg, Marie Watson, Lois Rideout. Senate President John F. Powers is second from right. Boston Herald.

led to the dump, right through the project—now set up the showdown.

In the midst of their protests, the women received a call from the law offices of F. Lee Bailey, who offered to represent them in their efforts to close the dump. When Bailey met with the mothers' group, he had been practicing law for less than two years but had already made quite a name for himself. In November 1961, exactly a year and a day after he began practicing law, he defended Dr. Sam Sheppard in Cleveland in a high-profile murder case. In August 1962 he represented the suspect in the Great Plymouth Mail Robbery, a million-and-a-half dollar heist that was the talk of the town. Shortly thereafter, he was retained by Albert DiSalvo, known as the Boston Strangler.

When Bailey became aware of the publicity about the dump's effect on the Columbia Point community and realized that the people there couldn't afford to hire a lawyer to take the issue to court, he offered to represent the residents free of charge. "In my view," he explains, "it was a worthy cause and it shouldn't fail for lack of money." Bailey was well aware of Columbia Point, having to drive by it every morning on his commute up the Southeast Expressway into town. However, his first visit there was to line up witnesses in his case:

I met with the representative group they had formed to try to spearhead the attack on the dump to get it closed. What I was looking for was the specific harm that would support an injunctive action to try and close the dump down. The ingredients for injunctive relief, which requires irreparable harm and an ongoing harm—both, in many cases—were certainly present.

That is about as far as we got before the city decided to take some ameliorative steps to avoid the litigation. An editorial was published in the *Boston Traveler* commending the whole effort to stick up for these people, and I think that had an effect on the powers that be in the city. They decided this was a battle that they didn't want to wage because the newspaper was going to kill 'em. Very frankly, this was a political issue as well as a legal issue, and the sad part is, as is too often the case, that the government would rather sit around and do nothing rather than get its hands dirty and go down and clean up that dump.

Getting as powerful a paper as the *Traveler* was then on your side was very helpful, because you could expect that if you did get a hearing and evidence was taken, it was going to be very prominently re-

ported—and probably in a way that would not be at all flattering to whoever it was in the city of Boston that had to walk in and try and defend their actions. I'm sure that my willingness to help caught some attention, but there was no question but that the newspapers were who they were afraid of. The message in the editorial was, "You're going to hear from us again if this thing goes forward." They had definitely taken an editorial stand on it, and that was the coup, I think, that made the lawsuit unnecessary.

A legislative committee touring the Mile Road Dump at Columbia Point, 1962. Senate President John E. Powers is sixth from right. *Courtesy of the Boston Globe.*

While the mothers picketed day and night, the headlines rolled out day after day in the daily newspapers: "Mothers to Pause Today When They Bury Little Girl," "Mothers Halt March, City Vows New Relief," "Will Mothers' Wall Be Raised Again to Halt Columbia Point Dump Trucks," "Mothers Plan Parties as Dumps Are Closed," "Mothers Dash Out of Kitchens and Keep Closed Dump Closed." Some of the servicemen who came home reported that they even saw pictures of the story in the papers over in Germany.

Meeting of Columbia Point residents to close the dumps, 1962. Boston Herald.

For years, the mothers had learned the hard way that "you can't fight City Hall." Now, practically overnight, City Hall learned that "you can't fight three hundred mothers"—not when the media are telling their story. Bob Quinn, who was the state representative for the Dorchester district that included Columbia Point, had filed bills to close the dump for years. He was well aware of the nuisances of the dump—trucks roaring up and down Mount Vernon Street; disease-carrying rats; even his wife's complaints, when the wind blew in a certain direction,

"Mothers Bully 10-Ton Trucks"

"They shall not pass" was the slogan as angry housewives formed a human barrier to halt the progress of trucks through the Columbia Point housing project yesterday. And last night, bone-tired but still determined, they vowed to continue picketing "until doomsday if we have to" in their fight to close two dumps at the end of the sprawling project. . . .

All day yesterday and until long after dark, a steady stream of women marched back and forth across Mount Vernon St. at Monticello Avenue, near the entrance to the dumps.

They won a partial, and temporary, victory when Mayor Collins ordered city trucks to stop using Mount Vernon St. for the time being while a solution to the problem was sought.

Little children marched with their mothers. Scores of the women pushed baby carriages. As marchers dropped out of the picket line to attend to household chores, others took their places. There were more than 300 in the ranks most of the day.

They marched until 10 last night, and they vowed to be back on the job at 6:45 this morning. The dumps open at 7.

—*Boston Globe*, April 25, 1962

Above: Children join the protest against the city dumps, 1962. *UPI/Corbis-Bettmann.*

Right: Columbia Point residents block trucks rolling past the project to the city dumps, 1962. Boston Herald.

that fly ash was dirtying the clothes hanging on her line more than a mile away in Savin Hill. And he was aware of the city's countless broken promises to close the dump.

Year after year, Quinn had shepherded his legislation through the House only to see it killed in the Senate. "This happened maybe for half a dozen years," Quinn recalls. "And sadly one day doesn't a big dump truck come and a little six-year-old black kid gets killed." This time, Quinn persuaded his colleagues on the Committee on Cities to "take a view"—make an official visit—to inspect the conditions at the dump firsthand. Quinn remembers the outing clearly: "They're walking around the dump area, and the chairman says, 'Quinn, you told us there were a lot of rats out here.' And he didn't get the word out of his mouth before a huge rat ran between us. He screamed. Almost on cue, my rat came out. So of course, the committee voted to report the bill favorably and the dump was closed."

James W. Haley, Boston's public works commissioner at the time, explains that the city was reluctant to close the facility because it was where the city dumped the ash from its incinerator. Two trucks ran back and forth between the incinerator and the dump, twenty-four hours a day. Although it had turned a deaf ear on years of protest, the city was finally forced to come to grips with the dangers of dump trucks on the Mile Road in the wake of Laura Ann Ewing's death. Haley explains:

[The day after the little girl was killed,] we had a meeting with the mayor [Collins] and it took us about ten seconds to decide that the dump out here was no longer a feasibility. So we just put on two extra trucks and started hauling it out to West Roxbury, where we had a big dump by then. And that was the end of it really as far as problems went. Twenty-four hours after the accident the press room wanted to know where were we going to take the rubbish, and the best that they would get out of me was, "Elsewhere." I wasn't going to upset the people in West Roxbury by telling them we were going to haul it all over there instead of over here.

The death of Laura Ann Ewing under the wheels of a city dump truck marked a turning point in the history of Columbia Point. Before the tragedy, the Mothers Club had been an informal group of women who met socially, for potluck suppers, fashion shows, and Friday night bingo. The tragedy politicized the mothers and indeed the entire Columbia Point community: for the first time, the community came together in a public protest and demanded that the city pay attention. The mothers learned the power of the media.

"Mothers to Pause Today When They Bury Little Girl"

The human barrier at the Columbia Point Housing Project in Dorchester that has blocked dumping and trucks for two days will halt this afternoon—but only for a minute.

The moving circle of women and children will stop at 2 p.m., when the funeral starts for the six-year-old girl who was killed beneath the wheels of a city dump truck Monday.

After a moment of silence, the picketing will resume and will continue, according to a spokesman for the angry project residents, "until both dumps are closed for good."

—*Boston Globe,* April 26, 1962

"Getting their point across . . ." Boston Herald.

Senate bill to close the dump. *Courtesy of Pat McCluskey.*

SENATE . . . . No. 787

[By Mr. Powers, petition of John E. Powers and Robert H. Quinn for legislation to prohibit the dumping of refuse or trash in a certain section of the Dorchester district of the city of Boston. Cities.]

The Commonwealth of Massachusetts

In the Year One Thousand Nine Hundred and Sixty-Two

AN ACT PROHIBITING THE DUMPING OF REFUSE OR TRASH IN A CERTAIN SECTION OF THE DORCHESTER DISTRICT OF THE CITY OF BOSTON.

Be it enacted by the Senate and House of Representatives in General Court assembled, and by the authority of the same, as follows:

1 The city of Boston is hereby authorized and directed to pro-
2 hibit the dumping of trash or refuse on land located in the
3 Dorchester district in the area commonly called the Calf pas-
4 ture, Mile road and Columbia point, said land being east and
5 west of Mount Vernon street and east of Morrissey boulevard.

When they took to the street, the newspapers and television stations came out to listen. Anna McDonald, leader of the mothers' effort to close the dump, recalls her husband complaining during this period, "I never see you anymore. I have to turn on the television to see you."

And closing the dump was only the beginning. The protest turned the city's attention to Columbia Point and its mounting problems. In September 1962 the *Boston Globe* published a seven-part series on the project. Editorials proliferated in Boston's major newspapers. Politicians began pointing fingers at one another. Columbia Point had a voice, and suddenly the city was listening.

Closing the gates at the Columbia Point dump, 1963. *Courtesy of the Boston Globe.*

Part 2
Columbia Point, 1962–1978

9 "Island of Isolation"

Laura Ann Ewing's death focused media attention on Columbia Point as never before. In September 1962 the *Boston Globe* followed up on the incident with a seven-part series on Columbia Point by reporter Richard L. Hurt, based on his experience living at the project for two weeks. Four years earlier, the paper had moved its offices from "Newspaper Row" on Washington Street in downtown Boston to a new plant on Morrissey Boulevard opposite Boston College High School. The housing project was now the *Globe*'s neighbor; the mothers' protest and its aftermath could not be ignored.

Hurt's series brought readers into a setting that was as highly visible as it was isolated. Although thousands of commuters driving up the Southeast Expressway to Boston passed by Columbia Point every day and may have wondered what life was like on the inside, they had no reason to get any closer. It wasn't on the way to anywhere and, if anything, the new highway, which was completed in 1959, cut it off further, intensifying the project's isolation.

The first installment of Hurt's series, entitled "6000 Isolated on 'Island'—in Heart of Hub," introduces this remote neighbor to the city of Boston: "From afar, the Island of Isolation appears as a cluster of rusty, brick rockets

poised at the throat of Boston Harbor. You don't notice details. But you approach, and you see what its residents try to forget, but can't avoid." Hurt goes on to describe some physical deterioration—broken windows, litter, and vandalism—at the housing project before continuing: "But residents can never forget the death of a little girl, struck by a truck

that was en route to a nearby dump they had tried in vain to close. And nobody seems to care—on the 'mainland' of Boston." The keynote Hurt strikes is the one that would echo through the coming decade: isolation. Columbia Point's isolation is not just physical but social. The people who live on the "mainland" have at best a vague notion of where the project is ("That's down by that big dump, isn't it?") or who lives there (the derogatory generalization "project people").

Above: The *Boston Globe's* new plant under construction, 1957, looking east across Morrissey Boulevard toward B.C. High, Columbia Point, and Dorchester Bay. *Courtesy of the* Boston Globe.

Right: "Coming . . . the most modern newspaper plant in the United States." The newspaper couldn't ignore its new neighbor. *Courtesy of the* Boston Globe.

What Hurt discovers when he "moves in" with residents of fifteen hundred apartments at Columbia Point is a more complicated picture: neat apartments next to apartments trashed by vandals. People who keep the hallways clean and people who don't. People who keep their kids under control and people who don't. A large elderly population—mostly white, mostly female—located in sunny, carefully kept buildings at the far corner of the project. The truth is that well-kept buildings alternate with run-down ones, good floors with bad within the same building, good apartments with bad on the same floor. One thing is clear: generalizations about Columbia Point are dangerous. In 1962 it is, in fact, both a decent place to live and a disaster.

Among other surprises at the Point, Hurt finds an extraordinary degree of racial harmony. He describes two neighbors, one white

Columbia Point II

City of Shame? Ridiculous Says 3-Year Dweller

(Boston is at the dawn of an exciting era. New buildings and highways planned almost everywhere—and with families being moved to accommodate these changes, the question arises, where should they go?

(Public housing projects? If so, what kind? Should they be like the Columbia Point Project where 6110 families now live in high-rise apartments?

(Because Columbia Point was one of the first projects of its kind in the country and a milestone in public housing in New England, the Globe sought to determine the good and bad things about such a development and sent reporter Richard Hurt to live among the people there to find the answers.)

By RICHARD L. HURT

For a lot of people, Columbia Point Housing Project is home—a good home.

Somebody once termed the project the "City of Shame."

"Ridiculous," scoffs one mother who has lived in the development for more than three years.

"Any city is a City of Shame for those who live shameful lives."

There are many people at the Point who love it there. But there also are many people who live for the day they can move away.

Why do people enjoy living at Columbia Point? Why do others want to get out? Which are its good sides, which its bad?

HURT

PROJECT *Page Nine*

Racial Tension Disputed

There is wide disagreement on the condition of racial relations at the project. Chandler W. Sharp, director of the Columbia Point Center, says a problem exists between Negro and white tenants, as well as between Southern and Northern Negroes.

Mrs. Ledonia Wright, president of the Columbia Point Inter-Agency Council, comprising private and social agencies working at Columbia Point, maintains, however, that Negro-white relations at the project are generally good.

Edith Babke, director of Dorchester House, of which the center is a branch, points to certain clubs at the center as among "the best integrated I've ever seen."

The recent protest movement was a study in interracial harmony. When it was necessary for the mothers to attend a hearing at the State House on the closing of the dumps, Negro mothers babysat with white children and white mothers reciprocated.

The present population of 1504 families includes 209 Negro families, or 14 percent. The Boston Housing Authority says that the figure approximates the city-wide racial occupancy for public housing, which is 17 percent.

—from Richard Hurt's seven-part series in the *Boston Globe*, September 12, 1962

Help for Columbia Point

The recent series of *Globe* articles on the
Columbia Point Housing Project, by staff
reporter Richard L. Hurt, outlined a pressing
problem for Boston, of whose existence
much of the public had not been aware.
With the spotlight now on it, action should
follow.

Here is a $20-million project housing 6110
residents, built 10 years ago, and yet still
lacking many facilities. Perhaps not much can
be done now about the fact that it was poorly located and designed. But other problems
can be solved.

The Boston Housing Authority's sorting
out technique has been criticized and should
be remedied. The project needs a library, a
bar, and more stores. Social agencies need
more help from the public to permit them to
do more.

The city Park Department might do more
about the project's unused, $250,000
recreation area. The residents' community
feeling is growing; their recent campaign
against the nearby dumps was inspiring.
Perhaps it is time now, with increasing prospects of Federal aid for such a pilot program,
for Mayor Collins and Redevelopment
Administrator Logue to make further history
at Columbia Point, whose people belong to
Boston, too.

— *Boston Globe* editorial, September 21, 1962

and one black, who "baby-sit for each other, exchange recipes, shop
together and have morning coffee together":

> "Isn't that the way it should be in America?" asked the white woman
> when I noted that despite the difference in races they seemed to be
> true neighbors.
> "She's poor. She can't afford to be prejudiced," said the Negro
> woman, wryly, and the two burst into laughter.

Hurt asserts that the Boston Housing Authority has begun assign-
ing a disproportionate number of "problem families" to Columbia
Point. He maintains that, among Boston's twenty-five public housing projects housing some fifty thousand people, "there is a status
rating—undrawn, unofficial, but real nonetheless." Hurt contends
that there are good and bad projects, white and black projects—and
the discrepancy is growing by the day. As evidence, he points to Old
Harbor Village—later called Mary Ellen McCormack—in South
Boston, the city's oldest housing project, which was built in 1938.
Like Columbia Point, it stands on a former dump. Like Columbia
Point, it is large, with 1,016 units in thirty-five buildings. Unlike Columbia Point, it has fewer families on welfare; more "intact," or two-
parent, families; and no blacks. In 1962, by contrast, 50 percent of
the residents of Columbia Point are under twenty-one. Six hundred
families, or 40 percent, are on some form of public assistance—aid
to dependent children, old age assistance, or disability assistance
from the City of Boston Welfare Department. Two hundred and
nine families, or 14 percent, are black. The turnover rate is 20 percent per year, compared with a citywide average of 12 percent.

In the last installment of his series, Hurt walks through Columbia
Point with Ed Logue, the new administrator of the Boston Redevelopment Authority, discussing what can be done to improve the project. Logue's suggestions are similar to those the City Planning Board
made back in 1953. Close the private dump. Build stores and recreational facilities. Provide phone booths. Plant more trees and bushes
for a less "institutional" look. Change the "social atmosphere" by allowing fewer problem families in the project. Logue flatly declares
Columbia Point a mistake. "This project is poorly located, badly designed, and never should have been built," he observes. "But it was
built and is here, and what we have to figure out now is what can be
done about it." At the same time, he tosses out sensible and innovative suggestions: Why not set up a library or open a pub? Why not
convert some first-floor apartments into retail shops? What about

limiting the number of families on welfare at Columbia Point to 20 percent?

Columbia Point is, Hurt concludes, "at a critical junction in its short, controversial life. One of the dumps already is closed; the other's future is under litigation. The attitude of the project's residents is positive, and ready to be transformed into constructive action. Opportunity to help bring about a balanced community at Columbia Point has never been better."

A week later, a *Globe* editorial reinforces Hurt's conclusion, issuing a challenge to the mayor, the Boston Housing Authority, and the Boston Redevelopment Authority: "The Boston Housing Authority's sorting-out technique has been criticized and should be remedied. . . . Perhaps it is time now, with increasing prospects of federal aid . . . for Mayor Collins and Redevelopment Administrator Logue to make further history at Columbia Point, whose people belong to Boston, too."

Columbia Point, the 1962 *Globe* articles and editorial suggest, is a project that has lots of problems; but it is not yet a project that *is* a problem. Its problems are not insurmountable; in fact, the time is ripe for identifying and solving them. There is a clear opportunity to build a bridge from the "mainland" to the "island of isolation"—to connect Columbia Point, physically and socially, to the city of Boston and its myriad resources.

Headlines from
Boston Globe *reporter*
Richard L. Hurt's 1962
series on Columbia Point

September 9: "6000 Isolated on 'Island' in Heart of Hub"

September 10: "City of Shame? Ridiculous Says 3-year Dweller"

September 11: "Neat Apartments Co-Exist with Others Hit by Vandals"

September 12: "Does Unwritten Law Segregate Families?"

September 13: "$250,000 Area Unused as Kids Play in Street"

September 14: "1951 Prospects of Bright Future Mostly Unfulfilled"

September 16: "Big Project Can Become Garden Spot — Here's How"

Ed Logue, Boston Redevelopment Authority administrator. *Courtesy of the* Boston Globe.

10 The Downhill Slide

The story of Columbia Point in the late 1960s and 1970s is a depressing one: a once-proud community disintegrating, torn by racial strife, drugs, crime, and neglect. An increasingly fearful community, where people retreat behind locked doors. Finally, a hopeless community, abandoned, defensive, and ultimately self-destructive. The project's decline is a story filled with frustration and failure that no one is eager or proud to tell. It's a story that the press outlined, sometimes with lurid detail. But perhaps it's best explained by the people who lived there: how they saw their community change, when, and why—and what it meant to them to see it change.

Sandy Young, a black woman who was one of the early leaders of the community, lived at Columbia Point from 1955 to 1971. In the early days of the project,

Young explains, being able to admit and identify your needs was a strength—the first step to getting them met: "Because we didn't have many, many things, we came together and developed the Columbia Point Community Development Council. . . . We came together out of sheer need. We were able to sit down and discuss exactly what it was we wanted. . . . We appreciated the fact that every six months somebody did come in and check your housekeeping."

In the 1950s public housing at Columbia Point worked, physically and socially. The residents had high expectations of management, of themselves, and of their neighbors. "We demanded cleanliness of the buildings and of each other," Sandy Young proudly recalls. Early Columbia Point residents have consistent memories of their clean, well-kept community: "If an elevator broke down, someone would be there to fix it in twenty minutes." "You couldn't find grass in the cracks in the sidewalk." "Mr. Steele used to drive around the whole project before leaving every day."

In the early days, tenants knew that if they didn't abide by the rules, the housing authority could evict them. But chance and policy combined to disrupt the cooperation between tenants and management. John Steele, the strict, hard-driving manager,

Erline Shearer, Tony
Peabody (wife of Governor
Endicott "Chub" Pea-
body), and Sandy Young at
a meeting of the Mothers
Club, Columbia Point.
Peabody was governor
from 1962 to 1964.
Courtesy of Erline Shearer.

died of a heart attack in 1960 and was succeeded by Leo J. Donovan,
"a good man," according to a BHA employee, "who walked into a
situation which soon would begin to deteriorate." According to
Sandy Young, things began to go downhill when the BHA abrogated
the authority of its on-site managers, "when they no longer could
tell me to pick up a piece of paper off the floor, or else I would be
moved out."

Now when a tenant picked up the phone and called maintenance
for something to be fixed, it would take weeks or months before
anything was done. Cooperation changed to antagonism. When

Below, left: "Mrs. Sandy
Young points to a hole
between asphalt and
concrete foundation of
building where rats enter
project apartments."
Columbia Point, 1969.
Boston Herald.

Below, right: "Mrs. Theo-
dore Sprissler, Columbia
Point resident and mother
of seven, points to wall
leak she claims has gone
untended for 10 years,"
1969. Boston Herald.

Soldiers in the War on Poverty

Lyndon Johnson declared "War on Poverty" on November 24, 1963, two days after the assassination of John F. Kennedy. The one-billion-dollar program was meant to be a comprehensive assault on poverty in America, not by putting more people on welfare, but by expanding opportunities for the poor through education and job training—giving the poor a "hand up" rather than a "handout."

One of the hallmarks of the War on Poverty was community involvement; the federal government required "maximum feasible participation" by the poor in designing and administering all federally funded programs. Action for Boston Community Development (ABCD), the local battalion enlisted to wage the war at Columbia Point, recommended coordinated health, welfare, and social services through the Columbia Point Community Development Council. Some of the programs established did mitigate conditions for some residents at the housing project.

But Columbia Point in the 1960s was also the sometimes reluctant host of a succession of well-meaning people who came into the community to study what was wrong and propose solutions. Sandy Young offers an interesting perspective on the War on Poverty—that of one of the "poor people" the war's soldiers were sent to rescue:

> I'll never forget the three gentlemen who came in from Washington, D.C. They had made prior arrangements to meet with the community development council and they came in to talk about how they were going to save the world. It was interesting: there was a black gentleman and two white men.
>
> First and foremost, they were very surprised to see the makeup of the council. We were all colors, all nationalities. That was their first shock. The second shock was the fact that we were an organized group of people. We didn't hold masters degrees; we were just a group of people who were involved out of concern.
>
> But they started to tell us how we were poor people, and we didn't understand what in the world they were talking about. Because as far as I knew, my kids ate every day. They had shoes on their feet. They were bathed. They were being educated. I loved them.

Sandy Young remembers one woman in particular who was sent to Columbia Point "to teach us how to live, how to shop." "You know," she says, "when you stop and think of it, the insult":

> By the time we finished with this poor soul, she left, because she was taking us to Filene's and teaching us how to buy curtains. Now, none of us shopped upstairs in Filene's. We went to Filene's Basement because we knew that anything that was upstairs over thirty days was coming down.
>
> The next thing she decided to do was to come into one of our apartments and tell us how to move our furniture around. Well, I decided to have her come into my apartment. Now, the couch I had was one of these huge Simmons hide-a-beds. The structure in that couch was you just didn't move that couch, you know. It could not fit in front of the windows; it couldn't fit on the second wall; it had to remain on the one wall that was the large wall, because of the size of it.
>
> . . . And there she stood in my living room. She was, number one, shocked by its cleanliness. She was, number two, shocked by its warmth and beauty and coordination.
>
> This poor soul had a doctorate and she was with us for about three weeks, and when she got ready to leave she said, "Somewhere along the way, somebody told me a big fat lie about how you people are supposed to be, what you are supposed to think, and how you are supposed to do."

Young may have been able to muster some sympathy for the young Ph.D. who finally recognized the "big fat lie" she had been told. But she had no such kind feelings for the psychiatrist who was interested in studying the "disadvantaged" women of Columbia Point:

> I can remember when the health center came in—I will never forget this—this psychiatrist decided he wanted to meet with all us women because we lived in this community, you know, and we must really have problems. And there was about fifty of us that he sat around in a group with . . . and he asked the question, "Now, in the evening, after you have had this hard day's work with these kids and living in this isolation, how do you relax?"
>
> And I just looked at him and I said, "You know what I do? I purchase Avon products, and there is a specific brand of a bubble bath powder, and I take and fill up my tub full of hot water, put this powder in there, and watch the bubbles just dance to the top, and then I sit into the bathtub and float

amongst the bubbles. That is how I relax. How dare you come into this community and insult us this way?" And he left.

Little did the doctor know he was surrounded by fifty savvy, resourceful women who saw right through him—and didn't hesitate to tell him so.

Erline Shearer recalls with some amusement her interview with what must surely have been the same psychiatrist, unless this brand of arrogance is characteristic of the field:

When the health clinic first opened at Columbia Point, one of the ways that the doctors approached setting up a community program was to try to determine what the needs of the people were, in terms of counseling and so forth. So they interviewed several individuals and families in the project.

When it was my turn, I guess they had done a little research, because they knew something about me. After I told him how I felt about living in the project, the doctor told me he was really kind of surprised and a little disappointed because he thought I would be more helpful.

I couldn't understand what he meant. He said, "Because you're not depressed." And I said, "No, I'm not depressed." I told him I knew I wasn't unhappy, but I didn't go around thinking, "Am I happy?" And therefore I concluded that everything must be okay.

I said, "I can tell you some things that give me pleasure. For instance, I can finally do the *New York Times* crossword puzzle in ink." And he said, "And that makes you happy?" And I said, "Well, it gives me a sense of accomplishment, yes."

So then he listed five reasons why I should not be happy: I was a single mother, I was black, I was living in Columbia Point, I was on welfare, and I can't remember the last thing. I told him that I was sorry to disappoint him.

They had a picture of what a "project person" was—what this profile was supposed to be. If you didn't fit the profile, they really in a sense were almost angry. Because then what were they going to do? Everything had been built on the profile. So we had a running joke among the mothers. One of us would ask another, "Are you depressed?" And she'd answer, "No, I'm not depressed. Are you?"

"Broken windows in this hallway door (note printed slogans on ceiling) are one of the many complaints of residents of Columbia Point." Dorothy Haskins (left), Sandy Young (right), 1969. Boston Herald.

management stopped fixing things, tenants stopped keeping the place clean. Instead, each began to point the finger at the other for the project's decline, and neither did their share. Sandy Young feels that the tenants often blamed the housing authority for their own failure to take care of their community: "One of the things that we didn't stop to realize in our attacks was that it wasn't the BHA who was dumping the trash in the hallways, it wasn't the BHA who was opening the windows and dumping trash in the yards. It was the tenants. We were blaming the BHA because they didn't clean it up . . . when, in all sincerity, it should have been the tenants cleaning it up because they were the ones that were throwing out the trash."

In the early days, the manager's job wasn't limited to fixing broken windows and leaky faucets. The manager was, in a sense, the "mayor" of a six-thousand-person town, working in close relationship with both the community and the police to mediate disputes and solve problems. Although Columbia Point tenants differ on exactly when things changed — or why — many saw the dilution of the project manager's authority as a turning point for the community. Sandy Young observes: "Somewhere along the way, somebody from

Below, left: "Mrs. Theresa Chatman shows damage to bedroom door in her Columbia Point apartment," 1969. Boston Herald.

Below, right: "Dour look of Mrs. Frances de Jesus is reflected in bathroom mirror as she studies gaping hole where plaster has fallen in her $90 a month apartment in the Columbia Point housing development," 1968. Boston Herald.

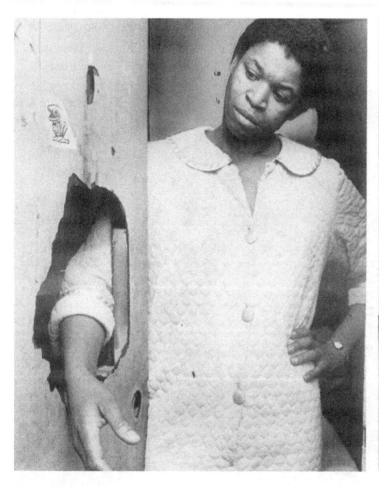

downtown said to the manager at Columbia Point, 'You no longer can go in and review a person's housekeeping, tell a person that they can be evicted, demand that they clean the hallways'—all of these rights were taken away from management. And when that happened, you started to see trash in the halls and the busted windows and the doors hanging off the hinges."

Without a manager willing to mediate problems, one resident explains, they all felt powerless: "You'd go to [the manager] and say, 'Look, there's a family here that we need to really sit down and talk about.' But now he says, 'I really can't do anything with that family.' So it's left to the tenants, and you don't want to harass your neighbor about some things; you want to be good to your neighbors. So you try to talk to them. But you have no backup. So you begin to get hollered at and screamed at."

In the 1960s, while the BHA manager was being "disempowered," tenant advocates were exhorting tenants to become "empowered." The BHA's rules and guidelines came to be seen by some as an invasion of privacy, an infringement of tenants' rights. Some tenants charged that the rules requiring them to do various chores—for example, cleaning the hallways—were unfair and demeaning. Outside tenant advocates challenged the BHA: What gave the housing authority the right to tell tenants they had to scrub the hallways? No other landlord could require tenants to do menial chores. Were these tenants second-class citizens just because they lived in public housing?

Sandy Young describes what happened to the project when tenants refused to comply with the BHA's rules under the rubric of "tenants' rights":

All of a sudden, it is an infringement upon your right for this, an infringement upon your right for that. What right does somebody from management have to come into your house and tell you your house is dirty? We *appreciated* the fact that the management could go around and tell you your house was dirty, okay? Because we were concerned about our community. We wanted our community to be clean, to be nice, and to be a family place for kids and for ourselves.

Can you imagine the BHA today saying to you, "If you want an apartment, first I have to look at your other housekeeping"? Why, that would be "an infringement on your rights."

In Sandy Young's view, even if some tenants felt the BHA's rules were strict and their enforcement autocratic, they were the key to the viability of the community. Once the rules were no longer obeyed, she recalls, she witnessed "the birth of a ghetto." She explains: "I remember one time a woman moved in on the first floor, Fanny moved in with her chickens and her goats. Until she realized that you couldn't live that way here. I remember how hard it was to try to keep the elevator clean. You know? Because other folks moved out. There was an exodus of people moving because the rules and regulations were gone." All of the checks on tenants—both on their "housekeeping" where they had lived before moving into public housing, and every six months after they moved into Columbia Point—stopped. In the new era of "tenants' rights," the BHA could no longer check on apartments, could no longer require tenants to clean the hallways or pick up their trash.

Roger Taylor, a leader at Columbia Point in the 1970s, recalls a similar transformation. Taylor, who moved into the project in 1963 with his wife and five children, remembers it as "a beautiful place":

Each building had its own little benches where you could sit out and get fresh air, and little flower gardens all around the building. Not only was it beautiful, it was quiet. We had nice elevators in the building. It was kept clean. At that time we had a manager out there, they had certain days to clean that hallway. And if you didn't do it, they would call you in the office. The man would be sometimes eleven or twelve at night, he would be out there seeing that you did what you were supposed to do. . . . Everybody just got along fine. Most families just kept to themselves.

Taylor's recollection of how and why things began to change is similar to Sandy Young's. One tenant group, he explains, felt that BHA rules requiring tenants to do various chores were unfair and demeaning: "A lot of them didn't like management coming around all the time, day and night, and they didn't think the tenants should be cleaning the hallways and the elevators. I disagreed with that because if you live in a building it's as much your responsibility to help keep up that building as it is the landlord's." Taylor describes what happened once the tenants refused to clean: "Well, nothing good came of it, because then the tenants began to think, 'I don't have to do this. Let management do it.' They would let the kids go in the little rose garden and dig it up and make mud pies and whatever. Then they began to tear up the benches that you would sit on outside. And from there it just started going downhill."

Ironically, even though refusing to clean the hallways was defined as "empowerment," tenants had much less control over the project

Renovation to prepare for
the Columbia Point
Health Center, the first
community health center
in the country, 1965.
Courtesy of the Boston
Globe.

once they stopped cleaning. Once they turned that responsibility over to the housing authority, the condition of the hallways was dependent upon the BHA. "The housing authority didn't put that mess down here," Taylor argues, "so why do you want them to pick it up? You live here, you pick it up. . . . Housing didn't live there. They'd go home at five o'clock."

In addition to poor management, residents of Columbia Point cite another change that had a profound effect on their community: tenant selection. Erline Shearer traces the deterioration of the community in the early 1960s to two root causes. The housing authority relaxed the screening process for selecting tenants. At the same time, they relaxed the rules for not only the physical but also the social maintenance of the community:

The changes that I saw I think really resulted from a change in the application and selection process. And it became a very sensitive thing. Because certainly most of the people who were moved in as a result of

The Columbia Point Health Center: The First Community Health Center in the Country

When the Columbia Point Health Center opened in December 1965, it became the first community health center in the nation. Born of the civil rights movement and the War on Poverty, the center marked a dramatic, if not radical, change in the delivery of health care services to low-income Americans. At the time, Columbia Point residents had to take at least three buses to get to Boston City Hospital for medical care; the new center would provide services to them in their own community.

Founded by two idealistic young doctors, Jack Geiger and Count Gibson, the health center opened on Mount Vernon Street in four renovated apartments in the public housing project. Geiger, who was on the faculty of Harvard University's School of Public Health, and Gibson, who was a professor at Tufts University Medical School, first met in 1964 in Mississippi, where they were members of the Medical Committee for Human Rights, a national organization that helped provide medical attention for civil rights workers. Geiger, who had worked as a medical student in South Africa, where community health centers originally developed, realized during his tenure in the South that this model could be modified and adapted in the United States in both rural and urban areas.

Geiger and Gibson approached the federal Office of Economic Opportunity to ask for a $30,000 grant for a yearlong feasibility study for two centers, one at Columbia Point and the other in Mississippi. "It became clear to me that if Tufts University Medical School was going to do a project fifteen hundred miles away, not only could we expect screams from the white power structure in Mississippi, but screams from Boston, asking why weren't we taking care of problems on our doorstep," Geiger, now a physician in New York, recalls. "Tufts had previously been involved with Columbia Point with some home medical care services, so we knew something of that community. And we were perfectly aware that Columbia Point was in the congressional district of the then Speaker of the House, John McCormack."

Much to Geiger and Gibson's surprise, the OEO offered full funding, provided that the health centers were up and running in less than a year. The Columbia Point Health Center opened exactly six months after the grant was approved and, soon enough, patients were streaming through the doors. According to Geiger, easy access to comprehensive primary medical care dramatically reduced the number of hospitalizations among the housing project's population. Despite some residents' misgivings about the preconceived notions and condescending attitudes some health care workers, particularly the psychiatrists, brought to the center, the general health at Columbia Point made steady gains.

The community health center idea caught on, and within a year other facilities were proposed and developed in Chicago, the South Bronx, Los Angeles, and Denver. The model has been replicated nationwide with varying degrees of success. Renamed the Geiger-Gibson Health Center on ts twenty-fifth anniversary in 1990, Columbia Point's first-in-the-nation is still providing a full range of medical and dental services and day care to a broader community in Dorchester and South Boston.

Not surprisingly, the original driving philosophy behind the health center still resonates today for Americans seeking medical care, no matter what their income level. According to Jack Geiger, the theme was simple and straightforward: involve the patients in their own care and achieve a better outcome. He explains: "What was needed in these low-income, poverty-stricken, high-illness communities was not just people to be passive recipients of medical care, but to be active participants in shaping and framing of programs to address their own needs, with a lot of emphasis on health education, environmental change, and behavioral change."

having to relocate when the housing shortage became so crucial had to have a place to live, too. We understood that. But we didn't see why you had to relax the rules.

When we were first moved in, they were very, very strict. And I can understand it. Like hanging things out the window. You couldn't hang your clothes out the window. I remember a neighbor was making a bed, and she put the pillows and the bedspread on the window while she was making up the bed. She got a knock on the door telling her to get the bedding off the window. It was very, very strict. They didn't come after you; but they let you know they would not accept that kind of behavior.

How and why did the housing authority relax the rules? "I would like to think it was sympathy and not apathy," Shearer comments. "People were allowed to stay when their rent got behind, or if the children became unruly or bothersome to other people. There was no sort of correction, or any attempt to rectify it; it was just allowed to go on. And it did. It bothered people because you'd say, 'Well, gee whiz, you know, I'm trying to keep my apartment looking nice. I'm sweeping the halls.'" As problems multiplied, Shearer recalls, the sense of community began to deteriorate: "Trash started piling up, or the street would be dirty, or around the building it would be dirty. It became more and more difficult to get people together to do things. People became more and more—I wouldn't say withdrawn, but not outgoing like they used to be."

Pat McCluskey saw a pervasive neglect—in the physical maintenance of the project, in screening applicants, in following up on tips about "troublemakers." All of the things that had been carefully attended to in the early days were neglected, and there seemed to be no one to complain to or to work with to solve the accumulating problems:

In the elevator buildings an elevator could be out of commission for a couple of days at a time, and nobody checked up on it. You know, and you're living on the fifth floor. You had to go up and downstairs with groceries and carriages.

Columbia Point Health Center, Dental Division, 1970. "The Manning family leaves the clinic after receiving dental care." Boston Herald.

Management would take our complaints and say that they would work on it, but they never really did that much. I think it was a situation where they knew that we were living there, and if we didn't like it we could get out. But if you try and improve it, don't look to them for help.

You could talk to management about people that were troublemakers and it would just go right over their heads. It was almost as if they were saying, "Well, they're troublemakers, and you're going to have to put up with it." And that's why a lot of people moved, because they figured, "Well, they don't care about us. All they want is their rent. And they don't care who the troublemakers are."

All of Columbia Point was painted with the same brush. And I guess they figured, "Well, one more troublemaker isn't going to make any difference." They didn't care that the good families moved out.

As the 1960s wore on, many of the most active residents of Columbia Point describe their feeling of burnout: too many years of working hard to improve the community, combined with a growing sense that "no one cares." In addition, there was the reality that their families were getting older, their children were growing up. Erline Shearer, Pat McCluskey, and a generation of mothers had moved into the brand-new project in the 1950s with brand-new families. They brought their babies with them in strollers to the Mothers Club for coffee each morning. By the 1960s, those babies were entering high school.

At the same time, the War on Poverty was making new education grants available, giving many of the women the opportunity to take courses. Some who had only a high school education took advantage of the new opportunity to pursue higher education. Others, building on their experience organizing the Columbia Point community, moved on to paying jobs in social services and community organizations. They had no more time for morning coffee in "the mini," for volunteering hundreds of hours to improving the community. The days of the Mothers Club were gone forever.

More and more, the families who had the resources to move out did—leaving the needier, less resourceful families behind. Ironically, as Columbia Point's problems became more and more serious, many of the very families that were the most capable of solving those problems felt unheard, overworked, and finally driven out. As Pat McCluskey ruefully concludes, "They just wear you down, you know?"

11 Housing of Last Resort

Although the tenants at Columbia Point were unaware of the inner workings of the Boston Housing Authority, much less of changes in public housing policy at the federal level, they could easily identify what caused their community to change for the worse, based on the evidence they saw all around them. Simply put, the community worked when the project was well managed and maintained, when tenants were carefully screened and selected, and when there were clear rules that were consistently enforced. When suddenly maintenance was virtually nonexistent, tenants were no longer screened, and the rules were no longer enforced, the project began to deteriorate, physically and socially.

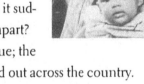

Why, when the Columbia Point community functioned so well in the 1950s, did it begin to go downhill in the 1960s and become a disaster by the end of the 1970s? Why, when the Boston Housing Authority had been doing a good job, did it suddenly stop doing that job and let a good community fall apart?

In fact, what happened at Columbia Point was not unique; the project was just one stage for a tragedy that was being acted out across the country. By the late 1960s public housing in the United States was in deep trouble.

PUBLIC HOUSING AT THE FEDERAL LEVEL

Although the public housing program was originally created to provide temporary shelter for working-class families, it increasingly became a program providing permanent housing of last resort for the hard-core poor. The mostly working-class families who moved into Columbia Point in the 1950s moved out as they got bet-

ter jobs, became financially more stable, and saw conditions worsening at the project. The new applicants for public housing who replaced them included a greater percentage of black families migrating to Boston from the South, people displaced by urban renewal in Roxbury and the South End, and later, Hispanic families. A greater proportion of these families had very low incomes or were on public assistance, and many of them had multiple problems.

By the 1960s it was becoming apparent in projects across the country that the method of financing public housing was problematic. A disproportionate amount of federal housing subsidies went to private housing. In 1962, for example, the government spent $820 million to subsidize low-income housing and $29 billion—thirty-five times as much—to subsidize middle-class housing with homeowners' tax deductions. Under the original terms of the public housing program, the federal government paid for the construction of public housing, but the local housing authorities were responsible for covering operating costs with the revenues they collected in rent.

In the 1960s housing authorities found themselves caught in a squeeze: by then, many of the buildings were almost twenty years old and were in need of costly major repairs. Inflation exacerbated the problem. And while operating costs were increasing, revenues were decreasing. The Brooke Amendment, sponsored by Senator Edward Brooke of Massachusetts and passed in 1969, was designed to protect tenants from rent increases by capping public housing rents at 25 percent of the tenant's income. The Brooke Amendment had the effect of reducing revenues coming into already-strapped housing authorities across the country.

Demolition of three buildings in the Pruitt-Igoe public housing project, St. Louis, Missouri, April 21, 1972. The remaining thirty buildings were razed four years later. *UPI/Corbis-Bettmann.*

The Public Housing Administration tried to make up for this shortfall with operating subsidies. From the perspective of the federal budget, however, the Brooke Amendment didn't save money; it just shifted it. The U.S. Department of Health, Education and Welfare saved money because rents were lower under the Brooke Amendment and welfare payments could be reduced. But the PHA had to spend more, providing operating subsidies to housing authorities whose reduced rents no longer covered basic operating costs.

Although the Brooke Amendment may have been a financial wash in terms of the federal budget, it tied the hands of housing authorities: they could no longer raise the money that they needed to operate and maintain their properties through rents. In the private market, a landlord who needs more money to maintain a property raises the rent. Public housing authorities, unable to do so, cut corners on maintenance instead. Projects quickly fell into disrepair as important capital improvements were deferred and problems worsened.

By the early 1970s public housing was in a state of crisis. In November 1971 the St. Louis Housing Authority voted to close its projects because it had no money to run them. The next year, it dynamited its most notorious project, Pruitt-Igoe, and photos of the imploding building appeared in newspapers across the country. Pruitt-Igoe immediately became a symbol of the failure of public housing.

In 1973 things went from bad to worse when President Richard Nixon's moratorium on all federally subsidized housing programs exacerbated the problem. By the early 1970s the promising program of the 1950s had become a nightmare.

PUBLIC HOUSING IN BOSTON

By the late 1960s Boston exhibited all of the local symptoms of the troubled federal public housing program. All of Boston's public housing projects were beginning to show signs of wear, both in the physical maintenance of the projects and the concentration of social problems.

While national housing policy was changing, the makeup of the population of Boston was changing, too. Before World War II Boston's minority population was very small—less than 10 percent of a total population of about one million. Moreover, many of the minority families in the city were middle class. After World War

Lucy Rivera with her daughter, Deborah, at 40 Tobin Court, Mission Hill housing project, 1970. *Courtesy of the* Boston Globe.

The Assassination of Martin Luther King Jr.: Two Perspectives

Kevin McCluskey was fourteen years old and a student at Boston Latin School when Martin Luther King Jr. was assassinated in Memphis on April 4, 1968. He and his family had moved out of Columbia Point just five days earlier and were still settling into their new house in Dorchester's Codman Square. He recalls that the situation in Boston remained relatively quiet in comparison with other American cities, where anger and grief triggered rioting and looting in many urban neighborhoods. There were problems in the city, but they were isolated. One major disturbance took place in Dorchester's Grove Hall, where a band of 250 youths grew to a mob of 800 that stormed the Jeremiah E. Burke High School on Washington Street and burned two flags.

McCluskey explains:

The assassination hit everyone pretty hard obviously, but not a great deal of unrest flowed from it. There were problems in Grove Hall, and we were aware of them. But our new neighborhood in Codman Square was like our old neighborhood at Columbia Point in that it was integrated as well. There weren't any problems in particular in Codman Square and there wasn't any significant trouble at Columbia Point either. . . . Then again, you only had a couple of stores down at the end of Mount Vernon Street, so what are you going to do? Start smashing windows of the store that provides you with milk and bread? . . . I was traveling around the city going to Latin School with my brother, and in the significant contact that I had with African American friends, teammates, and schoolmates, I don't remember whites being held accountable for Dr. King's murder. As far as playing it out in terms of individual confrontations between black and white youngsters, I don't think that's how people dealt with that tragic event.

Deb Shearer, whose family had been living at Columbia Point since 1956, was also fourteen years old when King was assassinated. She was a student at the Jeremiah E. Burke High School, near Grove Hall:

It was the afternoon and my next-door neighbor came by and said Martin Luther King got shot, so I know I was in the house when I heard. At that age I wasn't involved in civil rights things. The project was the project. Basically my friends and I—well, we weren't too young—but we weren't involved enough. I knew a little more maybe because my older sister was involved in civil rights. . . . I remember there were riots in Grove Hall. At Columbia Point things pretty much just went on as usual. Things weren't blown up. Things weren't chaotic. My best friend happened to be white, and after [King] died, her mother took her out of the Burke and put her in South Boston High. So that had a big personal impact on me. South Boston High was totally white. Dorchester High was integrated and the Burke at the time probably had more blacks than whites, and it was an all-girls' school. After the trouble in Grove Hall, her mother must have thought she would be a little safer at Southie, but my girlfriend hated it. Nobody wanted to go to Southie High. They didn't like us, black or white, because of Columbia Point. . . . But [at the Point] we all got along because we were living there and you either get along or you don't, and if you don't, you're in trouble.

Bromley Heath housing project, 1970. *Courtesy of the* Boston Globe.

Mary Ellen McCormack housing project, South Boston. *Courtesy of the* Boston Globe.

Bromley Heath, doorway at 640 Parker Street, 1971. *Courtesy of the* Boston Globe.

II, however, revolutions in technology and agriculture precipitated the largest migration of black families from the South to the North in the history of the country. Because this migration occurred between the censuses of 1950 and 1960, the city realized its magnitude only belatedly.

Within a matter of years, the predominantly white Mission, Bromley Heath, and Columbia Point housing projects became predominantly black—a phenomenon referred to as "tipping." Once a project had "tipped," its problems accelerated rapidly. By the end of the 1960s several projects in Boston were mostly black—Lenox Street, Mission Hill Extension, Annunciation, Bromley Heath, and Columbia Point. These projects also had the highest number of vacancies and the highest turnover rate. The projects that were mostly

Protest at Bromley Heath
housing project, 1969.
Courtesy of the Boston
Globe.

white—Mary Ellen McCormack, Old Colony, and Charlestown—typically had few vacancies and very little turnover. It was also common for certain areas of a large project to become segregated, as the BHA assigned white families to the "better" buildings and certain areas of a project tipped black.

Over the years, the Boston Housing Authority had become a highly political agency. The selection of sites and architects, the awarding of contracts—all of these regularly involved political favors. The political nature of the BHA was not unusual among housing authorities. The public housing program was deliberately designed to decentralize the administration of the program. Because local housing authorities decided where to build and how to assign applicants, they were naturally susceptible to local political pressures. The assignment of tenants was also highly political—in fact, it was considered one of major "perks" of membership on the board of the BHA. Ed Logue, who as head of the BRA was the only person with the legal authority to assign people who had been displaced by urban renewal to public housing, provides an insider's view on the politics of tenant assignment at the Boston Housing Authority:

There was a legal requirement that the housing authority was supposed to give priority to people displaced by the urban renewal program. . . . I would call up Ed Hassan, who was [mayor] John Collins's chairman of the housing authority, and I would complain. I said, "You're not giving me my fair share."

And he said—and I'll never forget it—"I have a list of the last four hundred people we filled. We gave a hundred and fifty to John McCormack." [McCormack was Speaker of the U.S. House of Representatives.] "We gave a hundred to John Powers." [Powers was the president of the Massachusetts State Senate.] Then he listed some other pals of John Collins. And then he listed me. I was last on the list.

Eventually, maintenance too became weighted down in the bureaucracy of the BHA and the unions. "If you needed a toilet to be put in," Elaine Werby, a former BHA employee, explains, "you had to get a licensed plumber. They didn't have enough licensed plumbers, so you had to wait. The tenants would get angry—and rightfully so."

In 1963 Ed Logue prevailed upon Mayor Collins to use his influence to have Ellis Ash, a respected figure in public housing, appointed chair of the Boston Housing Authority. The BHA board members, although not particularly supportive of Ash's efforts to im-

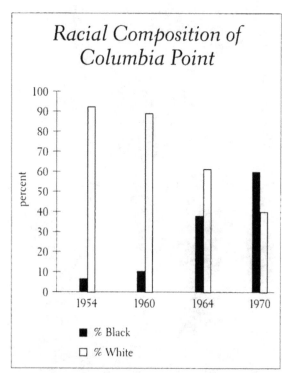

*Racial Composition of
Columbia Point*

% Black
% White

Tenant Leadership Transformed

Even as Columbia Point deteriorated and some of the earliest residents moved out, the next generation of tenant leaders emerged, new residents who were unwilling to give in, give up, and accept the conventional wisdom that nothing could be done to stem the tide. They worked at the community health center, worked with social service providers, and worked together to convince the Boston Housing Authority to do its job managing and maintaining the housing project.

The commitment of the Mothers Club was reincarnated in a succession of new organizations, including the Columbia Point Improvement Association and the Columbia Point Community Council. By the late 1960s Columbia Point residents, like public housing residents around the country, formed a tenants' task force, a representative body with formal elections, officers, and regularly scheduled meetings. When the Mothers Club went downtown in the late 1950s to meet with Mayor John Collins at City Hall, its members wore hats and gloves. When its successor organization set out ten years later to fight for Columbia Point, it did so in the more assertive style of that decade's political activists.

According to former resident and energetic task force leader Roger Taylor, rodents became an increasing problem for residents as conditions worsened in the project. Piecemeal extermination did little to solve the problem because it forced the mice from one building to the next and rats back to their nests near the waterfront. From the tenants' perspective, Boston Housing Authority management was ignoring resident complaints. Just before Christmas in 1969, the task force decided to take the issue before the housing authority board. Taylor explains:

I had my kids go down and gather up mice and rats and bugs. I went out and cut me a little Christmas tree. I think about it now and I tell you, it was terrible. I tied all of those rodents on this Christmas tree and I put a cloth over the top of it so they [the Boston Housing Authority board members] couldn't see what it was. So at first they wouldn't let us in for the meeting, so we demanded to go in there anyway.

So we go in and we're all standing around the wall and around the table and we were saying to them what we wanted. We wanted extermination, wanted to get rid of those rats, those big water bugs, and all that. And they were just going around the issue. I'm still standing there holding the tree. I got tired of it. I said, "Well, I'll tell you what, if *we* have to live out there with these rodents and big water bugs and things, *you* can live with them, too." And I took the cloth off and put it down in the middle of the table. And they were backing up. But it got the job done. You won't come to it; I'll take it to you. They exterminated all around the waterfront.

Mount Vernon Street led to Columbia Point, 1973. *Courtesy of the* Boston Globe.

prove the BHA and meet the challenges of public housing, didn't stand in his way. Even so, a colleague of Ash's at the BHA says he was "fighting an entrenched political authority with no support." As the 1960s wore on, the BHA's problems were mounting beyond any individual's capacity to solve them.

PUBLIC HOUSING AND COLUMBIA POINT

Columbia Point's problems may have been more prominent because it was the largest of Boston's housing projects and because of its isolation, but its problems were not unique. The story is told over and over of two Columbia Points: One had working-class families, black and white, who moved in in the 1950s, who remember a safe, clean, viable community—when no one thought twice about leaving their babies lined up in their playpens outside the building in the shade and fresh air. The other began in the 1960s, when the project was becoming increasingly black and increasingly poor; when racial tension began to build between neighbors and between black and white kids; when many of the community's stronger families had left and more were leaving every day.

Fidelis Way housing project, Brighton, 1977. *Courtesy of the* Boston Globe.

Why was the BHA dumping so many problem families at Columbia Point? Joseph Slavet, executive director of Action for Boston Community Development at the time, suggests that as the BHA had to place more and more families with multiple problems, they began concentrating them in the same projects. From his vantage point, the BHA's tenant selection process was an effort, however misconstrued, to contain the problem, to provide the greatest good for the greatest number. For Columbia Point, however, the BHA's policy of grouping all of the troubled families in the same project or even the same area of a project further burdened an already burdened community.

While conditions went from bad to worse in the 1970s, and Columbia Point deteriorated physically and its racial mix tipped from white to minority, the BHA put a moratorium on sending new tenants to the project. When tenants moved out, the BHA left their

Housing Time Line, U.S. Department of Housing and Urban Development

June 1934
> The National Housing Act creates the Federal Housing Administration.

September 1937
> The U.S. Housing Act creates the U.S. Housing Authority for low-rent housing and slum clearance projects.

July 1947
> The Housing and Home Finance Agency is established.

July 1949
> The Housing Act of 1949 provides federal funding to assist slum clearance, community development, and redevelopment projects.

September 1959
> The Housing Act of 1959 provides direct loans for elderly housing.

September 1965
> The Department of Housing and Urban Development Act creates HUD as a cabinet-level agency.

April 1968
> The Fair Housing Act of 1968 is enacted to ban housing discrimination.

August 1969
> The Brooke Amendment provides that low-income tenants of public housing projects pay no more than 25 percent of their income for rent.

August 1974
> The Housing and Community Development Act of 1974 establishes community development block grants and provides assistance for urban homesteading.

October 1977
> The Housing and Community Development Act of 1977 establishes Urban Development Action Grants, extends elderly and handicapped provisions, mandates the submission of an annual report on national urban policy, and establishes the Community Reinvestment Act of 1978.

July 1987
> The Stewart B. McKinney Homeless Assistance Act provides assistance to communities to deal with homelessness.

February 1988
> The Housing and Community Development Act allows the sale of public housing to resident management corporations.

October 1992
> The HOPE VI program is initiated as a demonstration program to revitalize severely distressed or obsolete public housing developments and promote fundamental changes in the way public housing authorities develop and administer public housing.

March 1996
> The Housing Opportunity Program Extension Act includes new drug and alcohol abuse provisions designed to help public housing authorities screen applicants and evict individuals with criminal records or those whose behavior is found to endanger other residents.

October 1998
> Federal legislation is proposed that would allow local housing authorities to open more than half of all public housing units to middle-income tenants.

Columbia Point, 1977.
Courtesy of the Boston
Globe.

apartments vacant, even though there was a long list of families waiting to get into public housing. Some have charged that the BHA deliberately left apartments empty because they had given up on Columbia Point. Joe Slavet, who later became a senior fellow at the McCormack Institute at UMass Boston, offers another view: "What [BHA chair] Ellis Ash was trying to do there was part of an overall effort to integrate the BHA's housing projects. . . . In order not to worsen the racial situation at Columbia Point we weren't going to take any more black families. . . . What is the most important thing: that people get housing, or that we integrate housing?" Whether the "mothballing" of apartments at Columbia Point was a deliberate effort to empty the project or an attempt to keep a bad situation from getting worse, in the end, all efforts to fix what was wrong with the project turned out to be exercises in futility.

"Despite Ellis Ash's good intentions," Slavet comments, "Columbia Point was deteriorating at a rate beyond his capacity to handle it. . . . It shifted from a working-class public housing project to a dependent family housing project." Although resources were coming into Columbia Point from a variety of places, the tenants "were getting poorer and poorer, and what we were delivering in the form of social services wasn't getting at the root causes of their poverty." Columbia Point's ills were accumulating faster than anyone could diagnose, much less treat.

12 Children of the Point: II

I remember two distinctly different Columbia Points. The Columbia Point that I recall as a very young person, early on in my life there, is vastly different from the Columbia Point that I recall in the last years I lived there before we moved.

—Charlie Titus, Athletic Director, UMass/Boston

The majority of the residents of Columbia Point were children, and their numbers grew every year. They saw the changes in the project from a unique perspective. Many grew up there; unlike their parents, they had known no other home. Many of these now-adult "children of the Point" talk about two different Columbia Points: the vibrant community they first knew, and the one they later saw disintegrate in the 1960s and 1970s. In many cases, the cast of characters for the two different Columbia Points is the same: kids who had grown up as close friends were suddenly antagonists. In many cases, they didn't understand why things had changed, but there was no doubt that things had indeed changed, profoundly and unalterably.

The isolation of the Point had in some ways made it an ideal place for a child to grow up. Cut off from the tensions and divisions of "the mainland," adults set

aside their prejudices. Children who grew up there never learned them. Catholic and Protestant, black and white, didn't matter; what mattered was that they were all from the same place. As one adult child says about his friends there, "We never referred to them and never thought of them as black or white. If you were a friend, you were a friend, and that was it."

The disintegration of the community can be traced in the personal stories of two people who grew up there, a white girl and a black boy. Carole Katz and Charlie Titus both moved into Columbia Point when they were four years old—Charlie in 1954 and Carole in 1955—and both moved out ten years later, in 1965. During those years, they saw

Columbia Point children
with Fire Chief James J.
Murphy, 1971. Left to right:
Mike Doren, 13, Jack
Gurry, 8, and Gregory
Dobson, 8. *Courtesy of the
Boston Globe.*

their neighborhood transformed utterly. Both of their mothers chose
Columbia Point because it was one of Boston's newest and best
housing projects, a good place to raise their children. Ten years
later, both mothers made the decision to move out because they
feared for the welfare of their children.

Carole Katz went to kindergarten in the "mini" building and to
first grade in the brand-new Paul A. Dever School just across Mount
Vernon Street. She remembers the project as a wonderful place to
grow up. There were two drum-and-bugle corps at the project, the
St. Christopher's Brigadiers and the Columbia Point Cadets. Carole
was a member of the church corps. Carole's mother was a single
parent, and to Carole, the families without fathers seemed better,
simpler: "This is kind of a funny thing to say, but most of the kids
there didn't have fathers, and in my experience the ones that did
have fathers had bad experiences. Like one girl whose father would
come around only once in a while and he'd be drunk and it would
be a real awful scene, and—I was really kind of scared of fathers. I
didn't see them much, but when I did they always seemed to be this
kind of depressing presence."

Carole remembers gangs in the late 1950s—the Gems and the

Playing hoops at
Columbia Point, 1973.
Courtesy of the Boston
Globe.

Gems Juniors, and a gang from Southie called the Saints—being
"sort of an elite clique" of white kids who would scratch their slogans
into the elevators. She was a close observer of the scene at the shops
just across the street from the project: "I remember that the coffee
shop was a real hangout in the fifties . . . where people like the Gems
hung out. . . . I remember them in like black leather and the greasy
hairdos and the teased-up hair and the girls in all the makeup and
peg pants. It's like right out of the movie *Grease* or something."

One of Carole's fondest memories is of swimming at the Point.
There wasn't a sandy beach that adults could use, but the rocks were
just the right size for kids. Swimming at the rocks, she recalls, was
entirely dependent on the tides: "When the tide was out, the area

was unusable, because the tide would go out like a hundred yards
and it would be all green muck. But when it was in, it was high
along the rocks and you could dive in, and then it was a fascinating
place. You know, living in an asphalt-brick environment, the shoreline was one of the few natural places to have some fun, with sea-
weed and barnacles and shells and just the ocean." Every year, Carole and her friends marched past the "No Trespassing" sign, broke
down the fence, and made a trail past the Firestone Tire Company
to the beach. "I knew the tides the whole summer long," she recalls,
"because it was so important. And I would be over there whenever
it was high tide."

Carole recalls that in the early 1960s Columbia Point became
known as a bad place to live—a reputation she traces to the publication of an exposé about the project in the *Saturday Evening Post*
on July 6, 1963, only ten months after the *Boston Globe* series by
Richard Hurt. Sensationally entitled "Tragedy of a Vertical Slum,"
the article, by Roul Tunley, begins from the point of view of a visitor
flying into Boston—not a vantage point familiar to those living in
the project. The opening paragraph is a tour de force:

> If you have flown into Boston lately, you've probably seen Columbia
> Point. It is a small, dirty finger thrusting itself into Dorchester Bay, a
> colorless peninsula of asphalt and marsh grass, relieved only by the
> rust-colored buildings of the Columbia Point Housing Project. Here—
> in the largest development in New England—live 7,000 not-so-proper
> Bostonians. Their home has been called "Alcatraz," "the Rock," "Sin
> City," and some earthier things. "They don't have red lights in the
> Point," says a 20-year-old girl who recently left the project. "They don't
> have to."

From the opening description of the geography of the Point as an
obscene gesture to the snide allusion to prostitution there, we can
only conclude that the author has an awful lot of smut on his mind.
No doubt, any member of the Mothers Club would have washed his
mouth out with soap and sent him to his room without supper. Roul
Tunley may have been surprised to know that among the 7,000 "not-
so-proper" residents of Columbia Point were more than a few readers of the *Saturday Evening Post*.

In fact, the article was a profoundly demoralizing event in the life
of the Columbia Point community. To thirteen-year-old Carole
Katz, its description of her neighborhood was confusing, untrue,
and hurtful in a very personal way. She vividly remembers the con-

Tragedy of a vertical slum.
Courtesy of the Saturday
Evening Post.

View of Columbia Point
from Carson Beach, 1967.
Courtesy of the Boston
Globe.

fusion of having her home described as a horrible place, and the
pain of suddenly feeling self-conscious about where she lived:

> I used to be kind of embarrassed about the fact that I had to get off at Co-
> lumbia Station, because everybody on the train would know that I lived
> in Columbia Point. I started to really have a hard time about living there.
>   And I blame that whole thing on the *Saturday Evening Post.* . . .
> You'd think it was a concentration camp. It just had all these horrible
> things that it said about it. You know, rats and barbed wire, and broken
> glass and everything, and up to that point I was completely oblivious to
> this. I said, What are you talking about? I'd never seen a rat in my life!
> What barbed wire? I never saw any barbed wire. The only barbed wire
> that was there was part of the Firestone Tire Company.
>   So it was really malicious almost. It was very damaging to me and
> I'm sure lots of other people who lived there. It became a real stigma
> to come from Columbia Point.

Although Carole deplored the article's stigmatizing of Columbia
Point, she did avoid certain areas of the housing project. "I remember Montpelier Street, the center street of the complex, being kind
of a scary place for me to walk," she recalls. Montpelier became the
predominantly black area of the project, with the whites mostly up
in the "front" of the project, on Mount Vernon Street. As time went
on, these lines of demarcation became more pronounced—probably, Carole guesses, as the housing authority put white families in
the "white buildings" and black families in the "black buildings."
  Carole's family moved from Columbia Point to the Hyde Park

Survivors

Stephan Ross was a youth worker at Columbia Point in the early 1960s, and he brought a powerful perspective to his work. Ross had come to this country at age sixteen, after spending eight "horrific" years in German concentration camps. Once here, he learned English, completed high school, served in the Korean War, went to college, and received a graduate degree in social work. Although he worked at Columbia Point for only a few years, his impact is felt to this day. Ross's name comes up again and again in conversations with former residents as someone who made a difference in their lives.

During his time at the public housing project, Ross developed sports programming, brought volunteer tutors from area colleges and universities to help with homework, recruited graduate students in social work and counseling to provide assistance to families, and made sure there was plenty of fun. After his own battered old car died, he persuaded the board of directors of the community center to put up some money for transportation for outings:

> I went and bought an airport limousine for two hundred dollars. I fixed it myself. I washed it and cleaned it and made it new. Once I took something like twenty-five children in that limousine to ride the police horses at the stables in Franklin Park. The kids loved it. Then I rented a bus and I got tickets at the Melody Tent in Hyannis. I persuaded them to give us any extra tickets for the kids and the senior citizens.

I would say, "I work in that poor housing development with the poor people. Can't you give them a night out so that they will see something beautiful and that there is another world?" They let us come twice a summer. From year to year, the kids were saying, "Steve, are you going to be able to take us to the Cape again this summer?"

Ross, who went on to work for the city for twenty-eight years in delinquency prevention and was one of the prime movers in establishing Boston's Holocaust Memorial, still keeps in touch with many of his former charges. As he looks back on his time at Columbia Point, a time when conditions were deteriorating dramatically, he points to the side-by-side existence of the good and the bad, but mostly the good:

> The people were coming from everywhere in the city. They were wonderful people. They used to make potluck suppers. Everyone brought things from their own ethnicity. We were eating food from different parts of the world. These people were eager and so willing to be a part of something. A lot of them came from the South, some people of color. But drugs were just starting, and there were incidents, bad things happening. The housing authority was losing control. But there were families who were surrounded by all the fire who had decency and religion and were able to manage to survive . . . and groups of kids who were able to extricate themselves. . . . I always remembered how difficult it was for me to survive in the [concentration] camps, and here are these kids who are free, and they are able to get the food and a place to live, and yet they are living in a horrendous world. I gave something to them, yes, but they gave something to me, too.

Youth table tennis
tournament at Columbia
Point, early 1960s.
Courtesy of Stephan Ross

Stephan Ross with kids in front of the community center, early 1960s. *Courtesy of Stephan Ross.*

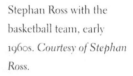

Stephan Ross with the basketball team, early 1960s. *Courtesy of Stephan Ross.*

Stephan Ross with a group at the State House, early 1960s. *Courtesy of Stephan Ross.*

Columbia Point youth worker Stephan Ross used an old airport limousine to transport his charges in the early 1960s. *Courtesy of Stephan Ross.*

section of Boston in 1965, when she was in the ninth grade: "I think that it was probably a little bit of not wanting to be part of a project that had a bad stigma, and my mother's economic situation got stable, and probably—I always have suspected, my mother never told me—she was getting worried about changes that I was going through at the time, getting me out of the project."

After the move, Carole recalls her mixed feelings about the place where she grew up: "It mostly had to do with what I knew outside people thought of the place. . . . I started to try and defend the project in my mind. . . . though while I was in Columbia Point I felt a lot of shame, I started in defense of that to become proud of it." Telling people she was from Columbia Point would get a strong reaction—one Carole wasn't always quick to dispel, even though she knew better: "It was considered to be a very tough neighborhood, so somebody who had come from there was assumed to be very tough. And I kind of liked that, though I knew I wasn't [tough] at all! And I knew that their perceptions were completely wrong." And yet, she was aware of certain ironies: "When I lived in the project, I had a three-speed bike, a Raleigh, beautiful bike, and I used to leave it outside, next to the stairs, unlocked, all the time in the project, in this so-called horrible place. And when we moved to Hyde Park, I had it on our front porch, and in the first month it was there it was stolen—in Hyde Park, the middle-class, wonderful neighborhood that we moved into." But mostly, she was relieved that she didn't have to "grow up too fast" in her new neighborhood: "I remember when I moved into Hyde Park and the first person to come and introduce herself to me lived next door and the first question she wanted to know was which church I'd be going to. . . . Everybody was sweet and 'good,' and it was a tremendous relief for me, because I was growing up much too fast at Columbia Point. I was thirteen and I was making out with boys and smoking cigarettes and kids were drinking. . . . And that was really tense. I didn't like it . . . I was so relieved I didn't have to keep that up."

Carole's feelings upon leaving Columbia Point are a rich adolescent mixture of sadness, shame, bravado, defensiveness, relief, and love. But her recollections of life there as a child are crystal clear: "I remember summer mornings the sun would make some beautiful lines on the buildings and in the shaded areas it would be nice and cool and it would just be striking-looking to me, and I would sit on the front steps and just enjoy it. It was just the sun on the buildings, but I liked it a lot."

Charlie Titus also has vivid memories of Columbia Point and

how it changed during the ten years his family lived there. Even years after he moved into a third-floor apartment in 110 Monticello, one of the seven-story buildings, with his mother and his sister, he can remember it clearly:

> You walked into a front room that was pretty small, and it had three windows across the front. As you walked from the front room, on your left was a small bathroom and on your right were two small bedrooms and a linen closet between them. And then at the rear of the apartment behind the bedrooms there was a kitchen. . . . The impressions I have of the atmosphere at Columbia Point are really strong and positive. I remember we had these little iron fences around grassed areas, and there was a field that we played baseball and softball on and that field was right next to the water. . . . This was my first experience, the first recollection I have of being around trees, grass, and water. It was a pretty place in those days.

But he continues: "The other thing that sticks with me is the isolation. . . . There was a city dump, and I should call it a dump and playground because it was our playground also. Where the Channel 56 TV studio is now was a First National supermarket, and part of the building where BankBoston is now was actually WHDH, the Channel 5 TV station. There was a liquor store next to the supermarket, and the *Boston Globe* was already there. That was essentially it on the peninsula."

There was a real sense of community among the residents of the housing project, but that began to deteriorate as the years went by. "Early on," he recalls, "we didn't do a whole lot of fighting—real hard negative fighting with each other. But that began to change. There was a tougher breed of kid out there, and it got to the point where at least for three or four years I must have fought every day of my life. I mean, that was just a way of life."

Titus recalls fighting against some of the same kids who had been his childhood friends. The fights were racial battles. "I found myself fighting against kids who I had been hanging out with and enjoying myself with," he remembers, "and that was a difficult time for me." The fighting became increasingly violent: "One of the fads in those latter days in Columbia Point was not only fighting but what we called 'stomping.' That's where you are fighting someone and you get them down and stomp them with your feet. That's a hard thing to talk about today, because it sounds so cruel and vicious, and in fact it was. But as kids, that was one of the fads we went through. I remember a number of real bloody, gory days out there, fighting as

Charlie Titus, director of athletics at UMass Boston, grew up at Columbia Point. *Courtesy of Charlie Titus.*

Cleanup at Columbia
Point, 1970. *Courtesy of the
Boston Globe.*

kids and policemen chasing us and coming into people's houses and
just taking folk out of the houses—just some terrible times."

Boys, he recalls, felt a "macho demand" to fight; his sister didn't
have as hard a time, he says, because the girls didn't "run the streets"
as the boys did. What kept Titus on track was the strong influence of
his mother. Pearl Titus saw to it that her son went away to camp—to
Camp Walden in New Hampshire—for a month in the summer,
the time when kids got into most trouble in the project. "When I got
back it was, let's prepare for school and reacclimate yourself to your
family," Charlie recalls. "I never really got a chance to get into a lot
of that summer activity at the Point. Which, you look back and say,
it was great. She was, again, right on time with that."

Titus has a keen sense of the very different fates of the kids he
grew up with at Columbia Point. They were all friends as kids growing up, but as they moved into their teens they went in separate directions. The difference, as he sees it, was family. His mother always
had her eye out for him, and he was well aware of her vigilance:
"When I look back on some of the guys that I spent time with out
there and some of them are since dead, there are some that are in

jail, some guys that have had drug problems, and some guys who have done very well. I think that the difference between those of us who have done well as opposed to those of us who did not have as much luck and success was probably the family influence. That told the difference for most of us."

Another strong influence in Charlie's life was his uncle. He owned a hand car wash, called the Blue Corral, on Washington Street in Roxbury, and Charlie worked for him from age eleven to fourteen. "He would come in and get me at four o'clock in the morning to go open the car wash by five," Titus recalls, "and catch the early-morning customers. The most amazing thing was that he made me cashier, when I was eleven." His uncle had no formal education past the sixth grade, and he would ask the boy to total up at the end of each day. "After an hour of totaling, I'd say, 'We have $564.75.' And he would say, 'You're wrong.' 'What do you mean I'm wrong?' He said, 'You should have $566.25.'" His uncle taught him, Titus says, to "be a man": "He taught me an unbelievable work ethic, he taught me a lot about being honest, and he taught me a lot about being true to yourself. Particularly, if you worked for yourself. And that's something that stayed with me."

Titus has thought long and hard about what caused his community to deteriorate. He sees a combination of factors, from tenants' feeling that management wasn't doing its job to what happens when long-oppressed people suddenly are offered the hope of a better life:

> You cannot put that many people into that type of a living situation—they have no pride of ownership at all. There is no equity being built; they are just living there. And then at the point that they perceive management is not doing a good job, it's all over. I didn't say whether management is actually doing a good job or not. The point is that when people *perceive* that management is not going a good job, then it's all over. . . .
>
> I also think that America changed drastically in the sixties. Now, no one could foresee exactly what was going to happen with the civil rights struggle. . . . I mean, you can't treat people like blacks were treated in this country in the forties and fifties and not expect something to happen at some point down the road. . . . I think that it was impossible for people to predict the impact that the Kennedys were going to have when they brought in Camelot and gave people new hope about the quality of life and what it could be about in this country. I think that all those greater things had an impact on the success and failure of a housing situation like Columbia Point.

Teasing apart the factors that contributed to the decline of Columbia Point is a difficult task. But Titus suspects that some of the problem with bad management at Columbia Point can be traced to Boston politics—contracts being given to "some politician's brother, sister, uncle, aunt, or friend." He notes that in the early days, residents banded together to make sure the community got the things it needed. But as they moved out, or became less active, the whole fabric of the community began to unravel: "I think that any time you have a management that sees that they have pretty much a docile clientele, then hey, there is not a tremendous amount of incentive to do the right thing, unless you're just a good solid person."

As a teenager, Titus came of age in a world that was increasingly dangerous. In the 1960s drugs became more and more prevalent at the Point, and each teenager had to make his or her decision about how to relate to them:

> I never dealt with the drug scene out there. I knew it was there. I guess I was just too afraid of it. Afraid of what my mother would do to me, afraid of what my uncle would do to me, and basically taking the position that if this is not something that is sanctioned by my family, or more importantly, if my family is so dead set and vehemently against it, there was nothing that I needed to do with it.
>
> I did have an ability to walk away from certain things, and I think that the strength to do that came from the family support again. It's one thing when you have to get a lot of reinforcement from your peer group. . . . But it's a whole other thing—and it takes your peer group's strength away—when the support from your family is so strong that you can say it doesn't matter what they think.

In negotiating the world of the Point, Titus was keenly aware of the expectations of his mother and his uncle. But it wasn't easy. "It led to some fights," he recalls. "You know, 'There goes Charlie, he's a punk, he can't hang.' 'Don't call me a punk.' You know." Charlie learned to fight with the kids who, as his mother said, were "throwing away time, finding ways to kill time." But the people he was closest to, most of them athletes still actively involved in football and basketball, were strong enough to stay away from drugs.

Kids also became increasingly involved with stealing and vandalism. In the late 1960s, as Titus describes it, the Point became virtually lawless territory:

> If you went in town and stole a car and brought it back to the Point, nine times out of ten you were over free. . . . It got to a point where even kids who lived in town would steal cars and bring them to the Point, because they could joyride for two or three days. They would

Distributing brooms and rakes on cleanup day, Columbia Point, 1970. Boston Herald.

ride around the Point, and then when it was time for them to go home, they'd turn the car off like it was theirs, park it, and go on back home, and come back the next day and joyride some more.

The cops were very cautious in those days, and one of the things that they wouldn't do was chase kids through hallways. So if a cop car spotted you, it would take you just a matter of seconds to stop a stolen car, get out of it, and hit a hallway. Once you hit the hallway, you were home free because the cops were not going to chase you through those hallways.

The hallways were the drug dealers' territory, the car thieves' territory, beyond the law. Hit the hallway, and you were "home free."

Titus's mother went back to work when the kids got old enough. "She was feeling real good about that independence," he explains. "And I think that made us a happier household. But I think she also began to become extremely concerned about how the Point was changing." With her new financial resources and her concern about the welfare of her children, Pearl Titus, like hundreds of other families who were able to, decided to move out: "I think it just became her final decision that for the sake of my sister and me it was time to make a move from the Point. And that was real difficult for me. Not so much for my sister because her and my mother had become very close and my sister wasn't the outgoing, extroverted type of person that I was."

In 1965 the Titus family moved to Columbia Road in Dorchester, close to where Charlie was attending the William E. Russell School. For Charlie, at age fourteen, the move was tough, especially

leaving his two best friends. For a few months, he went back to the Point whenever he could: "Although it was about a forty-five-minute walk, I could still get to the Point and visit my friends. It was hard on me because I didn't know anywhere else, I didn't know anyone else. I mean, Columbia Point was home, it was home, and it was the first time that we had moved where I was really old enough to understand and feel the impact of moving. . . . Once I got over it and began to make some new friends, I didn't spend as much time in the Point, which made my mother extremely happy."

Titus went on to graduate from St. Michael's College in Winooski, Vermont, and has been athletic director at the University of Massachusetts at Boston, right next to his old neighborhood, for nearly twenty years. "I firmly believe that we are all a product of our environment," he reflects, "the places we have lived, the experiences we have had, and the people we have known." Columbia Point made a positive contribution to the adult Charlie Titus became. The list of people who influenced him is a long one, with one real stand-out: "I think that I was fortunate enough to have a real, real strong mother who was committed to raising her children and giving them a better life than she had early on. And I think that foundation really made a difference. Because if that foundation wasn't there, all the people who have had a positive impact on my life probably would not have impacted it as positively. And I think the difference was the foundation that was laid by my mother."

13 Planning for Columbia Point

Beginning in 1962 and continuing for nearly twenty long and mostly frustrating years, a succession of urban planners studied what was wrong with Columbia Point and came up with proposals to remedy the problem. Everyone, it seems, was eager to study Columbia Point, to diagnose its ills and prescribe a cure. It was as if a procession of doctors came in to examine the patient, write their prescriptions, and charge their fees—while the patient grew sicker and sicker.

Largely in response to the *Boston Globe*'s September 1962 series on Columbia Point, housing experts began turning their attention to the needs of the community and pledging their help. The first comprehensive planning meeting was held in December 1962, bringing together a team of twenty consultants to explore "ways and means of improving the Columbia Point area." Among those attending the meeting were Herman D. Hillman,  regional director of the Public Housing Administration; Edward D. Hassan, chairman of the Boston Housing Authority; Edward J. Logue, administrator of the Boston Redevelopment Authority; and Ellis Ash, then deputy administrator of the BRA and later chairman of the BHA. Hillman pledged the support of his agency, provided that the city integrate plans for Columbia Point into an overall plan for private development on the peninsula. The BRA's new chief, Ed Logue, promised that his staff would develop just such a comprehensive plan for redevelopment of the area within six months. The experts were on the case, even if, as a *Boston Globe* headline soberly cautioned, "Columbia Point's Needs Could Take Five Years."

The city of Boston closed its dump on July 19, 1962; the private dump, known as the Mile Road dump, was also closed as a result of state legislation on the same day. Although the private dump appealed the decision and a restraining order resulted in its temporary reopening, the case was closed for good in February 1963 when the Massachusetts Supreme Court ruled against its operation. When the gates finally swung shut on the private dump, the *Globe* described "the big breath of fresh air sweeping through Columbia Point." The nine-year effort to rid the project of its most toxic menace had come to a successful conclusion, and hopes were high for the future of the peninsula.

There ensued a decade of planning for Columbia Point. The planning effort yielded very little. While the planners planned and the consultants wrote reports and the politicians postured and temporized, the community steadily disintegrated. In January 1963 Herman Hillman hired New York architect Albert Mayer, one of the original designers of the federal public housing program in 1934, to study the area surrounding Columbia Point. BHA chairman Edward Hassan hired the consulting firm of Adams, Howard, and Greeley to study the needs of the project itself. However, the BHA's recommendations, calling for such things as "physical revisions of the face of the buildings . . . to enhance the general appearance of the whole development," were mostly minor and superficial.

In addition, the BHA invited Action for Boston Community Development (ABCD), a Ford Foundation–sponsored social service agency, to help develop a comprehensive program of community and social services for Columbia Point. ABCD proceeded to conduct a "tenant attitude survey," interviewing 20 percent of the project's families, to determine their needs for social services and recommend "immediate and long-range programs for meeting them." The survey, entitled "Serving the People . . . at Columbia Point Housing Development: A Report and Recommendations," was completed in May 1964.

1963–64: URBAN RENEWAL

While the BHA focused on the problems at Columbia Point, the BRA's focus was broader: the development of the entire peninsula. In June 1963 the BRA received a $40,000 grant from the Urban Renewal Administration to assess the feasibility of developing the four hundred acres surrounding Columbia Point. The BRA enlisted the help of two consultants: Maurice A. Reidy, Engineers, in Boston, and Robert Gladstone and Associates, Economic Consultants, in Washington, D.C.

The BRA's application for urban renewal at Columbia Point provides a picture of the challenges and the limitations of the peninsula as of 1963, as the BRA saw them. "Columbia Point, an area of about 400 acres," it began, "has excellent access by subway and expressway, and scenically it is an outstanding site. Despite these advantages, it is bleak, underutilized, and largely undeveloped." The application went on to list several reasons why the Columbia Point area should be considered:

- The need to improve conditions at the housing project
- The fact that state legislation recently required the city to stop all dumping, and the likelihood that the private Mile Road dump would soon close
- The impending obsolescence of the sewage pumping station upon completion of new sewage facilities in 1965.

At the same time, the application warned of several "severe problems" at the site:

- Soil conditions, making costs of development high
- The dump's under- and aboveground fires and rodents
- Columbia Point's "unfavorable public image" and the "bleak and institutional character of the public housing project."

"These psychological factors together with the physical problems," the application concluded, "pose serious questions about the possibility of attracting private housing development to the area."

In 1964 the BRA reported the results of a year-long feasibility study of the Columbia Point peninsula. The BRA's solution for the housing project's isolation was to build an entire community around it, including a new citywide campus high school, new stores, a new post office, a new church, and private, moderate-income housing adjacent to the project. The plan proposed to balance the number of public housing units by creating a total of 1,520 new private units— 480 garden apartments built by private industry for moderate income families under the 221d3 submarket rate program, 550 row house units, and 490 seven-story elevator units. In addition, the plan called for reclaiming sixty-four acres for parks and recreation, including a fishing pier, tennis courts, boating facilities, and restaurants.

In short, the plan called for nothing less than a complete "new town" on the peninsula—an idea that would resurface again in the years to come. "The concept coming into view," the *Boston Globe* reported, "is to connect the housing project with the rest of the Dorchester–South Boston community area by new developments including private housing, roadways and recreation areas."

In assessing the marketability of the proposed private housing, the report identified two liabilities: the stigma of the housing project and the soil conditions. However, the "unique values made available" would offset the stigma, the report concluded, and the added construction costs due to the soil conditions would increase the average rental by no more than $4.80 a month.

ABCD's 1963 Survey of Columbia Point Residents

According to a survey administered in 1963 by Action for Boston Community Development, there had been 679 "intact" families, 449 single-parent families, and 194 elderly living at Columbia Point in 1961. By 1963 the intact families had dropped to 582, the single-parent families to 404, and the elderly population to 136.

Some of the following questions from the survey produced these answers:

Do you own a car?
Thirty percent said yes and 70 percent said no.

Do you have a telephone?
Sixty-five percent said yes and 35 percent said no.

Do you feel your move to Columbia Point is a step up or a step down from your old neighborhood?
Forty percent said a step up, 38 percent said a step down, and 19 percent said about the same.

Sign points the way to Columbia Point. *Courtesy of Marie Kennedy, Columbia Point Oral History Project.*

The BRA's vision was not to become a reality—the concept had never been backed by a realistic plan for financing. Even more important, the key obstacle, it turned out, was getting the site designated as a qualifying area under the federal urban renewal program. As Ed Logue had anticipated, the New York regional office of the Urban Renewal Administration rejected the BRA's proposal, saying the site failed to qualify for renewal funds because it was not a slum packed tight with poor people and dilapidated tenements. The "blight" on the peninsula was not a matter of too many buildings that needed to be razed, but of too much empty land that needed to be filled. Ultimately, that desolation would prove to be as deadly as conventional urban blight—but it was not a category recognized by the federal government.

Once the BRA's plan for comprehensive urban renewal of the peninsula was rejected, Ed Logue turned his agency's attention and energy to major urban renewal efforts that would change the face of downtown Boston. At Columbia Point, only far less ambitious plans would go forward.

Right: Two aerial views of site of University of Massachusetts' new Boston campus shows its relationship to Columbia Point and the pumping station, early 1970s. *Archives and Special Collections Department, Healey Library, University of Massachusetts at Boston.*

1965: THE BAYSIDE MALL

For the most part, the residents of Columbia Point were oblivious to the grandiose plans for redevelopment of the peninsula; their needs were more immediate. They pressed not for a "new town," but for shops that would enable them to buy groceries and clothing nearby. In 1962 more than fifty Columbia Point tenants lobbied at the State House for passage of a $3.5 million allocation to build a shopping center next to the housing project. Although the Boston School Committee was also considering building the new English High School on the site, in the end officials decided that a large shopping center should be built by a private developer adjacent to Columbia Point.

In May 1965 Mayor Collins presided over the groundbreaking for a twenty-seven-acre, thirty-four-store shopping center, declaring it "another important step in the development of the New Boston." Even though the Columbia Point community might have been surprised to hear itself included in the "New Boston," the shopping center was an exciting and long-awaited new neighbor. Anchored by Zayre, Almy, and a Stop & Shop supermarket, it was the fulfillment of a promise the city had made more than a decade earlier, to provide convenient shops for the six thousand residents of the housing project.

Some were skeptical. Although BRA administrator Ed Logue decried the lack of stores at the housing project, he never believed that stores alone would solve Columbia Point's problems. "I don't count

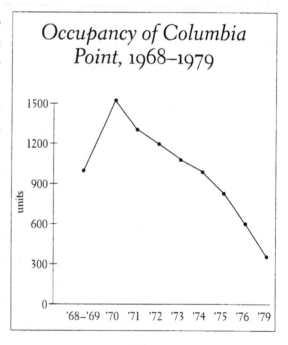

Occupancy of Columbia Point, 1968–1979

a shopping center as part of a neighborhood," he told the *Boston Globe*. Others were wildly optimistic. State representative Bob Quinn, whose district included the housing project, cited the precedent of ancient Greece and declared that Columbia Point residents would "be connected with the rest of society by the marketplace."

1967: THE UNIVERSITY OF MASSACHUSETTS

The state legislature voted to open a Boston campus of the University of Massachusetts in 1964, and a year later classes began meeting in a leased office building, the old Boston Gas headquarters, in the city's Park Square. As the search for a permanent site for the university's new campus took place, additional buildings were leased nearby to accommodate the growing number of students.

By 1967 more than fifty potential sites had been identified and all but two eliminated. In the end, the trustees decided between Copley Square, favored by university students, faculty, and staff, and Columbia Point, a site that some planners felt was too isolated. Ed Logue recalls that the BRA determined that the in-town site—including air rights over the Massachusetts Turnpike where Copley Place now stands—was too valuable to the city's tax base to allow the tax-exempt university to build there: "They were going to put it in the South End . . . around the old Boston Gas building. I found out about it and said, 'You're not going to do that.' I had federal contracts and plans all

University of Massachu-
setts completed, early
1970s. *Archives and Special
Collections Department,
Healey Library, University
of Massachusetts at Boston.*

around it. They said, 'Where else should we go?' We said, 'How about Columbia Point?' Of course, they then proceeded to design the university so that there was no connection between it and the housing. It was our recommendation but their decision."

In fact, in 1967 the BRA issued a report touting "an exciting concept and a site for the development of a great public university—an Urban Campus by the Sea." The report ticks off the benefits of the site. "Comparisons clearly demonstrate the superiority of the Campus by the Sea," it declares:

- The site is accessible to rapid transit and the Southeast Expressway
- It is immediately available, with no disruption of family or business, and no threat to an existing community
- No tax-producing properties are impaired
- Land acquisition costs are low; the site offers ample space for student housing, outdoor athletic facilities, and parking
- The site offers unique access to Boston's shoreline

Perhaps anticipating opposition to the site, the report exhorts in conclusion: "A university must be bold, imaginative and resourceful in its site planning, as well as in its curriculum and programs."

In 1968 the trustees voted for the Dorchester site. Some local residents were heartened by the choice because they felt the new university might help stem the tide of deterioration on the peninsula and prevent additional low-income housing from being built. But others worried that an influx of students would threaten the more stable neighborhoods in the area. UMass students, faculty, and staff were uneasy about the location's physical and psychological isolation.

Questions surfaced and stirred controversy. What impact would six thousand students—with as many as twenty thousand projected students in the coming years—have on the community? Would the relatively inexpensive rental housing be driven up by student demand for apartments, as it had in Allston-Brighton, Back Bay, the Fenway, Cambridge, and Somerville? Would students, faculty, and staff be safe and secure on the peninsula? At Columbia Point, where conditions were deteriorating, the worry was even more acute. Would the housing project be taken over, or perhaps even demolished, to make way for student housing? The initial vision for the university included plans for the construction of such housing on the peninsula, and residents of the project feared that the university wouldn't tolerate its down-at-heel neighbor.

When the university finally opened in 1974, relations between the university and housing project residents remained wary. For starters, the university did not appear open and inviting to the community. According to architectural writer Ellen Perry Berkeley, one of the reasons UMass looks like it does today is that it was built like a fortress with security in mind. Boston architect William Rawn, who was then assistant chancellor for community affairs and physical planning at the university, wryly described it to Berkeley as "overbearingly brick." That it still is today.

1970: REHABILITATION BY DESIGN

One of the few planning efforts that directly involved the residents of Columbia Point was their collaboration with a design class at the Massachusetts Institute of Technology taught by Jan Wampler. Wampler, an architect and social activist, first became involved with Columbia Point in the late 1960s when the Boston Chamber of Commerce decided to enter the competition to have Boston selected as the site of the 1976 Bicentennial World's Fair. Wampler's proposal, which was one of several, was that the fair should serve as an "urban laboratory" where countries would exhibit their solutions to social problems. He planned to use Columbia Point for his own exhibit, which would demonstrate that public housing could be redesigned to improve physical and social conditions for residents. In 1970 Wampler worked with a group of tenants to study the buildings and devise solutions. They determined that the project's apartments were designed for the typical American family with 2.8 children—perhaps appropriate for the original tenants of public housing, but much too small for the large, often single-parent families typical of public housing in the 1960s and 1970s.

At the time, HUD had given Columbia Point a nominal grant of $8 million to modernize all of the bathrooms at the project. Wampler maintained that fixing the bathrooms would do little to ameliorate worsening conditions at Columbia Point or any of America's public housing projects. "The problem was the whole place didn't work," he explains, "either the apartments or the community." Instead, he devised a plan to modernize the bathrooms for less than the amount budgeted, and to use the remaining funds

The *New England Real Estate Journal* announces a proposal to locate the 1976 World's Fair in Boston. *Courtesy of Corcoran, Mullins, Jennison.*

to rehabilitate one building as a demonstration project that would include one apartment for ten people, elderly apartments, small apartments, a day care center, and a community center. Wampler's core design idea was that each family could customize the layout of its apartment to suit its own needs. The key was to design the interiors as flexible spaces that could expand and contract to accommodate families of different sizes. He listened carefully to the ways in which tenants used space, discovering, for example, that often there was no single room in the apartment large enough for a family to sit down together for a birthday party. Many large families, he discovered, often ate dinner in shifts because the kitchens were so small.

"The whole intention was to give people more input into their physical surroundings," Wampler explains. Although the buildings were well built structurally, what didn't work were the individual apartments. Wampler developed what he called a "home model kit," a system of walls made of movable closets that would allow families not only to customize their apartments to meet their needs but also to modify them as those needs changed: "The intention was that every family . . . could design their own apartment with this kit. . . . They could make some changes and they could continue to make changes. The point is that people need to invest somehow in their housing—not economically, but emotionally."

Although the BHA supported Wampler's efforts for a time, in the end the housing authority pulled the plug on his plan, claiming it was too expensive.

1974: THE THOMPSON PLAN

In September 1973 Ben Thompson Associates, the Cambridge architectural and planning firm best known locally for masterminding the redevelopment of Quincy Market during the 1970s, was commissioned by the University of Massachusetts to draw up an overall redevelopment plan for the peninsula. With construction at the university's Boston campus by now well under way and impact studies predicting that as many as 35 percent of students would be seeking housing close to the campus, residents of Dorchester and the housing project were increasingly anxious. The redevelopment plan was meant, in part, to quell their fears.

In January 1974 Thompson's plan, *The Columbia Point Peninsula: A Program for Revitalization*, was published. Predicting that the university would have 12,500 students by 1980, the plan asserted that "a tremendous potential exists at Columbia Point: its location, accessi-

Shopping Trips

Shortly after the Stop & Shop supermarket closed its doors and left the Bayside Mall in the early 1970s, a small, informal group of *Boston Globe* employees decided to volunteer to shop for senior citizens at Columbia Point. Former *Globe* reporter Nina McCain recalls:

When the supermarket closed, the elderly residents who had been shopping there had no place to go. I remember reading about it and talking to people about it. There was nothing formal. No edict from on high. A group of us simply got together and decided to approach the woman who ran the senior center at the project, a wonderful woman named Mrs. P. We called and told her we would like to help out. Since she was the one with the contact with the seniors, she canvassed the group and found out who needed what and she assigned us various people. . . .

We operated pretty much independently. We didn't all shop together. We just contacted our senior folks and then figured a time that would be best for them. At that time the seniors were mostly clustered in a building at the end of the point, almost in the water . . . but there was one woman that I shopped for who was left in one of the major buildings. She had been one of the original tenants and she would tell me how wonderful Columbia Point once was, like paradise, clean and beautiful. She was a small black woman, maybe five feet tall, and very active in the Baptist Church. She had no use at all for all those bad kids who had come to the project. But she was left in one of the high-rise buildings and it was truly a nightmare. The plumbing was ripped out. The elevators didn't work. Going up the stairs was an adventure. And there were always bad dudes hanging around. . . .

I remember there were a couple of periods that were tenser than others. . . . I had a tire iron in my Volkswagen Beetle that I used to keep next to me on the front seat, and I occasionally slipped it up my sleeve as I went in the building. I wasn't afraid, I was wary. I always figured I'd manage somehow or other, but I was really more worried about getting her in and out. If somebody grabbed her, it might have been the end for her.

Other than these volunteer shopping expeditions, McCain says the relationship between the *Boston Globe* and the Columbia Point housing project at the time was "virtually nonexistent." She explains:

We were right across the street, but other than our effort, which was certainly not promoted or organized—the publisher didn't come out and say go do it—there wasn't much contact. It was pretty much they're over there and we're over here, and if somebody murders somebody, we'll go cover it—though there was one *Globe* photographer who always refused to go to Columbia Point. So when we would tell people we were going over there, we'd get, "Oh, my God, you're taking your life in your hands."

bility and amenity could be used to create one of the most desirable locations for new development in the City of Boston." Although the report decried the lack of planning on the peninsula, it argued that the investment of more than $300 million to construct a major new university "has changed the image of Columbia Point and created new opportunities for well-planned commercial, residential, educational, and recreational development."

But the good news about the desirability of the peninsula was a double-edged sword for the residents of the deteriorating housing project. On the one hand, the siting of UMass at Columbia Point indicated that the peninsula had real development potential. On the other hand, once the property was seen as valuable, residents feared that it would no longer be available for low-income housing.

Like Ed Logue's plan for urban renewal on Columbia Point a decade earlier, the Thompson plan called for additional development on the peninsula, in effect building a new community around the housing project and the university. Major elements of the plan included the following:

- Four thousand dwelling units—a combination of new units, rehabbed existing units, and "selective removal" of existing units. The units would include "a variety of housing types and costs without any visible distinction between low, moderate and medium income housing."
- A "Town Center," including a Little City Hall, post office, library, and youth center.
- A major shopping facility.
- A new main street, a public transportation link, and a road circling the outer edge of the peninsula.
- Recreation facilities, especially along the shoreline; shared sports facilities with UMass; and continuous waterfront access along the perimeter of the peninsula.

The plan called for the BRA to assemble the site, the Massachusetts Housing Finance Agency to finance residential development, and the Boston Housing Authority to upgrade the housing project. Mayor Kevin White announced the Thompson Plan at City Hall on January 17, 1974, declaring that the site could be transformed into "one of the handsomest neighborhoods in the city."

Nine days after the mayor unveiled a large model of the "New Town," as it was dubbed in the *Boston Globe*, the university opened. Ben Thompson's grand scheme and impressive architectural model materialized just in time to create positive press for Mayor White and highlight the opening of the new university. The *Globe* reported that "the sight of the university's brick red towers rising from the old city dump seems to have inspired everyone," and the mayor's office reassured Columbia Point residents with a guarantee that they would not be forced out. Yet the people living at Columbia Point had immediate problems that were rapidly worsening, and no one was doing anything about them.

Columbia Point residents protested that they had no role in devising the Thompson plan. Moreover, they charged that the proposal to redevelop the entire peninsula distracted from the real problem of improving or upgrading the housing project for existing tenants. In fact, the Thompson Plan ignored these efforts, calling for demolition of 110 Monticello, the building Jan Wampler had proposed to redesign. Reacting to the Thompson Plan, Wampler commented, "In order to attract a developer, they'll have to move the poor out of Columbia Point."

Although the *Boston Phoenix*, an alternative weekly newspaper, concurred, claiming that there was "nothing to discourage fearful visions of a middle-class invasion at Columbia Point," neither the Thompson plan nor the student or middle-class invasion ever materialized. Like Ed Logue's plan a decade earlier, the Thompson plan died a quick death. It required a $150 million investment, and there was no financing. In fact, a footnote, easily missed among the architectural drawings in the plan, quietly admitted as much: "As of this writing, federal housing programs have been suspended and new legislation has not yet been approved by the Congress."

1975: MODERNIZATION

In October 1975 the Boston Globe reported that Columbia Point received $10 million for "modernization" as part of HUD's federal Target Project Program. Yet Columbia Point manager Andrew L. Walsh was not sanguine about the prospect of modernization: "I feel frustrated, especially for [the tenants]. Most are good, decent, law-abiding people just trying to live their lives." Walsh knew that, despite plans for modernization, the vandals—"midnight plumbers," as they were called—would come in and strip the apartments in a matter of minutes.

Only three months later, that happened. On January 9, 1976, the *Globe* reported, "It takes about five days for glaziers, plasterers, carpenters and painters to rehabilitate a gutted apartment at the Columbia Point housing project. But it takes only a few hours for van-

Left: The architectural firm of I. M. Pei & Partners' plan for the Kennedy Library, 1976. *Courtesy of the* Boston Globe.

Right: Kennedy Library site (looking east, pumping station at left, UMass Boston at right), 1977. *Courtesy of the* Boston Globe.

dals and thieves to ruin it again." Overnight, the story reported, vandals broke into an almost-finished four-bedroom unit at 360 Mount Vernon Street: "All the windows but one were broken; new window sashing was ripped out; the new medicine cabinet and light fixtures were torn out; radiators were pulled out; sinks were stripped of plumbing fixtures. And then the apartment was set afire."

Reviewing the various plans to solve the problems at Columbia Point in the 1960s and 1970s is like watching a Greek tragedy. Events unfold with a slow, tragic inevitability as people make the same mistakes over and over again. A planner presents ambitious plans and hopes are raised. But there is no financing. Token funding is allocated for token repairs. And conditions worsen.

1976: KENNEDY LIBRARY AND MUSEUM

Before his assassination in 1963, President John F. Kennedy had decided that his presidential library should be built in Cambridge near Harvard University, where he hoped he might teach upon leaving office. After his death, the Kennedy family proceeded with planning for a complex at Harvard that would consolidate the university's school of government and add a museum to the library that together would create a fitting memorial to the slain leader.

After more than ten years of planning, the proposal triggered heated community opposition from Cambridge residents who feared that swarms of tourists would invade Harvard Square and threaten its tweedy academic character. In fact, in 1975 an environmental impact study indicated that more than a million visitors a

The Kennedys dig in. Left to right: Jacqueline Kennedy Onassis, John Jr., Ted, Rose, and Caroline. Kennedy Library groundbreaking, 1977. *Courtesy of the* Boston Globe.

year would make their way to the library and museum. That was the last straw. In the face of mounting resistance and possible litigation, the Kennedy family decided to look for another site.

According to Bob Wood, the president of UMass Boston at the time and a Kennedy family friend who had served in Washington under both presidents Kennedy and Johnson, Stephen Smith, Kennedy's brother-in-law, called him and asked for some assistance. "He said, 'We're having a little trouble with the sherry group in Cambridge and we think we should find alternatives. Are you interested?'" Wood recalls. "And I said, 'You bet your boots I'm interested.'" Wood tells the story of lobbying the Kennedy family to locate the library out on the Columbia Point peninsula. He recalls the day he escorted Ted Kennedy and Jackie Onassis and some others to look at the site:

It's a lovely October day, and the sun is setting on the harbor, and Jackie falls in love with it. She says it's got to be here. On the drive back into town, Ted is rubbing his hands and saying, "How do I tell Harvard? How do I tell Harvard?"

And Jackie, in that wonderful, deep voice of hers, says, "Ted, there are three things an Irishman says when he gets to Boston. He says, 'Where's Harvard?' and 'How do I get into Harvard?' and then, if he's wise, he says, 'Screw Harvard.'"

Ted almost drives off the road.

In 1976 the Kennedy Library also committed to building on the peninsula, which only added to the apprehensions of the Columbia Point tenants. What they did not realize is that while the coming of the library and the university appeared to threaten the very existence of the housing project, they were also its only hope of salvation.

EPILOGUE: THE BAYSIDE MALL

As much as the opening of the Bayside Mall in 1965 raised the hopes of the Columbia Point community, its closing ten years later was a devastating blow. The opening of the mall wasn't just a matter of finally having good stores convenient to the project, although that was certainly something the community had sorely needed all along. It also signaled new life for the besieged project: good stores wanted to be located out on the peninsula. The residents of Columbia Point were customers they wanted to do business with.

Eight years later, the brand-new mall was as blighted as the project. By 1973 the *Boston Globe* reported that twenty-two of twenty-eight businesses at the mall were closed, including Woolworth's and Almy—because of shoplifting, vandalism, and inadequate patronage. The mall was described with "doors and windows all plywood, its long corridors the playground of stray dogs and gulls from Dorchester Bay. . . . The atmosphere was that of abandonment before disaster."

By 1976, according to a BRA study, the mall had become lawless territory: "Since the mall is practically open on all sides and is borderless, protection becomes practically impossible. Youths apparently did not hesitate to lift shops, mug customers and snatch purses and grocery bags from pedestrian shoppers or from inside their cars." The report dryly recommended that "Bayside should alter its identity as an unsafe center for shops and shoppers."

After years of struggling to get stores and finally getting the mall they always wanted, the community in 1976 was back to where it had been in 1954. The community didn't blame the stores for leaving; residents were well aware of half-drunk soda bottles on the store shelves, of kids shoplifting and disappearing into the project. As one resident noted, "It was closed because so much was stolen." Another said the closing of the shopping center was a turning point in the history of the community: "Everything died for the people."

Finishing construction of the Kennedy Library, 1979. *Courtesy of the* Boston Globe.

So it was that Columbia Point, perhaps because of its isolation, or its reputation, seemed to have a psychological life of its own. Certain events in the life of the community stand out as tragic, triumphant, traumatic, defeating. The death of Laura Ann Ewing. The closing of the dump. The opening of the Bayside Mall. The coming of UMass. The closing of the mall. The coming of the Kennedy Library.

Because it was a community acutely aware of its vulnerability—a community without power or legitimacy—these events took on special significance. The coming of the mall had conferred legitimacy. Kids remember walking over to the new stores with their mothers to pick out their brand-new Easter outfits. Conversely, the closing of the mall erased that legitimacy. The stores didn't want the people of Columbia Point as customers, with their shoplifting and vandalism. Adding insult to injury, once the mall was closed, the city was quick to appropriate its parking lot for the yellow school buses that were dispatched twice daily to implement the court-ordered citywide school desegregation plan.

Perhaps in the fate of the boarded-up stores and vacated supermarket the community saw prefigured the fate of the housing project. This was a community that had to create itself, to bring itself to life. A community that fought hard against dissolution, against overwhelming odds. A community that suffered terribly and that keeps some secrets to itself even to this day.

The Bayside Mall, mostly closed and boarded up, with Columbia Point in the background, 1977. Boston Herald

14 Moving Out and Moving In

Different people mark the beginning of Columbia Point's demise at different times. Many of the early families describe moving out in frustration and fear while others were moving into the same community with fresh energy and optimism. Yet their stories are remarkably similar. At first, families find and build friendliness and cooperation and support within their building, or on their floor, in spite of the obvious and growing problems with maintenance, vandalism, and drugs. Gradually, each family's life becomes circumscribed more and more tightly, until it reaches a point at which the project has become unlivable. Eventually, those who can move out, do. Those who stay do so only because they have no other choice.

MOVING OUT

Many families moved out of Columbia Point with deep regret. Many had worked hard to build a strong, nurturing community. They left with the memory of what

it had once been, with sadness at what it had become, and with a sense of the futility of their efforts to stop its slow and painful demise.

For many, the decision to move came down to a decision to protect their own children. Although they had devoted years to making the community a good one, a single incident in which their child was harmed, or faced the threat of harm, changed their minds in an instant. Back in 1962, it was the threat to all of the children of Columbia Point—and the tragic death of one of them—that had mobilized the community to action. Once again, it was the children that mobilized people to action. But now the families no longer came together to make common cause. Each had to make its own decision, in part because the community was breaking down.

Many of Columbia Point's parents were young and starting families when they moved in, in the 1950s. By the 1960s their children were growing up, many of them teenagers, the project was developing more and more serious problems, and the adults

"A new patrol was installed at Columbia Point yesterday to give added protection," 1970. *Courtesy of the* Boston Globe.

"A new patrol was installed at Columbia Point yesterday to give added protection," 1970. *Courtesy of the* Boston Globe.

were getting tired. When they perceived that their children were in danger, that was enough to tip the scales. Each of them has a "moving out story"—the moment when it became clear that it was time to leave.

Jim Duffy, 1967

I moved out because it got to a point where it was getting nasty if you were white down there. In my building there were twelve units. Only two of us were white, which is not a big deal if everybody is happy, you know. There were some great people there, the Austins and the Joneses.

They were good people, but you had situations that really bothered you. For instance, my younger son. His playmates were all black, and he'd hear a young black kid calling another black kid "nigger," so he would do the same, but now next thing you know you have somebody knocking on my door, saying that my son is calling his son a nigger. And, you know, it was so stupid, but if you understand what I'm saying, it's just a bad situation. . . .

We'd always wanted to get our own place, and then I had a chance to get one, so we bought the place that we have now [in Mattapan]. We're very happy here, and half of our neighbors are black. And they're great people. It's not perfect, but everyone minds their business, they take care of their voices, they smile, say hello. No one is nasty.

It's something like the first years at Columbia Point. . . . I often used to think that it was a model, really a model for the whole country because blacks and whites were living together and minding their business, and not hurting anybody.

Pat McCluskey, 1968

My son Stephen used to go and visit his godparents out in Dorchester, and they'd bring him home. They would never come into the building. They were that afraid of it, believe it or not. But anyway, they'd drop Stephen off, and he'd come in the lower hallway. And we were on the third floor, so he had to walk up two flights.

This particular Sunday night they brought him home. He came in the lower hallway and there were kids there that he didn't know. They said, "Who are you, whitey?" And he said, "I live here." There were some words exchanged, and there was a knife pulled on him. He got away from them and came upstairs, and he was just white as a sheet. And when he told me I just went crazy with the thought that I'd lose one of my children.

And I said to my husband, "We have to do something. I don't know what we're going to do, but we have to do something to get out of here." And that wasn't the first instance. I mean, there was such a changing population. The person that didn't know him of course wouldn't have known him because the person didn't even live in the project. That's what was happening, too. A lot of people were coming from the outside and causing problems. They'd get into an argument or a fight with somebody, and cause a lot of trouble, then they'd just go back to where they came from.

I think a lot of the people ran into the same thing that I ran into. Their children got older and were not able to stay right in their own area. And you'd worry about them. I thought to myself, "Well, my son couldn't even enter his own hall area and come up to his apartment without somebody threatening him. What would happen to him if he had been further up the street, and no place to go when they pulled a knife on him?" So I said to my husband, "The children are getting older now. We have to make some kind of decision." When it comes down to worrying about one of your children being killed—I said to John, "It's not worth it. We have to get out." So we bought a house in Dorchester on a wing and a prayer. We borrowed a hundred dollars for the purchase and sales agreement.

When we look back on it, my youngest daughter was very withdrawn. She was very quiet in school—almost too quiet. And we found out years later that she was afraid. She was afraid all the time. And we moved at just the right time. She was seven years old. And she just blossomed after we moved. So there were a lot of things that were going on with the children. They were afraid of different things that were happening, I guess, maybe that we weren't aware of.

Sandy Young, 1970

I moved out because I could just no longer fight. I had always planned to go from 119 Monticello down to 179 with the senior citizens. I wasn't going anywhere else. But it became so difficult to continue to live here. . . . And in 1970 I moved out, tears in my eyes.

I will never, ever forget my years at Columbia Point because I made some friends that no money on this earth could buy. We laughed together, we cried together, and I think that was the kind of strength that kept us going because of the needs that we had here. When you talk about closing the dump—that was a swinger. I'll never forget the day when they told us, "If you come out here tomorrow to protest we're going to turn the hoses on you," and we all came out in bathing suits. I'll never forget the day they said, "We're going to take you to jail if you continue to march," and we all came out with our kids all packed, lunches, diapers and everything: "We're ready."

Father Larry Wetterholm, 1975

When I left Columbia Point in 1975, of the fifteen hundred or so apartments maybe six hundred were occupied. At that point it was a project of minorities. The golden days from my point of view were the days when the projects were so heavily filled. When I left it was half filled, and really interest in the sports program began to wane, and at that point it was a matter of keeping peace.

When I left in 1975, it was at the time of the busing and everything was in turmoil. I suppose we could talk forever on the busing. It's something that never should have taken place. It was counterproductive and it really bankrupted the city of Boston, it certainly caused white flight to the suburbs, and it polarized the region.

I look back with great pride. And satisfaction. Periodically we have in Boston or elsewhere in the area a Columbia Point reunion, and I love it. I see so many of my protégés, and we make so much of one another. Frequently, I'm involved with the graduates as it were of Columbia Point, either marrying their children or baptizing their grandchildren or even burying them.

What am I most proud of? Well, I think I'm proud of the achievements of the former Columbia Point residents. The former youth of Columbia Point. Many of them are firefighters for the city of Boston, police for the city of Boston. Many have gone on to college and have done well for themselves. Those are my laurels, if I may word it that way.

The Aylward Family, 1977

John Aylward, who lived at Columbia Point with his parents and eight brothers and sisters from 1954 to 1977, marks the change in his com-

Above: Tot lot, Columbia Point, 1972. *Courtesy of the* Boston Globe.

Right: "Vandalized benches add to mood of desolation at Columbia Point housing project," 1978. Boston Herald.

munity as a single event: the Vietnam War. "Almost everybody I knew in the project went to Vietnam," he says. "They got drafted, spent two months in basic training, thirty days' leave, and they're off to Asia."

Although some did go on to higher education, for most Columbia Point men in their late teens and early twenties, college was unheard of. "Nobody had the expectation to go to college," Aylward says. "Nobody had the money to go to college. Somehow it just wasn't built into our psyche that that was the next step in life. Consequently, the next step was to the military." Starting in the late 1960s, many young men left Columbia Point for Vietnam; the few who returned found a completely different place.

Before going off to war, Aylward recalls, "I lived in the second building in the project, on the first floor of 264 Mount Vernon Street. I could stand out on the curb in the early sixties, and every single person who came walking down the Mile Road I would know and have something to say to and something to chat about." Coming home to Columbia Point from the war, however, was like "being in a foreign country":

You'd watch people walk by and say, "Gee, who's that? I don't know him." The close-knit groups all broke apart; you stayed close with a smaller niche of kids. The complex, intertwined neighborhood model all broke down. It became more of an independent place to live. You didn't have the security of knowing you could walk through the project any time you wanted, day or night, and everybody would know who you are and nobody would bother you. All that was lost in the late sixties; it became a dangerous place to live.

At one point, you thought you had total control of everything that was going on around you, including the direction the project was going. And then you come back and realize you don't have any control over anything. And once the structure broke down, many of the people who were stable, living there year in and year out, decided to move out.

John Aylward came home from the army in January 1970 and in May 1971 became a police officer. For him and many of his friends, he says, "Civil service was the way to go to stabilize one's life." His family stayed at the project while they saw many of their friends move out. By 1977, however, "the risks [of staying] were too great." Although Aylward and his brothers were big, athletic types in their twenties who were able to defend themselves, his mother was a small woman who attended mass every day, walking to church. One day she was knocked down, her bag was stolen, and the assailant "ran off into the project and vanished." Shortly thereafter, John Aylward bought a three-family house in Dorchester for his family. They still live there: his sister on the third floor, another sister on the first floor, and his father on the middle floor. Aylward remains in touch with Columbia Point people to this day. "Although they didn't have a lot of money and didn't get great educations," he says, "they still remain loyal friends. They're good people."

MOVING IN

Esther Santos, 1962

Esther Santos and her husband and family of five kids were "burnout victims." In August 1962 they were burned out of their apartment on a quiet street of triple-deckers in Dorchester, and the Boston Housing Authority sent them to Columbia Point. Esther remembers her initial, horrified impression of her building at Columbia Point: "Seven stories, twenty-eight families, oodles of kids. Dirty, roach-infested. I just didn't believe there was anything like that, and I knew no way was I going to stay there. As soon as we found a way to get out, we were leaving." Before long, however, the Santos family became friends with the other families in the building. They all helped one another. They baby-sat for one another, they cooked for one another. If someone was sick, everybody pitched in and helped. In no time, the dirt and the roaches meant nothing; Esther Santos was staying put.

At first, Santos was mildly irritated at the housing authority's requirement that each tenant clean the hallway—"Of course, they couldn't wait to knock on my door and say, 'Your week is such and such and you have to do this and do that'"—but the four families on her floor decided to take the cleaning one step further. They got together and scrubbed the hallway floors, washed the windows, kept both sets of stairwells spotless. Soon enough, their hallway drew the attention of the rest of the building. "So the other folks," she recalls, "the other six floors, they all decided to do the same thing too because our floor was so spotless. . . . We had a great time doing it. We took real pride."

The problem was that the building was wide open. No matter how clean Santos and her neighbors kept it on the inside, they couldn't keep trouble out. Not when the front door was hanging by only one hinge and the back door was missing altogether. The elevator was broken, and not only the residents but also, annoyingly, many outsiders were continually going up and down the stairwells. Santos and her neighbors soon identified the problem: "It took us a little while to find out. One family on the seventh floor was selling drugs out of their home; that's why the traffic was so heavy."

"Alex and his sister Severthia Carr walk home to the Columbia Point projects where they live with their mother." Boston Herald.

According to Santos, by 1978 "most of the people had no faith in the Boston Housing Authority": "Some people had horrendous-looking apartments, no fault of their own, with leaks, mildew that they never came and repaired. If you had a leaky faucet, it went on for months because they just didn't come to repair it." Santos's community expanded in concentric circles: the fourth floor, the building, the entire project. The smaller circles were more manageable; but eventually, the safety of even the smallest of those circles—her family—could not be ensured unless the larger community was safe.

Ruby Jaundoo, 1965

Ruby Jaundoo moved into Columbia Point with her husband and three children in 1965. She had come to Boston from Washington, D.C. She recalls her first impression of Columbia Point: "It was a nice place to live in the sixties—fifteen hundred units, all filled, the buildings were kept up, the landscaping was nice, a lot of open space. It was a nice community."

Ruby Jaundoo taught preschool at the P. M. Hassett Day Care Center right across Mount Vernon Street for fourteen years, and she saw the effects of what was happening at Columbia Point on the children there. "Their physical needs and their mental needs were being met," she says. "But their housing needs weren't being met. If we want to raise children up to be healthy and productive people, we need to give them decent housing, and in my opinion that wasn't happening." The way Jaundoo saw it, it was a simple matter of the BHA failing to fulfill its responsibilities. Like the other tenants who were hanging on at Columbia Point, she was trying to do a good job raising her children, and she felt the BHA had an obligation to them.

After a while, Jaundoo recalls, the political forces seemed to be ready to let Columbia Point fall apart: "Once the word got out that the police weren't going to come in, that's when the negative element started to erupt here. The only way to get a police officer out here was you had to say another police officer's in trouble. . . . You still had a sense of community here. People joined together to help one another. But if you take just a handful of folk that allow negative activities to go on in the community, it's just setting the tone for the whole community. That's what happened at Columbia Point."

According to Jaundoo, the media didn't help either: "They would never write that a kid left here and went on to college, a kid went to Europe to go to school. But if somebody got arrested for drugs, if somebody got shot here, those were big headlines. People began blowing things out of proportion. Anything good that ever came out of Columbia Point never got any mention; but if anything bad happened, it made the headlines."

Even some local clerics abandoned the Point. Jaundoo recalls attending a community meeting at the *Boston Globe* to discuss the redevelopment of Columbia Point. When a local minister stood up to speak, his words took her breath away. "He said, 'It's never going to materialize. It's never going to happen. People go to Columbia Point and walk over dead bodies in hallways.' I could not believe he could say a thing like that. This is an ordained minister. Those were some of the forces we had to deal with."

There was no doubt that Columbia Point had problems. "I have to reinforce the fact that there was a negative element here," Jaundoo says. "A lot of bad people—no, maybe not bad people—a lot of negative people who knew they could come to Columbia Point and do their negative things and get away with it."

"Some people who like to tell the story don't really know the history," she says, "and they're making this a dreadful, awful place to live. There was some dreadful, awful things going on here, if one wanted to describe it that way." But the problem, Jaundoo says,

Life at Columbia Point captured by photographer Linda Swartz for her documentary, "Columbia Point." © 1985 by Linda Swartz.

wasn't dead bodies in the hallways. It was that the BHA and the Boston police should have been out there doing their jobs.

She knew of only one gang operating out of Columbia Point—the so-called Detroit gang: "A young lady that lived there allowed them to come and stay in their apartment. The police knew the gang was there. And they didn't do a damn thing about it. They knew exactly where this gang was. They did raid the apartment once, but it came up empty. I said to myself, sometimes, I think they wanted to find nothing, so they wouldn't have to deal with it. Let it take care of itself."

As long as Columbia Point's problems didn't spread to the rest of Boston, the police, in Jaundoo's opinion, were content to turn their heads: "It's not erupting over at Savin Hill. It's not erupting into South Boston. So just let it alone. Columbia Point is isolated out there; just let it take care of itself. The majority of people who were living here were black, probably eighty percent, another eighteen percent were Hispanic, and two percent were white. Most of the white people were our elderly people—somewhat of a forgotten group. I don't mean to sound cold. I mean, it wasn't the good life, but it wasn't as dreadful either as some people would say it was."

Etta Johnson, 1967

In 1967 Etta Johnson moved north from Virginia, sharing an apartment with her sister at Columbia Point. At first she wasn't involved in community activities but kept to herself. In 1969 she moved into her own unit at 5 Belvoir and immediately fell in love with it: "It was beautiful. It was gorgeous. I loved it. It was my dream house." Etta took turns with her neighbors cleaning the hallways, even waxing the floors and decorating the walls with pictures.

Johnson's building was mixed racially, with a white family, a Hispanic family, and two black families on her floor. All of the kids would sit on the floor in the hallway, playing with their toys. The families closed off the stairs and the kids used the hallway as their play area. Like hundreds of families before her, she and her sons enjoyed living at Columbia Point: "I had a wonderful time. There's a little corner beach on the end over here. It was nice sitting in it, and we had a good time every day during the summertime. We had a wonderful time; we went swimming in that water. We'd take our lunch over there and everything. We'd have a ball every day, in that little corner. . . . We used to go down there all the time. The kids used to play basketball. They roller-skated on the tennis courts and stuff like that. It was wonderful."

Johnson began to see the community change around 1973. The major change she noticed was in maintenance: "At first, when you called in a work order or said something's wrong, maintenance was out there just like that to fix it. All of a sudden that stopped. That came to like a halt. No one came for work orders. I have no idea why. It was just like they didn't care."

Before long, Johnson recalls, squatters began moving into the empty apartments. "They would just break the lock on the door," she recalls, "put their own lock on it, and they were in." She and her neighbors watched helplessly as management failed to take action to evict the squatters or fix things that broke: "If a person would come out and visit a friend of theirs, they'd look how many doors was empty, and if they needed an apartment, sooner or later, [they'd move in]. You know, you could even call the BHA and tell them there's squatters in that apartment, but I don't know if anybody ever investigated it. The squatters never left."

Soon Johnson no longer felt safe. She and her children kept to themselves inside their apartment: "There were people living there with all kinds of noise, they were in and out all night long, and it got to the point where I wouldn't even let my sons outside by themselves. David was maybe twelve years old at that time, and I wouldn't let him go outside by himself. I went outside with him and I stayed outside with him until he got ready to come back in."

By the late 1970s, Johnson recalls, there were only about 350 families left in the fifteen-hundred-unit project:

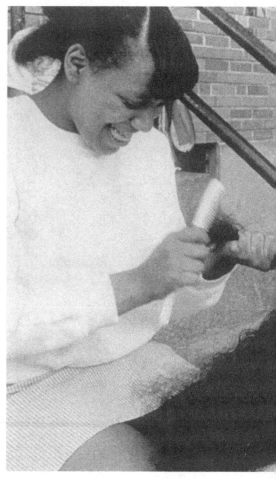

Life at Columbia Point captured by photographer Linda Swartz for her documentary, "Columbia Point." © 1985 *by Linda Swartz.*

Everybody was scattered. It was awful because you could come to my building and there would be ten families in that building, a seven-story building, and all the other windows are boarded up. So you go to the hallway, and there's no main door any longer, somebody took that all the way off and left that on the side. The lights are out; it's pitch black, and you have to walk up five flights of stairs. You don't know who you're going to meet in those corners.

I went out early in the morning, and I always got home before it got dark. I did everything I had to do before it got dark, and whenever it got dark, I was in my house.

My sons had to stay in. They couldn't go out unless I was going out with them. But our hallway was still intact, we were taking care of it every month, and still doing the cleaning until they moved us to a different building.

Why did families stay at Columbia Point when things had gotten so bad? Because they had no other choice. Johnson recalls what it was like for her to watch as more and more people moved out:

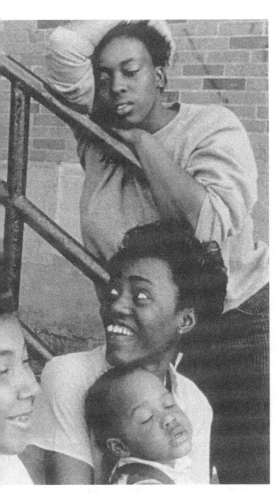

Through the seventies I watched it go down. Right down. I watched people moving out, and I could not afford to move out, because I had checked out apartments outside and the rents were so outrageous, there was no way I could get out there. If I got out there I was going to fail because I couldn't afford to pay that rent, and then I'd be on the street anyway, so I said, no, I was going to stick it out.

By 1974 my sister that I came to when I first moved to Boston moved out, I had another sister who moved out, I had a brother who moved out, my Mom had moved out. They all were living in Columbia Point, and a lot of other friends I knew, and all of them moved out. All of them moved out because it got so bad, they had to get out. They just said, "Forget it, I'm gone."

By the 1980s Johnson was one of the few residents left. She spent a lot of time inside her apartment, looking out the window at a community that had been completely abandoned—by the Boston Housing Authority, and even by the Boston police:

I always watch out the window, so I was watching out the kitchen window one night, and I see this guy get out of this white car, and all of a sudden a bunch of guys come up and they jump on him, start beating him up, and they took his car. I got on the phone and I called the police and something just dawned on me, you've got to say a white man is getting beat up.

So I said, "There is a white man getting beat up," and then it still took them about a half an hour to get here. If I would have said there was a guy getting beat up and left it alone, they would have never come. They would have never come. Let them kill themselves.

They just pulled back and let it go to hell. You can do whatever you want to do at Columbia Point. You could, I don't care what it was, you could do it. And no one ever said anything to you. No one.

When the housing authority began consolidating families in the buildings in the front of the project and mothballing the buildings in the back, Johnson and her children were relocated to 19 Brandon. Even though the other people on her new floor wouldn't clean the hallway, Johnson did it herself: "I didn't mind because I wanted to have a clean hallway. I didn't want to track it into my apartment." She still wouldn't let her sons, the oldest now fifteen, go outside by themselves. "He comes back to me now," she says of David, "and says, 'Ma, I know you kept me in a lot, but I want to thank you.' You know, he didn't realize it when he was growing up. He thought I was being mean to him. But he tells me now how proud he is of how I brought him up."

Erline Shearer and her
extended family at their
home in Dorchester.
Courtesy of Erline Shearer.

A Columbia Point Family Moving In and Moving Out

Erline Shearer moved into Columbia Point in 1956 and lived there for seventeen years, raising her five children. Her family's story spans the history of the project from its earliest days to its decline.

Like the journalists and the housing experts, Shearer felt that Columbia Point's isolation was its biggest problem. But it was her opinion that, to some extent, people in the project brought that isolation on themselves. She was determined to overcome that, both for herself and for her children.

Shearer had grown up in Roxbury, taught to feel that the whole city was hers to explore. As she explains, "My Mom said, 'It's out there. Go get it.'" She brought that spirit with her to Columbia Point—"Once I got to the MBTA station, there wasn't anything to keep me from going where I wanted to go"—and she instilled it in her children:

Wednesdays in the summer I used to take my kids down to the Esplanade. The Pops used to do their rehearsals there and do children's concerts. And each one of my kids could bring a friend. I remember the first time I took some kids other than my own to the library at Copley Square. They had never ever been outside of what used to be called Columbia Station. That had been the extent of leaving the Point. And it wasn't until a lot of kids started going to middle school that they got on something other than a school bus or the shopping bus.

I remember taking some kids that were having difficulty in reading. We combined two things. We took them to Ashmont Station, and we would ride the train from Ashmont to Harvard and the kids had to learn to read the stops. And they also learned how to get home, and things like how to make change to get on the subway. We were trying to cut into that feeling of isolation—we could go anywhere in the city, and at that time it was only a dime, and there were a lot of things out there.

As Shearer's children got older, they explored farther and farther afield:

My son Chuck was interested in sports, so we found a bike and put some wheels on it. And he and his friend Richie Long—who's now captain of the police out in Denver—would take turns riding over to Fenway Park to get tickets. They'd take a bunch of kids and go to the bleachers. . . . When Chuck was sixteen and he thought he was going to become a Red Sox player, he saved his money, took a bus, and went to Red Sox summer practice in Scottsdale, Arizona. And when my daughter Jackie was seventeen, she went to Mississippi and she worked with Marian Wright—now she's Marian Wright Edelman—with the Children's Defense Fund. She worked there in the Head Start program and helped with voter registration.

Although Columbia Point had been largely free of racial tension in the 1950s, the upheaval of the 1960s—the civil rights movement, the black power movement, desegregation—was felt even out there on the edge of Dorchester Bay. Erline Shearer watched as her children dealt with racial tensions for the first time: "They certainly knew that they were black kids. But it didn't seem to matter to them, and it didn't seem to matter to the kids that they were with until the whole desegregation thing started coming up. And then they became aware of how it was affecting other people, and what other people's view of their friendship was. You know, 'Why are you friends with them? Why aren't you with your own?' Things like that."

Shearer felt that the changes were most difficult for her youngest child, Debbie. "These were kids that she had known all her life," Erline explains, "because she was only two when we moved there. Obviously, she couldn't understand why it was wrong, or supposed to be wrong, for them to be friends." Debbie's best friend and constant companion, Dylan, was a white girl who lived in the apartment next door. Shearer recalls the subtle ways in which their relationship changed:

On Sundays they used to go in town and go to the Prudential Center. They'd ride the elevator all the way to the top, and take the soap from the washrooms, things like that. And then they'd come home and talk to each other through the bedroom windows. Neither one of them knew what was exactly happening, and why all of the sudden they shouldn't be playing with each other.

It was strained there for awhile. Not to the point that they stopped seeing each other, but they just became more aware that there was a difference. But they didn't know what it really was. . . .

I remember little Linda one time coming home, and she said, "I didn't know I was disadvantaged." And I said, "I didn't know it either." And she said, "Well, in school they told me that I was." So it was things like that. . . .

But nothing changed between the parents either—at least the ones that mattered, let me put it that way. To this day, some of those kids when I meet them on the street, I don't always remember their names, but they remember me. Sometimes they remember me as Chuck's mother, or Jackie's mother, whatever. And there's no restraint, no hesitation, no nothing. Kiss you wherever you are.

Debbie was the only one of Shearer's children to participate in the Metco program, in which children from the inner city were bused to suburban schools. Every morning, Debbie got up at five o'clock and had to go to Roxbury to get the bus to Lexington High. Shearer recalls that Debbie's adjustment was doubly difficult. All of the Metco kids had to face the challenge of fitting into a mostly white, affluent suburb. But Debbie, coming from the Point, didn't even fit in with the black kids:

Deb was the only one who didn't live in what I would call the inner city. I mean, she was out at the Point. She didn't live in Roxbury, she didn't live in the South End, or where larger groups of blacks were living. So this was new to her. All of a sudden she didn't know the latest slang, she didn't know how to dance, she didn't know any of those things. So she had a rougher time in Metco than she did in South Boston. She got over that pretty quick because she learned quick. But she wasn't sure she liked it. Some of the kids at Lexington wanted her to be more like the others because they knew how to deal with that. They didn't know how to deal with her if she couldn't talk like them, if she didn't dress like them, and if she didn't have interests similar to theirs.

Erline Shearer moved out of Columbia Point in 1973. "I moved on the spur of the moment," she recalls:

I was in the supermarket, and I met somebody who used to be the assistant manager down at the Point. And he just mentioned that he had to go home and clean up the apartment in his house because the tenants had just moved out. And I said, "Really? How many bedrooms?" And he said, "Three." I said, "Where is it?" So I went home, and I thought about it, and there was no one home then, just me. So I called him up, and I said, "I'll take it." So I knew that I had to do something because I was becoming stagnant. I mean, I was going to work, coming home, I was becoming less and less involved within the housing project.

Never one to stagnate, Erline Shearer moved on. However, twenty-five years later, she still thinks of Columbia Point as her home. Shearer and her children have good memories of the place where they grew up: "We talk about the Point a lot. I have a very close friend. I don't see her that much, but I consider her still my friend and we still see each other once in a while at the supermarket or at the mall. Her oldest daughter never, ever says that she lived at the Point. Never. She says she lived in Dorchester. That's as far as she would go. My kids say they lived at the Point."

The kind of community Shearer remembers has a richness that seems to belong to a time gone by, whether a housing project or a street in suburbia:

I'd move back in a minute. In fact, I think a half an hour after I was gone I wanted to move back. Yes, I really missed it. It's the little things, like I think I was the only one in the building who had a meat grinder. And that meat grinder used to make the rounds around Christmas time. People would be grinding up their giblets and things. I'd say, "Well, I don't know who's got it. But Helen had it last. Go check with her."

My oldest son, Chuck, was one of the first in our building to graduate from junior high. And his jacket made the rounds. Every year that was the graduation jacket. "Who had it last?" "Who graduated last year?"

I still have the one set of encyclopedias that went through the building. I had only one rule: Your hands had to be clean. *The World Book Encyclopedia.* My grandkids are using them today.

Erline Shearer had clear expectations for her children, which she felt she shared with other members of the Columbia Point community. She also had a few simple rules: "Don't ever let a policeman knock on my door. That basically is how we did it. You do what you have to do, and you do it well. You do the things you have to do whether you like it or not, like homework. And you will go to school, and you will graduate. And be on time for supper."

Erline Shearer's five children grew up true to their mother's expectations:

Chuck went to Boston University. He was in the service. He was trained in economics and went into the banking business. He found that was not to his liking. I think Chuck was the only loan officer who never found anybody home to collect on their loans. In banking he dealt mostly with elderly who had loans on their mobile homes. And he said, "Momma, how can I take their home away from them?" I said, "I think you're in the wrong business." And he now is working in the Brookline court system.

Jackie went on to Brandeis, and she was a history and English major. And she did all kinds of things. Her first independent film, dealing with the problems that came up due to the busing situation, was called *A Minor Altercation.* She worked on *Eyes on the Prize* with Henry Hampton. Linda went to Northeastern. C.F. went to Brown to study geology, and to the University of California at Santa Cruz. Now he's a dean at Carleton College in Minnesota. Deb's my freelancer. You name it and she did it.

"I gave them all a key when they left," Shearer concludes. "And I said, 'If you're ever in the neighborhood, you know you can come home.'"

"WE HAVE TO BE REALISTS"

Erline Shearer Represents Hopes For Poverty Program

Mrs. Erline Shearer doesn't have to live in the Columbia Point Housing Project anymore. But it's been her home for more than 10 years, and she's going to miss it.

But she's got to move out, because she's a financial success. She's not only earning her own way, she's making a good salary, $9,000-a-year, and expects an even better one, $12,000. Yet, she came to ABCD as an employee in January of 1966 as a $6,500-a-year resource analyst.

No one is more pleased for her than her boss, Robert Coard, executive director of Action for Boston Community Development (ABCD), antipoverty agency for the City of Boston.

"Mrs. Shearer represents almost the sum total of our hopes for the poverty program," Coard said recently, "a program not only serving poor people, but actually run by them, not just as unpaid board members, but as top executives."

Mrs. Shearer was recently appointed to run one of ABCD's five major service programs. As the new director of the Urban Training Division, Mrs. Shearer directs some 12 staff employees assisting the board, staff and volunteers of ABCD in acquiring skills as community organizers.

The division also works with affiliate agencies and interested representatives of business, labor, and industry.

The training itself runs the gamut from indoctrination in parliamentary rules of order to briefings on the nature and

Shearer had another responsibility, an even more important one, as a mother.

"Maybe it's a little strange," she observed the other day, "but there was never any question about it. We all knew the children were going to college. We were on welfare, and living in a housing project, but we didn't worry about money, rather we were concerned with the choice and selection of the college. We just assumed they were going to college, and a way would be found."

And four of her five children already have — all on scholarships. Charles, the oldest

She has technical expertise but that's not what she was most to get over to the people, both the poor and the not-so poor.

"To be poor means one thing — not having enough money." Mrs. Shearer said, "Sure, many poor people don't have as good education as middle class people. That doesn't mean they lack the intelligence or the ambition or the willingness to improve their lot. Give them the chance and the opportunity to help themselves. That's what I've tried to do all along. That's what I intend to keep

MRS. ERLINE SHEARER

Erline Shearer, working for Action for Boston Community Development (ABCD). *Courtesy of Erline Shearer.*

15 The News from Columbia Point

One way to trace the fate of Columbia Point through the 1960s and 1970s is in the pages of Boston's newspapers. Although by no means the most accurate account of life at the project during these years, it is the version of Columbia Point of record—the only version most people knew. Newspaper accounts give a sense of two parallel universes: the world of the planners and the politicians, and the world of the people struggling to live at Columbia Point amid steadily worsening conditions.

Boston Globe articles alternate between optimistic reports on life at the project—"Project Families Very Cooperative," "Isolation on Wane"—and more negative reports—"Sniper, 9, Wounds Dorchester Boy," "Rats in Project, Mother Charges." For example, the Columbia Point Improvement Association, formerly known as the Mothers Club, continues its efforts to get basic services for the Point:

> **December 1963.** "500 Sign Demand for Buses" reports that Columbia Point residents are protesting the lack of bus service between the project and Andrew Station. The improvement association presents a petition signed by more than five hundred residents of the project, calling for affordable bus service instead of having to wait at a wooden shelter they called "the shanty" at Columbia Circle.

At the same time, reports of violence at the project are a steady theme throughout the 1960s:

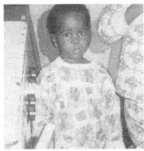

> **December 1967.** "Dorchester Youth Held in Robbery" reports the robbing at knife point of ABCD director Don Strong and two Harvard students as they walked through the project to a meeting.

> **February 1968.** "Sniper, 9, Wounds Dorchester Boy" reports that a nine-year-old boy, aiming his father's .22-caliber rifle out of his apartment window, shot a five-year-old boy in the back as he walked home from the candy store.

> **October 1968.** "Youth Gang Nailed in Breaks" reports a series of break-ins at Columbia Point, culminating in the arrest of eight boys living in the housing project.

Optimistic articles are interspersed with the dire news from the Point:

August 1967. "Isolation on Wane" reports that the project is "fast overcoming a collective sense of inferiority and isolation." The article recounts the tenants' successful efforts to improve their community: picketing to get the dumps closed; demanding traffic and street lights, better bus service, and improved police protection; opening the Columbia Point Federal Credit Union; and opening a community library. Although the housing project continues to have problems, the tenants are portrayed as resourceful in taking the initiative to solve them.

April 1968. "Boston Housing Plan Due for Vote Today" reports on a proposed plan to turn over the management of Columbia Point from the housing authority to the tenants. Attorney Frederick Wiseman, better known for his documentary filmmaking, including the exposé *Titicut Follies*, once banned in Massachusetts, is a member of the Organization for Social and Technical Innovation, Inc., of Cambridge, the consulting firm proposing a tenant management corporation for the residents of Columbia Point.

In 1968 the Columbia Point tenants initiate a lawsuit against the Boston Housing Authority in an effort to hold it accountable for conditions at the project:

April 1968. "Public Housing Tenants Sue to Hold Rent: Want Repairs" reports that a Columbia Point tenant, Alfredo De Jesus, has brought suit against the Boston Housing Authority. De Jesus, executive director of *Centro de Acción*, brings the suit against the BHA, charging that four Columbia Point apartments are "unlivable." As evidence of the charge, the suit mentions that the ceilings leak, plaster is falling off the ceilings, the toilet is unbolted, and there is no ceiling in the bathroom.

The pressure is on the BHA. The six thousand residents of Columbia Point are holding it accountable as their landlord. The lawsuit is soon followed by a rent strike:

November 1968. "Heatless Columbia Point Tenants Threaten Rent Strike" reports that, for days, only three of the project's seven boilers were operating, while temperatures dipped as low as 39 degrees in some apartments. The project is beginning to lose "our best families," one resident claims. The article quotes Ellis Ash, director of the BHA, who admits, "Those conditions do exist and some for an intolerably long time." Columbia Point manager Jeremiah Sullivan adds, "We've got only two carpenters, and they're doing so much to repair the vandalism that we're hard pressed to do the other things."

Columbia Point
Community Youth Center,
*1980s. Courtesy of Marie
Kennedy, Columbia Point
Oral History Project.*

Despite the tenants' protests, conditions worsen:

January 1969. "'Terror' Cited at Columbia Point" reports on "a reign of terror that has erupted" at the project. Residents are assaulted and property is vandalized. Vendors and tradesmen are refusing to serve the Point. The article documents that a major milk company has canceled deliveries to the project and taxicabs are refusing to take calls.

June 1969. "Arrest of 16-Year-Old Ends Columbia Point 'Lone Bandit' Terror" reports the arrest of a teenager who had been terrorizing elderly members of the community.

July 1969. "Project Called a Menace" details the increasingly nightmarish conditions there. Mothers can't treat their children's strep throats because so many apartments are without hot water, and elderly residents are near collapse from having to carry groceries up several flights of stairs in buildings with broken elevators.

Life at Columbia Point captured by photographer Linda Swartz for her documentary, "Columbia Point." © *1985 by Linda Swartz.*

The litany of troubles culminates in the Columbia Point tenants' ghoulish Christmas present to their landlords at the Boston Housing Authority at the close of a dismal decade:

December 1969. "Tenants give BHA roaches for Christmas" reports that tenants interrupted a meeting of the BHA board. "In solemn procession," the article recounts, "the tenants came bearing gifts":

"On a long table, in front of [the five BHA board members], they placed jars of holiday goodies.

"Dangling from green branches amidst the sparkling silver tinsel on the Christmas tree were half a dozen tiny dead mice.

"Carefully stored in the clear glass preserve jars were scores of dead cockroaches and a handful of squirming live black bugs."

The tenants leave a Christmas list of fifteen items needing urgent attention, ranging from extermination to control of wild dogs at the project and to repair of unsafe elevators in which children had been injured or killed. The list itself is a sad testament to the disgraceful conditions in which BHA tenants are being forced to live.

In 1962, when Columbia Point first grabbed the attention of the outside world, its prospects had seemed hopeful in spite of the problems the community faced. The consultants were called in, and the problems did not seem insurmountable. But now, at the end of the decade, hope has all but evaporated. The urban planners' grand schemes have been replaced by the tenants' rodent-festooned Christmas tree. The BHA board members express no denials or defenses; they send exterminators to the project the next day.

By the beginning of the 1970s people live at Columbia Point only if they have to. Social service offices at the Point are routinely burglarized, building cleanups by tenants cease for the most part, and people continue to move out:

> **January 1971.** "An Edge of the Universe: Traveling a Hard Road at Columbia Point" paints a bleak portrait of the project that many want to flee. The lead paragraph sets the discouraged tone: "It's bad, bad. It's very bad. A young woman I know came up to me a few weeks ago and she said, 'You know, I get the saddest feeling when I come around the corner on the bus. I feel like there's nothing left.' I told her we all have felt it."

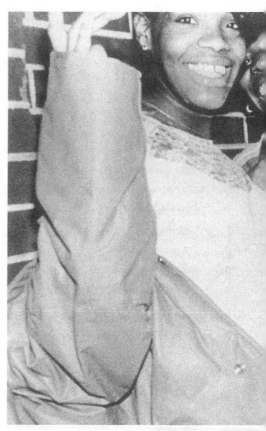

Life at Columbia Point captured by photographer Linda Swartz for her documentary, "Columbia Point." © 1985 by Linda Swartz.

The remaining tenants struggle to make the community livable — now a matter not of adding wished-for amenities but of trying to achieve a modicum of basic safety. Residents form a "community patrol" that follows the mailman with a loudspeaker on the first and fifteenth of the month, when the welfare checks are delivered. In an attempt to cut down on shoplifting at the Bayside Mall, stores including Stop & Shop, Zayre, and Almy hire teenagers from the project as "monitors" in the stores, paying each monitor twenty-five dollars per week.

In March 1971 in a column entitled "An Explosive Solution for Columbia Point," *Globe* columnist David B. Wilson makes a not entirely facetious proposal: "The solution to the Columbia Point 'problem,' is, of course . . . to sell the damned thing and give the money to the tenants." Indeed, the city and its services — police, fire, ambulance — appear to be in full retreat:

> **July 1971.** "Harbor View Masks Night Warfare by Columbia Point Gangs vs. Firemen" reports that Boston fire commissioner James H. Kelley has asked for police protection for all fire engines entering the project, citing "many incidents of rock and bottle tossing from rooftops."

Firemen report that they are afraid of going into the project, saying that it is common to get at least three alarms from Columbia Point, most of them false, on Friday and Saturday nights. The reporter, riding a fire truck into the project, describes the grim scene: "[Buildings] are littered with crushed beer cans, melted ice cream, papers of a thousand varieties, old auto parts and sometimes some garbage. For

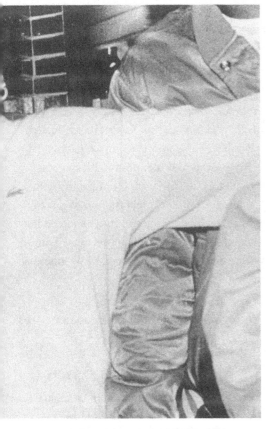

the most part, the doors leading into the first floor corridors have been taken off their hinges. . . . As the fire truck pulled into Monticello Avenue, bricks and bottles began to pelt the truck from all sides." A follow-up article reports that Columbia Point residents are incensed about the previous article, charging: "When good things happen they're not written up. The fact remains that it's no different here than any place else." That article, in turn, is followed with countercharges from the Fire Department that conditions at Columbia Point are indeed "the worst in the city."

As crime escalates—a 70 percent increase from 1970 to 1971—and residents continue to desert the project, the possibility of demolition is real. A BHA official notes that "Columbia Point has often been referred to as the Northeast's Pruitt-Igoe," the St. Louis housing project that was ultimately demolished:

> **March 1973.** "Columbia Point: Can It Be Saved?" describes the deep sense of apathy at the project. Maintenance is virtually nonexistent, and President Nixon is reducing federal funding for public housing. Columbia Point residents fear students will displace them. The Bayside Mall is on the verge of death, with most of its stores already closed. One-fourth of the units at Columbia Point are vacant. A proposal to turn over management of Columbia Point to the tenants is met with suspicion. As resident Thelma Peters explains, "I think the government has had so many hassles across the country with the way public housing is set up that they're looking to unload it."

In October 1973 the mood at Columbia Point shifts from apathy to horror when the project is again the scene of senseless violence and death. In 1962 the death was that of a six-year-old girl crossing the street in front of the project. In 1973 the death is that of a sixty-five-year-old man fishing off the rocks behind the project. This time, the context for violence is the escalating racial tension in the city, fueled by the busing crisis:

> **October 1, 1973.** "Rigid Security at Dorchester" reports that classes would resume that morning at Dorchester High School after a two-day shutdown was ordered to ease escalating racial tensions. On September 27 and 28, the high school was the scene of a number of violent incidents, with many students injured and substantial property damage. Pressure was mounting in the city and the prospect of court-ordered busing to desegregate the public schools loomed. The previous February the State Supreme Judicial Court had upheld the lower court's order requiring a racial balance plan for the Boston public schools. In April, the city erupted: some four thousand antibusing advocates led by Louise Day Hicks had marched on the State House. The violence at Dorchester

Detectives investigate the crime scene where Ludovico Barba was stoned to death while fishing behind Columbia Point, October 1973. *Courtesy of the* Boston Globe.

High foreshadowed what would follow almost a full year later when U.S. District Court Judge W. Arthur Garrity's June 1974 ruling requiring busing was implemented and the schools opened that September.

October 4, 1973. "Woman Slain by Torch" reports that, on Tuesday night, October 2, Evelyn M. Wagler, twenty-four, a white woman who had just moved to Boston from Chicago, was walking on Blue Hill Avenue in Roxbury with a gas can because her car had run out of gas. She was attacked by six black youths who forced her to pour gasoline on herself and set herself on fire. She died several hours later, on Wednesday morning.

Within twenty-four hours the violence rips into Columbia Point:

October 5, 1973. "Boston Man Stoned to Death" reports that on Thursday afternoon, October 4, gang violence erupted at Columbia Point. Sixty-five-year-old Ludovico L. Barba was fishing on the rocks behind the shopping center adjacent to the project when he was set upon by a gang of forty to fifty black teenagers. Barba was stabbed in the back and then stoned. He was found lying face down, half in water, his eyeglasses knocked into the water, a broken fishing rod at his side. Near his body was a wallet-sized wedding picture of a man wearing glasses and a woman in a wedding dress. Barba had been fishing at Dorchester Bay for years, and his wife often joined him. He was born in Boston and had received a law degree from Northeastern University.

Father Larry Wetterholm, the priest at St. Christopher's parish at Columbia Point, remembers that day with a terrible clarity:

There was a lot of friction in the schools, and on this given day a busload of students [from Columbia Point] were driven into Andrew Square. There was a fracas, and the black youngsters got back on the bus and told the driver to drive them back to Columbia Point, and some of them went berserk.

I had just finished saying mass and I heard an awful noise outside. . . . Then I wondered just what was going on. I left the rectory and went down towards the water. There was a goodly number of people on the edge of the water. A man who was down there fishing was killed. He had been stabbed and I crawled on my stomach over the rocks down there to pray over him and there were maybe thirty or forty people and many of them had witnessed the murder.

Above, left: "Cleaning out an apartment," Columbia Point, 1973. *Courtesy of the* Boston Globe.

Above, right: Columbia Point, 1973. *Courtesy of the* Boston Globe.

Two suspects, ages fifteen and sixteen, were sought, both from Columbia Point. The boys were arrested but never convicted.

Within hours of Barba's death, two other people are attacked at Columbia Point. Ronald Leonard, thirty-seven, a furniture delivery man from Revere, is attacked in front of 11 Brandon, knifed in the back. He is rushed to Boston City Hospital and reported as still in critical condition a week after surgery. At around the same time, Claire Oates, twenty-eight, a white woman from Quincy, is knocked down, slashed, and robbed of her handbag as she is walking her dog behind the Bayside Mall.

The only hope for a community that is all but dead—except for the few hundred people still living there—will come some two years later on February 7, 1975, when a tenant in the Mission Hill public housing project, Armando Perez, brings the Boston Housing Authority to court with an unprecedented lawsuit.

"T.P.F. [Tactical Patrol Force] officers aid Boston police. Housing detail officers investigating an attempted handbag snatch in elderly section of Columbia Point project," 1972. *Courtesy of the* Boston Globe.

"Soul and Sorrow in the Project"

On Sunday, July 1, 1973, Walter Haynes's article in the *Boston Globe* reported on his experience living in Columbia Point for a month. The article echoes the seven-part series written by Richard Hurt in 1962 that first alerted the city to conditions at Columbia Point. Ten years later, the picture of the Point has changed—from optimism to despair.

Haynes, a young black reporter and a member of the paper's urban team, describes the project's profound isolation "from the city, from food services, from social agencies, from other communities." His is no exposé of a "vertical slum," but rather an elegy for a forgotten neighbor, dying a slow and lonely death less than half a mile from the newsroom at the *Boston Globe:* "I didn't see the blatant violence I had heard about. I didn't see the 'sin city' someone had written about. What I did get was a glimpse into the lives of people. What I did hear were the voices of these people who have made Columbia Point home. And from what I saw and heard, I got an idea of how it is to be killed softly by broken promises and dreams. It's a way of dying you often read about but find hard to believe, especially when it's happening across the wide streets of Morrissey Boulevard."

Haynes describes the constant background of soul music in the project; elevators that never work; two women in the thrift shop debating whether it was a good thing that the Boston Housing Authority stopped screening applicants. ("I came in here with my four children and they didn't ask me any questions," one woman says. "I'm glad they didn't because my husband had our marriage certificate and he was in the army down in Texas.") "Neither of them agreed on just when the project changed," Haynes notes, "when the people moved in who threw trash out the window, or when the dope addicts arrived in the hallways."

He describes a young man known as Snake, age twenty-five, who grew up in Alabama and had once been the kingpin of heroin at Columbia Point, taking in close to two thousand dollars

a week selling to addicts who mostly came from the city to the housing project to buy. Snake explains why he stopped selling: "The reason I got out was because I realized the effects heroin had on the people I was selling it to."

Haynes describes the scene on "welfare day," when people crowd the hallway waiting for the postman; lots of dogs crowd the hallways, too, mostly German shepherds, none on leashes. Jack Driscoll had been delivering the checks since the project opened. "Driscoll starts his route in the high-rise section on Montpelier," Haynes explains, "because he says deliveries there are harder. All the mailboxes in the project seem to have been mangled by some madman."

One woman advises Haynes, "If you want to know Columbia Point, knock on the doors of the people you never see. The ones that stay locked up behind closed doors." Haynes takes her advice and starts knocking on doors of apartments in his temporary home at 26 Montpelier: one woman came from Helena, Arkansas, another from a small town in North Carolina. They tell Haynes that they mostly stay to themselves; no, they haven't had any problems; but when they call the housing authority about broken windows or water backing up, no one ever comes.

Haynes listens to the woes of the BHA maintenance man, Bo, who sweeps the project from 24 Montpelier back to Monticello: "'I'll never finish, man,' he said. Bo probably has the most permanent job in the city. He leaned on his broom almost like a soldier leaning on his rifle. 'I lay in bed at night and listen to the trash fall from the floors. Crash!! The people are probably saying we ain't going to give old Bo a break. Gotta make him work hard.'"

Like a character in a play who's seen it all and sweeps across the stage in the last act, Bo comments, laughing and shaking his head: "People ask me if I'm ever going back to the South. Sure, man, soon as I get the money to buy some land. I'll buy six pork chops and my little girl eats three . . . people up here are crazy, hear. As soon as I get some money I'm gone."

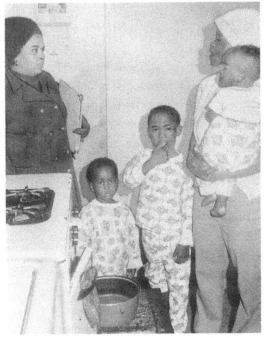

Above, left: "11 Brandon Ave., scene of a stabbing," Columbia Point, 1973. *Courtesy of the* Boston Globe.

Above, right: "State Rep. Doris Bunte talks with Columbia Point resident Mrs. Jannie Robinson and her children," 1975. Boston Herald.

Left: "Black Caucus and news media tour Columbia Point housing project," 156 Monticello Road, 1975. Boston Herald.

Below: "John Santos, 19 Brandon Ave., Columbia Point Building Captain, experiments with building patrol," 1973. *Courtesy of the* Boston Globe.

Busing at Columbia Point

Columbia Point residents were no different from residents of other Boston neighborhoods in their attitudes about "the busing," as U.S. District Judge W. Arthur Garrity's 1974 desegregation plan is often called. Before the Dever elementary school and the McCormack middle school opened on the peninsula in the 1950s, the children of Columbia Point attended schools in South Boston and Dorchester, largely without incident. Once the court order was issued and implemented over a two-year period, however, the atmosphere became highly charged, and many parents at Columbia Point felt as though their children were victimized by their new school assignments.

Betty Quarles, a Columbia Point resident, remembers that three of her children were bused on the first day of busing, September 12, 1974. At the end of that school day, the buses did not return to Columbia Point until after 5 p.m. That worried Quarles, and as a result, she attended a meeting in Roxbury where Mayor Kevin White called for volunteers to ride the buses as monitors. She did so for three years. Although Quarles was never on a bus when rocks were thrown, the threat of violence was almost always palpable. "I would tell the kids to watch me and if they saw me duck, they should duck, too, and fast," she recalls.

She and many of her friends at Columbia Point believed that busing could have worked more smoothly if it had been implemented gradually, starting with elementary-age children and proceeding one grade at a time. To Quarles, requiring Boston's teenagers to leave their friends, activities, and teams made no sense. "Taking kids out of high school and forcing them to go someplace else was bound to cause trouble," she says. "Anybody could see that."

School buses leave the abandoned Bayside Mall parking lot, 1974. *Courtesy of the* Boston Globe.

Part 3
Columbia Point, 1978–1987

16 Unlikely Partners

Mount Vernon Street led to the Columbia Point housing project and nowhere else; there was one way in and one way out. The three white men driving down Mount Vernon one evening in the fall of 1978 were an unusual sight. As their gray Oldsmobile slowed to make a left turn into the project, a Boston police officer stepped out of his patrol car and signaled them to pull over.

In 1978 nobody entered Columbia Point without a police escort. Most simply refused. Taxis, fire engines, even ambulances waited at the entrance—for as long as it took—until a patrol car was available. The men in the Olds had to be told: you don't go in or come out unescorted, not if you want to come out in one piece.

In the last light of day, the patrol car slowly led the car through the project, past three- and seven-story buildings, yellow brick blocks lined up in great monotonous flat-roofed rows. The Columbia Point they drove through that evening showed no signs of life; huge squares of red plywood stared blankly where windows should have been. The playgrounds and basketball courts were deserted. Here and there a swing still hung from a chain, a rusted hoop was still attached to a backboard. Everywhere the asphalt was strewn with rubbish and broken glass. The smell of salt air was the only signal that Dorchester Bay lay just beyond.

The police car pulled over next to a three-story building and the three men stepped out of their car. The officer wanted to know how long they planned to be there; he told them a cruiser would be waiting when they came out. Easily pulling open the front door, its lock broken, the three men climbed the dark stairwell. Their destination was the office of the Columbia Point Community Task Force. They brought with them a plan for nothing less than the complete transformation of the Columbia Point housing project.

At the top of the stairs, behind a heavy metal door, a made-over apartment served as the task force office. Three members of the task force, the elected representa-

"Boarded-up high-rise
building at Columbia
Point stands vacant, the
victim of vandalism and
poor maintenance," 1978.
Boston Herald.

tives of the 350 families still living at Columbia Point, were waiting. Terry Mair, Esther Santos, and Ruby Jaundoo—three black women—had given their children early dinners that evening. They didn't have a long walk to the task force office, but they made a point of arriving before dark. They had not been given a police escort; Columbia Point was their home.

Terry Mair, president of the task force, was the twenty-six-year-old mother of six children. Esther Santos had been living at Columbia Point for sixteen years, raising five children. One of the first tenants elected to the task force, she had worked for years in her steady and

Esther Santos, Columbia
Point Community Task
Force, early 1980s.
*Courtesy of Corcoran,
Mullins, Jennison.*

determined way to try to stop the community from deteriorating.
Ruby Jaundoo, a handsome woman in her forties, had lived at Columbia Point for thirteen years, raising four children and teaching at
the Patricia M. Hassett Day Care Center, across the street from the
project. Jaundoo hadn't been eager to join the task force. For years,
people who were already involved had been after her to run for election, but what finally persuaded her were her preschoolers and her
own children. She felt she owed it to them to see to it that the
Boston Housing Authority lived up to its obligations.

She and the other members of the task force were well aware that
the city of Boston was beginning to recognize the potential value of
the Columbia Point peninsula, even as the housing project was deteriorating. The University of Massachusetts had put a chain-link
fence across Mount Vernon Street to block off its new campus from
the increasingly dangerous housing project; yet its proximity was an
unavoidable geographical fact. When there was talk of locating the
Kennedy Library on the peninsula, the tenants were the first to recognize that the juxtaposition of a decaying, racially segregated housing project and a gleaming white memorial to John F. Kennedy
would be an irony of the highest order.

The tenants of Columbia Point watched the arrival of these two
respectable new neighbors with apprehension. "When the Kennedy
Library went up, in our opinion this became prime property for
everyone. It scared me," Ruby Jaundoo says of the institution whose
formal dedication on October 20, 1979, drew luminaries including
President Jimmy Carter, Jacqueline Kennedy Onassis, and Lady
Bird Johnson to the peninsula. After all, if the onetime garbage
dump turned public housing project was suddenly to become valu-

Columbia Point, 1979.
Courtesy of the Boston
Globe.

Ruby Jaundoo, Columbia
Point Community Task
Force, early 1980s.
*Courtesy of Corcoran,
Mullins, Jennison.*

able real estate, would the Columbia Point tenants be cleared out with the rest of the debris?

Although the task force had fought successfully to secure a $10 million HUD grant, it soon became apparent that "modernization" wasn't enough to fix what was wrong with Columbia Point. The project was fast approaching what looked like a dead end. The task force members recognized the futility of modernization, but they had no better idea with which to replace it. The city seemed to be in retreat, withdrawing even essential services such as garbage collection, fire, and ambulance. The tenants of Columbia Point were not being treated like citizens entitled to city services. Gradually, they came to be treated more like prison inmates, stripped of ordinary rights, isolated in fear within their apartments, even though they had committed no crime. That evening in 1978, assigning police protection to the three white men entering the project was not unlike assigning a guard to to accompany visitors into a prison.

The men climbing the stairs to the task force office were Joe Corcoran, Joe Mullins, and Gary Jennison—partners of a six-year-old real estate development company. They brought with them a proposal based on two core ideas: they would convert the low-income public housing project into a private, mixed-income community; and they would do so in partnership with the tenants.

Joe Corcoran had been waiting for this meeting for a long time. Columbia Point had always been on his horizon; as he says, "I grew up with it." The youngest of eight children of immigrant parents in a working-class Irish family, Corcoran grew up in Uphams Corner, only a couple of miles from Columbia Point. He was on the peninsula even before the housing project, attending Boston College High School when there was nothing out there but the new school, the old pumping station, and the dumps. In the summer of 1951, when ground was broken for Columbia Point, Corcoran went over and tried to get a job as a laborer. Just sixteen, he was turned down for being underage and not a union member.

Over the years, Corcoran had kept an eye on conditions at the housing project. For the first ten years or so, it had been a viable community. Back then, families would qualify for public housing at a low-income level, but they would not be forced out if their income increased. The way Corcoran saw it, public housing really began to go downhill when public officials reversed that policy and insisted that public housing be reserved for the poor, setting income limits for tenants. He explains:

Life at Columbia Point
captured by photographer
Linda Swartz for her
documentary, "Columbia
Point." © *1985 by Linda
Swartz.*

[They argued that] even if some guy's making only fifteen grand a year, he shouldn't be in there because there are poorer people waiting. So the laws get changed. Only the poorest of the poor can live in public housing, and the working families must move out. Then the Brooke Amendment comes along, saying you can't pay more than 25 percent of your income to live in public housing—and suddenly the housing authority doesn't have enough money to run the place. For years, mayors would make political appointments to the housing authority board, many of whom knew nothing about housing.

In the early 1960s Corcoran met frequently with Columbia Point resident leaders such as Jim Duffy and Pat McCluskey, and with Donald Strong, who staffed Action for Boston Community Development's neighborhood-based antipoverty agency at the housing project. The informal group invited John Giuggio, an executive of the *Boston Globe,* Columbia Point's new neighbor, to join them. Together, they went to see Ed Logue to discuss the BRA's 1964 plan for urban renewal on the peninsula. Incorporating as a nonprofit, the Dorchester Landing Development Group, they worked to build public support for the plan. Corcoran and the others believed that the BRA's vision of a "new town"—with more housing, more retail stores, and a range of facilities—was the solution to the peninsula's problems. But the plan went nowhere. Columbia Point continued to deteriorate while Corcoran established himself in the real estate business in Dorchester, working with his two older brothers building conventional apartments before striking out on his own in 1971 to develop mixed-income housing.

Several times in subsequent years, Corcoran had driven through Columbia Point, walking around "reconnoitering" and talking to tenant leaders. He couldn't understand how anyone could build something so wrong. In his opinion, it was wrong architecturally and it was wrong socially. From an urban design standpoint, it made no sense—just a bunch of tall, ugly buildings jammed together, blocking the water, which anyone could see was the best feature of the site. It was just plain wrong to put all those poor people out there; fifteen hundred units of warehousing, that's all it was.

By 1978 both Joe Corcoran and Columbia Point had come of age. His company, Corcoran, Mullins, Jennison (CMJ), was six years old, a little short on cash but strong on experience, with a good track record. He knew he could make Columbia Point better, maybe even turn it around, if he could persuade the powers that be. It might take years to put the pieces together, but Corcoran could be very patient if he had to—because he had a clear vision of what Columbia Point could become and he wanted to be the one to make it a reality.

Joe Corcoran, Joe Mullins, and Gary Jennison took their seats opposite Esther Santos, Ruby Jaundoo, and Terry Mair. These women were the new players, successors to a previous generation of resident leaders at the housing project. The three men were well aware that they were only the last in a long line of white men in business suits who had walked in and told these black women they were going to make their world better. Al-

Left to right: Joe Corcoran, Gary Jennison, and Joe Mullins. *Courtesy of Corcoran, Mullins, Jennison.*

though they had complete confidence in what they had to offer, the partners knew it would be a hard sell. All they hoped to get out of the meeting was the chance to explain their proposal and invite the task force to visit one of their developments and see for themselves. "We could show them our product," Joe Corcoran explains, "how people live in our developments versus what the housing authority can show them. That's what we had to sell."

Joe Mullins went first. Tall, red-haired, and outgoing, Mullins was a proud son of South Boston from the same Irish Catholic working-class background as his partner, Joe Corcoran. Before joining Corcoran, Mullins had worked for the Federal Housing Authority. He knew all the ins and outs of government-assisted financing and had established good working relationships with the bureaucrats. As a project director, he brought the experience and the drive that would be necessary to get a complicated project like Columbia Point done.

Their company, Mullins explained to the task force, wanted to transform Columbia Point into a private, mixed-income community. They had already developed several successful mixed-income communities. In 1973 they had begun developing the first phase of Queen Anne's Gate in Weymouth, Massachusetts—544 units with 25 percent low-income, 25 percent moderate-income, and 50 percent market-rate tenants—the first successful mixed-income project in Massachusetts and one of the first in the nation. In 1976 they had taken America Park, a badly deteriorated state public housing project in Lynn, Massachusetts, a blue-collar community fifteen miles north of Boston, and transformed it into a viable mixed-income community renamed King's Lynne.

Gary Jennison was up next. Compact, clipped, and efficient, Jennison was a no-nonsense guy, the numbers guy. A CPA formerly with Coopers and Lybrand, Jennison formed and oversaw CMJ's construction and management divisions. He brought precisely the same matter-of-fact approach to the challenges at Columbia Point as to the other properties CMJ had developed. They had a prototype that worked, so why not apply it? "Somebody was going to do Harbor Point," Jennison recalls. "If it wasn't us, it was going to be somebody else. We felt confident, based on our experience, that we could do it just as well or better than anyone else."

When Jennison looked at Columbia Point, he did not see a complex problem that had defied solution for years. "It was a prime piece of real estate," he explains. "You knew the market was there, as long as you did it right. Everyone wants to live on the ocean.

Once you brought the tenant group on board, you had the whole package. You just had to employ the principles."

Their company, Jennison explained to the task force, had already demonstrated that mixed-income housing could work. Market-rate tenants would live side by side with low-income tenants, as long as the development was well built and well managed. To make a mixed-income community work, he went on, you had to build it and operate it as a market-rate development—then everything else would fall into place. You had to give market prospects value that was better than anything else in the area. The formula, Jennison explained, was simple: build the best apartments, have the best landscaping, provide amenities like swimming pools and tennis courts, and make sure the pricing is right. CMJ was confident, Jennison concluded, that the same prototype that had worked so well at Queen Anne's Gate and King's Lynne would be successful at Columbia Point.

Although the three members of the task force listened politely and attentively while Mullins and Jennison explained their proposal, they had a hard time believing what they were hearing. "I thought it was a bunch of white men coming in and trying to pull a snow job on a bunch of black women," says Ruby Jaundoo. "That's exactly what I thought." Why would these developers want to come in and pour millions of dollars into a place like Columbia Point? Since when did anybody think black people should be able to live in such a nice place as they proposed, side by side with white people? Since when would people who had the money to rent an apartment *choose* to live next to poor people—not to mention in a place with the stigma of Columbia Point? Jaundoo kept her thoughts to herself.

Terry Mair was more outspoken. Why did these developers want to get involved with Columbia Point, she asked. They must be in it for the money. Joe Corcoran expected her question and answered it directly. There were lots of ways his company could make money, he told them. It was building second homes down on Cape Cod for affluent people at that very moment. He hadn't come to Columbia Point to make money; he thought the place was a nightmare, and he knew his company could turn it around.

No wonder the task force was skeptical. One minute, the entire city seemed content to sit by and let the community destroy itself. The next minute, the tenants were being courted by a developer to become their partner and completely transform the place. What scared the task force was not that Columbia Point might become a

Life at Columbia Point
captured by photographer
Linda Swartz for her
documentary, "Columbia
Point." © 1985 by Linda
Swartz.

nice place to live. It was, Ruby Jaundoo explains, that the tenants
they represented wouldn't be a part of it: "They were saying that
they're going to come in and do this to Columbia Point. That wasn't
easy to accept. It wasn't easy for me, and it definitely wasn't easy for
the residents that remained here. The only thing we could think of
was displacement, of being relocated to someplace else. . . . The
thought was in my mind that if they were going to come in and do
all that, the people who were here now were not going to be there
then." The price of making Columbia Point livable, Jaundoo feared,
would be losing the place where she lived.

Joe Corcoran took over for the last part of the presentation. Yes,
his company wanted to make Columbia Point better. But the real
difference was that they wanted to do it in partnership with the tenants. Not only would the original residents remain at Columbia
Point, but they would also become full partners with the developer.
Together with CMJ, the tenants would write the rules for Columbia
Point: Who would be the architect? How many units would be
built? How big would they be? What kinds of kitchen cabinets, windows, carpeting would there be? In all issues requiring a decision,
they would be equal partners. Until and unless they could reach an
agreement on every single issue, the project wouldn't go forward.

It was ironic that Corcoran was the one making this pitch. Just a few years earlier, when he heard that a precondition of the redevelopment of King's Lynne was a partnership with the tenants, he walked away from it. At the time, Corcoran had thought the idea was totally crazy. Turning around a failed public housing project would be difficult enough without having tenants as partners. But the tenants had pursued them, and by the end of the King's Lynne project, CMJ was sold on the concept of fifty-fifty partnership.

CMJ's "conversion" wasn't a matter of altruism as much as pragmatism. Corcoran explains: "When you've got the tenants as partners, then you overcome the bureaucratic wish to do nothing, the political wish not to take risks. The political establishment can ignore us as money-hungry developers, but they can't ignore the plight of these people who want something better." In the course of the project, CMJ had come to see partnership with the tenants as the best guarantee of getting the job done and overcoming inevitable hurdles. "We knew that what we had done at King's Lynne

"Mrs. Marie Forsythe, left, and neighbor Lillian Riley check broken stove," Columbia Point, 1979. Boston Herald.

would be possible to do at Columbia Point," Corcoran added: "We were convinced that the way to approach it was not through the bureaucrats but through the people. Generally, developers sell grandiose ideas to the political people. But we knew that the power of the tenant organizations would carry the project against the political and bureaucratic opposition we would face."

The fifty-fifty partnership that CMJ had reluctantly agreed to at King's Lynne was now the centerpiece of what they were offering the tenants at Columbia Point. Instead of a landlord-tenant relationship, Corcoran explained, CMJ proposed joint ownership: "We told the tenants, 'We want to be your partners. You'll be in control. It won't be the housing authority saying how it's going to go. We'll say how it's going to go together.'"

The offer of fifty-fifty partnership was something the task force hadn't heard before. They liked it, but they didn't believe it. Esther Santos was particularly skeptical. "What developer in their right mind would want to come in to redevelop buildings," she asked, "and have residents—people who have no idea what is going on—at their elbows questioning them at every turn?" He knew how she

Apprehensive Neighbors I:
UMass Boston

Richard Hogarty, a senior fellow at the McCormack Institute and former professor of political science at UMass Boston, maintains that the relationship between the university and its neighbors has been uneasy ever since the university announced its plans to move from downtown Boston to the Columbia Point peninsula. Hogarty, who chaired the Campus Impact Study Group, formed to respond to community concerns in 1973, a year before the new campus officially opened its doors, explains that there were issues on both sides. The community, which included South Boston and the Savin Hill section of Dorchester as well as Columbia Point, worried that nearby streets would be clogged with traffic and rents strained by student demand. For its part, the university saw the public housing project as a threat. He recalls:

> Some faculty and students perceived it as a real danger and focused on the social pathology that was manifest there. They were scared, and they thought about possible muggings at night and so on. There was genuine fear and anxiety combined into one.
>
> Some saw it as a kind of a Pruitt-Igoe and were saying that the best way to handle Columbia Point would be to blow it up, too. . . . Others were more enlightened and really wanted to be good neighbors. While there was a lot of rhetoric going on about good fences and good neighbors, the Robert Frost

thing, there was also some genuine spirit on the part of some faculty and a commitment to the urban environment.

Hogarty's committee made a series of recommendations to address transportation and housing questions as well as to increase numbers of low-income and minority students, increase financial aid, and provide educational opportunities for students from the surrounding neighborhoods at the new campus. By the late 1970s the university had closed the field office it had established at the housing project to coordinate some of these efforts. In Hogarty's view, the university has fallen short over the years despite several initiatives, including a series of reports and studies from the College of Public and Community Service:

> We [the Campus Impact Study Group] did not want to turn our back on the community. We wanted to keep the doors open and be a good neighbor. But the university fumbled the ball and paid more lip service to our vision of what could be done. . . .
>
> I just don't think it has worked out the way it could have, and I guess I really have to fault the university. They pulled back internally and were consumed with their own administrative problems. Maybe that was inevitable. But I think we really hoped that there would be more of a communal relationship and more positive interaction.

felt, Corcoran answered, because he had felt exactly the same way before King's Lynne. There he learned that if a community is going to succeed, the residents have to be involved. If you're building a house with an architect, he told the task force, you're not going to tell the architect to design and build it, only to move in and discover that the space doesn't work at all. No, the client knows best what works, so the client should have a say in the design. Nobody knows better than the people who live at Columbia Point, Corcoran went on, what works and what doesn't work at the housing project. "He said it was a challenge," Esther Santos recalls. "He enjoyed working with the residents. Even if we were not learned people in the eyes of the development world out there, we had what he needed. And he had what we needed."

Joe Corcoran, Joe Mullins, and Gary Jennison knew the tenants had no reason to believe them; that's why they told the tenants they should visit King's Lynne and see for themselves. Don't take our word for it, Joe Mullins recalls telling them; take a look at what we do: "We said, 'Come on over to King's Lynne because we've got a partnership with the tenants over there. We bought public housing that was state owned, and we turned it around with a partnership with the residents—and we kept the existing residents there. . . . See for yourself that low-income people can live with market-rate people as we say they can. And don't believe anything until you listen to residents who live there.'" This project isn't for us, Joe Corcoran concluded; it's for you. In fact, if the tenants didn't want to work with CMJ as partners, CMJ wanted no part of the deal. The company wouldn't go to the housing authority or HUD or anywhere else. If CMJ couldn't work with the tenants, it didn't want the job at all.

As the night deepened and the Olds made its way down Mount Vernon Street, the three men had a feeling they'd be back. Joe Corcoran was sure that the women had enough curiosity to go to Lynn, and that was the most he had hoped to get out of the meeting. Even if the tenants were skeptical, the partners had planted the seed. In fact, they had planted two seeds: first, the idea that Columbia Point could be transformed; and second, that the tenants could be equal partners with the developers. Over the coming years, even as Columbia Point deteriorated, those two ideas would grow with the tenacity of weeds through asphalt.

"Vandalized, vacant apartment at 6 Blair Road," Columbia Point, 1975. Boston Herald.

Apprehensive Neighbors II:
John F. Kennedy Library and Museum

John Stewart, who retired as director of education at the John F. Kennedy Library in 1999, recalls that the library was flooded with proposals from forty to fifty different communities including Amherst, Concord, and Brookline once it was "kicked out" of Harvard Square by neighborhood opposition. In the end, there were really only two serious contenders: a site near Brandeis University in Waltham and Columbia Point in Dorchester. "It became very, very clear very quickly that Columbia Point was superior primarily because of its location vis-à-vis downtown Boston and accessibility to the airport," he says. The downside, of course, was the proximity of the Columbia Point housing project:

Columbia Point, Christmas Day, 1976. Boston Herald.

I remember going to one of the first meetings that Bob Wood [then president of the University of Massachusetts] organized to talk about Columbia Point. It was at a bank downtown, a very informal group of business people and bankers and others that met a number of times. This must have been the mid-seventies because the library was under construction. . . .

Clearly Columbia Point was going to be a bit of a problem in terms of selling the library. It was the unspoken thing that the library was leaving nice, safe Cambridge to go to not-so-nice, not-so-safe Dorchester. It was a significant concern, the perception of Dorchester as an unsafe place and you were going to be in a bad neighborhood.

According to Stewart, visitors to the library would be not only put off by the library's location but also unable to ignore the blighted housing project, which would stand as an embarrassment for the city and a symbol of the failure of government to provide for the very people that the Kennedys championed. In fact, Stewart believes that this concern ultimately provided some broad, positive impetus to "do something" about Columbia Point.

Even though the housing project has been transformed, the Kennedy Library has had only a limited relationship with the community to this day. But Stewart points out that its youth corps, a volunteer community service group, has long had a unit, one of four in the city, at the McCormack Middle School: "We have never done as much as I would have liked to have done with the community [that would become Harbor Point]. . . . From time to time we have done programs with the Dever School and with the new Harbor School [a "pilot" public school on the peninsula]. Several years ago we were part of a major grant to do a big project . . . with young people at Harbor Point, but it never happened. We didn't get the grant."

17 Seeing Is Believing

The minute I met Joe [Corcoran]—way back, before Columbia Point—he said to me, "The reason I want to do King's Lynne is because I want to do Columbia Point." Because he's a Dorchester boy. He's a Dorchester boy.

—Eleanor Wessell

Terry Mair, Esther Santos, and Ruby Jaundoo left the meeting with the developers curious enough to take them up on their invitation to visit King's Lynne. There they could see for themselves what Corcoran, Mullins, Jennison had done to turn around a public housing disaster called America Park by taking it private and forming a partnership with the tenants.

Although America Park and Columbia Point were both public housing projects built in the early 1950s, in some ways they were very different. America Park was originally built as veterans' housing and was owned by the state; Columbia Point was not restricted to veterans and was owned by the federal government. America Park, with 408 units, was only a third of the size of Columbia Point. While America Park's two-story walkups were scattered over a sixty-acre hillside adjacent to a middle-income residential area, Columbia Point's drab brick high-rises were densely packed on less than forty acres of land isolated on the edge of Dorchester Bay.

By the 1970s, however, the fates of the two projects had become cruelly similar. While Columbia Point had achieved national notoriety as one of the worst federally owned housing projects—in a class with St. Louis's Pruitt-Igoe and Chicago's Cabrini-Green—America Park had earned a local reputation as the worst state-owned project. The place was strewn with junked cars, old mattresses, and packs of stray dogs and, like Columbia Point, was rapidly emptying out. In 1970 only 125 units were still occupied; the rest were boarded up.

Like the task force at Columbia Point, a small group of determined tenants at

America Park, Lynn, Massachusetts. *Courtesy of the* Boston Globe.

Below: Dogs roamed America Park, 1974. *Courtesy of the* Boston Globe.

America Park had told the state that they didn't want to put any more "modernization" money into the project. It would only be a Band-Aid on an open and infected wound. Instead, the America Park tenants received permission to use their modernization money to hire a nonprofit housing consulting group, Greater Boston Community Developers, to help them figure out how to rehabilitate their community.

The tenant group began working with a young planner named Langley Keyes. Keyes, who later went on to become the head of MIT's Department of Planning and Urban Affairs, recalls the picture of life in public housing as the America Park tenants presented it to him:

> The tenants felt that they never would be part of Lynn as long as they were part of America Park. If you lived at America Park, you couldn't get a checking account. Your kids ended up in the back of the bus. It was mostly a white project; it wasn't as though it was black. But it was housing of last resort for people from all over New England. There was a lot of other public housing, but this was the place that nobody wanted to live in.
>
> The argument the tenant leaders made—and they made it very forcefully—was, "We're always going to be outsiders in this town as long as we're identified with America Park. So we need to do something more dramatic than just fixing up the units."

The tenant group was led by the intrepid and outspoken Eleanor Atkins, a self-described "Lynner, born and bred," who moved into the project with her four children in 1961. She later married Dan Wessell, another tenant at "the Park" and a father of five, and together they raised nine children there. By 1970 Dan and Eleanor Wessell were sick and tired of living in public housing and determined to work for change. Together they were a formidable pair. In Langley Keyes's words, "Dan and Eleanor knew how to cut a deal; Eleanor knew how to throw a fit." Eleanor Wessell was convinced, then as now, that low-income housing was doomed to failure:

> I probably shouldn't say this, but I don't believe in public housing— not all low-income, anyway. And the reason that I don't is because you have no dignity. There's a stigma to it. Besides that, nobody wants to put any money in it. In America Park, if I didn't repair my own apartment, I didn't get it repaired. We used to get together and hire an outside contractor to come in and fumigate our units. Because we really felt the housing authority was feeding the roaches vitamin K. Largest roaches in the world.
>
> You couldn't get a job because you lived in America Park. You were charged more deposits by the telephone and the gas company because you lived in public housing. The school systems frowned on you. So that was not my idea of housing. At least with mixed-income, the school systems don't know whether you're a doctor's child or an unwed mother's.

The women on the Columbia Point Task Force had heard about America Park even before the meeting with CMJ. In fact, Esther Santos had met Eleanor Wessell when they sat together on a committee made up of residents representing several public housing projects in the Boston metropolitan area. All of the projects were facing the same problems—bad management, escalating crime, empty units being taken over by squatters and drug dealers. Columbia Point's problems seemed worse only because the project was the largest.

Like the residents of Columbia Point, Eleanor Wessell had some choice words for the succession of people who had tried to "save" America Park during the War on Poverty:

> Who needs these pompous, overeducated liberals who never had to worry where their next meal was coming from, telling us how programs will be run and who they will serve and why—like we can't figure that out for our-

Left to right: State Representative Jim Smith, Eleanor Atkins, and Dan Wessell review plans to redevelop America Park into King's Lynne. *Courtesy of Eleanor Wessell.*

selves. I don't want any of those patronizing smart-asses around here anymore. They're the ones who got us into this mess, and frankly it's in their best interest if we stay in the mess. Then they can go out and tell the world how wonderful they are helping the poor while they take their paychecks and go live in the tony part of town.

The tenant group at America Park knew better than any outsiders what they wanted, and they worked with Langley Keyes to make it become a reality. The first hurdle was drafting state legislation that would allow state-owned public housing to be sold—the first such legislation in the country. Drafting the legislation was something of a balancing act. "We wanted to create an act," Keyes explains, "which would make it possible to take a rundown public housing project that was judged to be substandard and deteriorated beyond repair, tear it down, and replace it with a private, mixed-income development." At the same time, Eleanor Wessell emphasizes, they wanted to define the legislation narrowly enough so that it couldn't be taken advantage of by cities that wanted to unload their public housing: "We knew that if there was a way cities could dump public housing, they would. So we had to make sure they had to go through a whole process before they could sell. A project had to be more than a third 'unsuitable for living'—and the State Department of Public Health had to declare it—and the tenants had to be involved in planning what happened next."

The legislation, which became known as Chapter 884, laid the foundation for the new community. Ownership of the property would be conveyed from the state to a private development corporation. That corporation would be a joint venture between the tenant task force and a private developer, with equal control over every aspect of the development. The new development would be mixed-income, with one-third low-income, one-third moderate-income, and one-third market-rate families. Finally, the state would provide funding to the task force for independent planning and social services.

The next hurdle was getting the legislation passed. Fortunately, it had the blessing of state representative Tom McGee, who would later become Speaker of the House—himself a "Lynner." McGee shepherded it through the legislature. The final hurdle was financing. The Massachusetts Housing Finance Agency, or MHFA, created in 1971 with the purpose of making low-interest loans to private developers building mixed-income housing in the state, would make a tax-exempt 7.5 percent loan to the private developer. In addition, subsidies for low-income units were expected to be made available through the federal government's new Section 8 program, which provided subsidies that paid landlords the difference between low-income and market-rate rents.

It took only a very small group of tenants—six or seven—to form a core group to plan the redevelopment. As Langley Keyes explains, "The tenants' organization at King's Lynne was not only Eleanor and Dan but six or seven other very, very thoughtful, heads-up people. And basically everybody else, to be perfectly honest, just wasn't there." The tenant leader's role, however, was often a difficult one. Keyes recalls going with Dan and Eleanor Wessell to meet with local neighborhood groups and put on a slide show explaining the new community. "The folks would say how awful people in the Park were," Keyes recalls. "Eleanor would sort of bite her tongue and yell at me when the meeting was over." Eleanor Wessell had to shuttle between meetings at the State House and tenants at the Park railing about the politicians. She would say to Keyes, "'I'm up there promoting how bad the place I live is in order to get this legislation passed'—she was terrific. She would play a role. It wasn't easy."

Once the legislation was passed and the financing arranged, the way was clear for requests for proposals. In 1973, when the state announced a competition for developers interested in redeveloping America Park, Joe Mullins and Gary Jennison went up to take a look. "The place was a nightmare," Mullins recalls. "It seemed like the animal population was greater than the human population. One tenant, a member of the Hell's Angels, had three pit bulldogs, an alligator, and two boa constrictors. He had had a lion, but the previous year he sliced the lion's throat because it clawed one of his three children." Mullins and Jennison reported to Corcoran not only that the project was severely deteriorated but also that the developer would be required to enter into a partnership with the tenants. As a company, CMJ was firmly committed to the mixed-income concept—as Joe Corcoran says, "It seemed to me that this was the right way to house poor people"—but they weren't prepared for the "tenant as partner" concept. They were convinced that lack of strong management control was the main reason for every housing failure, public or private. If they were required to share that control, they felt, then they couldn't guarantee the physical or financial future of a project. As far as the partners were concerned, they wanted no part of America Park.

While Mullins and Jennison were checking out America Park, the America Park tenants were doing some checking of their own. Determined to find a developer who would turn their community around, the tenants visited several developments in the area—among them, Queen Anne's Gate in Weymouth, Massachusetts, a mixed-income community built by CMJ in 1973 under the MHFA program. They liked what they saw—a beautiful, well-managed community—and what they heard, especially from low-income residents who were proud of their community. It wasn't a "project," they said, and they weren't looked at as "project people." "We saw good management," Eleanor Wessell recalls. "We saw people who were interested in good housing. We talked to the low-income residents, who said they loved living there. In other developers we saw, 'Oh, well, we'll romance the tenants and we'll get it and then it will be ours and they'll be gone.' We didn't see that in Joe, Joe, and Gary."

When Eleanor and Dan Wessell learned that CMJ had decided not to submit a bid, they called and asked them at least to give them a chance to talk. CMJ agreed to the meeting. "They asked us why we weren't submitting a proposal," Joe Corcoran recalls:

> We told them there were two reasons. The first was that America Park was in deplorable shape and the second was that we didn't believe that we could really partner with the tenants. We told them that we had a very strong private management company with strong principles, and that we really weren't sure that we could be compatible.
>
> But they went on to convince us that was exactly what they wanted. They wanted strong management, and they wanted to get rid of the bad apples on site, and they wanted a development they could be proud of, and they wanted to have people of other income levels living with them.

Eleanor and Dan Wessell's persistence won the day. They persuaded CMJ to submit a proposal. Corcoran observes that the ten-

"Living room floor of apt. #28 at Whipple St., Lynn, America Park housing project, scene where two boys suffocated in a refrigerator," 1974. *Courtesy of the* Boston Globe.

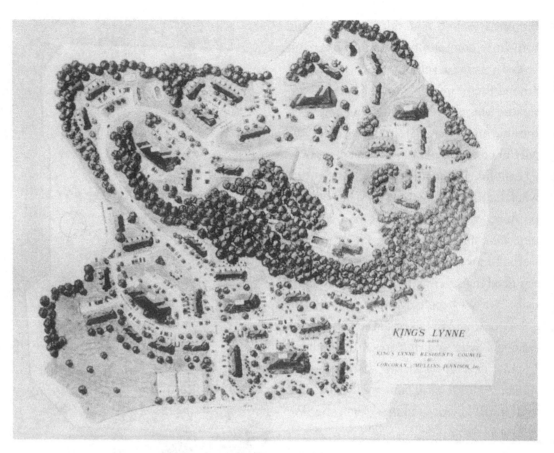

ants "had exactly the same objectives that we had." Langley Keyes
explains that the tenants were convinced that the best developers of
mixed-income communities are precisely those who are *not* special-
ists in subsidized housing: "It was clear that the people who built the
best mixed-income communities—one-third low, one-third moderate, one-third market—were in fact conventional builders who
found themselves having to do that because they were approaching
it from conventional building, having to compete in the market
side. And Eleanor and company said, 'We don't want somebody
who's used to building subsidized developments, because they're
not going to make it appeal to the market.'"

After agreeing to submit a proposal, CMJ visited America Park
again—Joe Corcoran's first visit. He found the site much more depressing than Columbia Point, an entire hillside piled with garbage,
abandoned buildings, and dogs roaming in packs. Corcoran's
brother John also toured the site and later said to him, "Joe, these
dogs, there are hundreds of them, and none of them wag their tails."
Those unhappy dogs, CMJ decided, could be the first "test case" of
the tenant-developer partnership. CMJ's management company
had a strict no-pets policy, and they asked the resident council if
they would support that policy if they submitted a proposal. The resident council didn't answer until a week later, after they had a

chance to meet with their residents. Yes, they would definitely support the no-pets policy.

Agreeing to the tenant-developer partnership in principle, however, was different from working out the specific terms of that partnership on paper. "We were sitting down to negotiate the partnership with our attorneys and their attorneys," Eleanor Wessell recalls. "I don't know whether you know about attorneys, but I have a son who's an attorney. No attorney ever settled anything. So we decided to throw the attorneys out of the room. And that's where we got the partnership. We decided that we would have a fifty-fifty partnership. And that's what we did. And Joe's attorneys were not happy with that. But he stuck with it and defended it."

The terms of the partnership were simple: the tenants would have 50 percent ownership control, 10 percent of the syndication proceeds, and 10 percent of the cash flow, following the format that Langley Keyes had created. The tenants and developers would be fifty-fifty partners on all policy decisions—how many units, how big, kitchen appliances, and so on—with day-to-day operations carried out by CMJ's professional management company. Both sides would have to sign off on all decisions before moving forward.

The city of Lynn resisted, first rezoning the property for industrial use in order to prevent the redevelopment of America Park from going forward, then opposing the fifty-fifty agreement. Eleanor Wessell explains that the developers stood by their new partners in the ensuing fight: "The city wanted us to have 49 percent and CMJ to have 51 percent. I went to the meeting and I said, 'Look, this is crazy. I might as well have none as have 49 percent.' And Joe, Joe, and Gary agreed with me. They said, 'Well, the city is going to have to accept fifty-fifty or we're not going to go ahead with it.' I'd have fought them to a standstill, but I didn't have to—which made it nice. We had to fight the city. But we didn't have to fight each other."

CMJ's proposal was one of only three submitted. The general consensus among developers and policy makers was that a mixed-income development was risky enough without making the tenants equal partners. Although the two competing firms were more established, the America Park tenants on the selection committee favored CMJ. The company was ultimately selected, and ground was broken for King's Lynne in 1974.

But that wasn't the last of the hurdles at King's Lynne. The 1973 Nixon moratorium on federal housing subsidies meant that there was no longer a mechanism for supporting low-income residents. Joe Corcoran knew the only recourse was state funding through

Proof Positive

King's Lynne proved to be so successful, and in some areas the impact on the people, including the existing tenants and their kids, was measurable.

There was a junior high in Lynn where the kids from America Park went to school, and many of them had severe learning and behavioral problems. I remember some of the teachers telling me that the kids changed after moving into those new apartments. The teachers could actually see it in school. It was this fabulous new development with the pool and the tennis courts and the landscaping. That's what those teachers said. The change in behavior and attitude and performance in school was dramatic once they had this new opportunity.

—Michael Dukakis, former governor of Massachusetts and now a government professor at Northeastern University, 1998

leased housing programs administered by the Massachusetts Department of Community Affairs. He recalls:

The current year's allocation had been spent, and our only hope was to tap the following year's allocation. Obviously there was tremendous demand throughout the commonwealth, and the chances of obtaining what we needed were almost nonexistent. We met with Eleanor and Dan and decided to see Mike Dukakis, who was the new governor, and ask for the allocation we needed.

Dukakis had defeated the incumbent attorney general, Robert Quinn, in the primary and upset the incumbent governor, Frank Sargent, in the final election. I was concerned because I'd personally supported Bob Quinn. He was from Savin Hill, and my family and I had known him and supported him when he first ran for the state legislature. I worked for him delivering campaign flyers when I was in high school.

I'd never met Dukakis until that day. He listened intently, asked many pointed questions, and at the end of the meeting, obviously impressed with the persistence of the resident council, he indicated that if his housing budget for the new fiscal year was approved, that his administration would make America Park funding a priority.

This was an enormous commitment, and in my view, it was entirely due to the tenant partners, who presented the situation as only they could. Dukakis clearly responded to them. We were there as the developers, but it was the tenants who made the case.

Despite a two-year zoning battle with the city of Lynn, the partnership plowed ahead, withstanding growing pains from within and skeptics from without. Halfway through the design stage, for example, the tenants said they did not want Sasaki Associates, the international architectural firm selected by CMJ to do the site plan for King's Lynne, to design the new apartments for the new community. They preferred the local architect, Claude Miquelle, who had designed the buildings at Queen Anne's Gate. The partnership made a joint decision to switch architects.

Eleanor Wessell recalls a workshop she conducted with Joe Corcoran at a multifamily housing convention when they were first planning the partnership: "Joe was laughed at for even thinking that mixed-income housing and a tenant-developer partnership could happen. We went back to the same conference ten years later after it was all over and we were doing well. And Joe gave a speech at the conference and said, 'Ten years ago someone at this same conference told me to come back when I could sell refrigerators to Eskimos. Well, I'm back.'"

Another key component of CMJ's approach to redeveloping

America Park was providing social services to members of the community. CMJ and the social service providers involved the families in all aspects of designing the new community, from getting their input in designing floor plans, to choosing appliances for the kitchens, to planning playgrounds. Social service workers explained the development process step by step. The place had to work not just as a housing development but as a community. Joe Corcoran explains: "One, the tenants are immediately afraid that they're going to get re-

King's Lynne, Lynn, Massachusetts, 1985. *Courtesy of the* Boston Globe.

moved, and two, they're afraid that they aren't going to be able to make it in this new privatized development. Often they're second-generation public housing folks, and the social service people come in and tell them that they are guaranteed a unit as long as they comply with the lease. If you pay your rent and don't interfere with the rights of others and take care of your housing, you have nothing to fear."

King's Lynne was an eye-opener for CMJ. The developers had been totally skeptical about becoming partners with the tenants before doing the project. The experience made them true believers. From then on, the company made such partnerships an essential component of its public housing turnarounds.

When the Columbia Point Community Task Force visited King's Lynne, they had clear concerns. "I remember that they were skeptical," Eleanor Wessell recalls. They were concerned that there wouldn't be a guarantee that the tenants would be able to move back after the community was redeveloped:

They were concerned that their elected board might not stay low-income people. That these smart market people would come in and move them out. I don't understand why low-income people don't think they're smart. But they were concerned that smart people would come

An early rendering and model of Goody & Clancy's initial plans for Harbor Point. *Courtesy of Goody & Clancy.*

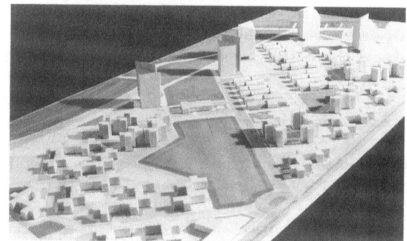

in—lawyers and that—and take over their board and they'd lose control. You have to understand America Park was like 20 percent minority and the rest white. Columbia Point was almost 100 percent minority at that point. So they were saying, "You are different than we are. And you're smaller than we are." I think they were very skeptical. And rightly so.

What they found at King's Lynne was a thriving mixed-income community with 441 units: a mixture of handsome, varied buildings on a wooded hillside; beautiful landscaping; several miniplaygrounds scattered about; tennis courts, two swimming pools, a fitness center, and a large community building with meeting and function rooms. Beyond the physical community, they found a proud, hard-working Resident Council whose members told them in no uncertain terms that they were indeed co-owners of the community, that they were indeed fifty-fifty partners with CMJ in all decisions affecting King's Lynne. And that was the reason the place looked so good and worked so well.

The residents told the visitors from Columbia Point that they, too, had been skeptical at first—with good reason. They had lived through the same broken promises from the local housing authority. But they had taken matters into their own hands. They had persuaded CMJ to submit a proposal. They persevered for a fifty-fifty partnership because they wanted a permanent say in running the new development.

The Columbia Point visitors learned that the partnership was real. It wasn't easy, but it was real. The tenants would have to be tireless. They'd have to educate themselves in every single aspect of planning the new community. They'd have to put in a lot of work preparing the tenants for life in the new community. And the work wouldn't be over once the new community opened; it would be just beginning.

The task force returned from King's Lynne impressed with what they had seen: an attractive, mixed-income community, and tenants who were truly partners with the developers. "They said, 'We still think you'll never be able to pull it off,'" Joe Corcoran recalls, "'but we're with you.'"

With the tenants on board, CMJ then approached the architectural firm of Goody, Clancy, & Associates to work with them and the Columbia Point residents to create a preliminary master plan. Architect Joan Goody shared Joe Corcoran's vision of a mixed-income community—because, like him, she had grown up in one:

Joan Goody. *Courtesy of Goody & Clancy.*

Joe Corcoran arrived in our office one day in 1978. We had just designed some subsidized housing for seniors in Winthrop and he liked the design. He had just turned America Park in Lynn into King's Lynne. He had known Columbia Point as a boy living in Dorchester, and a long-term goal of his was to do the same thing here. He was working with a small group of tenants, and he had to sell the idea first to the Boston Housing Authority and then to get federal funds. So he asked us to develop a new approach to Columbia Point.

At that time the secretary of HUD was Patricia Harris, and the federal policy was very much against demolishing any public housing. It was after Pruitt-Igoe had been demolished, so one of the constraints was to minimize the amount of demolition—exactly 180 degrees from where the federal policy is now. And I think because I had grown up in Brooklyn, New York—in an area not dissimilar to some of the parts of Dorchester with one- or two-family houses, front porches, all the kids playing in the street—Joe and I both had similar images of what a neighborhood was.

I'd grown up in a completely mixed-income neighborhood. In fact, before World War II almost everything was mixed-income. There were rich folks living in my block—the doctors lived in the brick houses at the corner—then everything from laborers to professionals to business people lived in between. So mixed-income seemed like the most normal thing to me. It was just part of my innate thinking.

The group of tenants we worked with included a woman named Terry Mair. I frequently quoted one of the things I remember her saying about the importance of making this a mixed-income community from the perspective of the low-income tenants. She said, "If it takes rich folks to get the services we need out here, bring out the rich folks." Having a mixed-income community wasn't a matter of the low-income people needing role models. It was simply that a community that was entirely poor and isolated was never going to get the attention and the services that a mixed-income community could.

Armed with the tenants' support, a legal and financial framework, and architects' plans that reduced the project's density and demolished some of its original buildings, CMJ then embarked on a serpentine journey through the political process, trying to muster support for its redevelopment plan. CMJ intended to use the same legal model for Columbia Point that they had used at King's Lynne: the government—in this case, the federal government—would sell the public housing project to a partnership of the tenants and the private developer.

The first stop was the BHA, which flatly rejected the plan. "They thought it was impossible," Corcoran explains. Undaunted, CMJ took the plan directly to the local office of the Department of Housing and Urban Development. HUD's regional director, Edward Martin, was interested but said the plan needed the political blessing of his superiors in the Carter administration. There HUD secretary Patricia Harris objected that the redevelopment plan would reduce the total number of low-income units at Columbia Point. Martin recalls that these objections were overcome only when she visited the site in person in October 1978 and saw for herself that the project, situated on "the most wonderful piece of real estate in New England," was too dense. "The site visit turned her around," Martin says.

Even so, Steven Coyle, an assistant to Harris who would later become director of the Boston Redevelopment Authority, believed that in order to succeed, the plan ultimately needed the blessing of local political powers in Boston. So Joe Corcoran went back to Boston and made an appointment to see Mayor Kevin White. White's secretary told him the mayor would not have time to see the King's Lynne video and that he would see him alone. Corcoran recalls:

> We met in the afternoon in his office at City Hall overlooking Quincy Market. It was a beautiful June day, and he suggested we go out for an ice cream cone. As we crossed Congress Street, I told him how we had turned America Park into King's Lynne and how we could do the same at Columbia Point.
>
> As we returned to his office, I made my move for his support. I painted a picture of how politically advantageous it would be to be the first big-city mayor to turn around a deteriorating public housing project. At that point, he looked at me sternly and said with a sarcastic tone, "Corcoran, I don't need political advice from you—you stick to real estate, and I'll handle my political well-being." He made it clear that he was not in a position to be out front as a supporter, but I did feel that he was receptive to the idea, and that was important.

CMJ's plan to privatize public housing and create a mixed-income community failed to win the broad support of the controlling Democrats, who were reluctant to antagonize public and assisted housing advocates at either the local or national level. CMJ was forced to put the Columbia Point project on hold. However, the seeds had been planted in Washington and in Boston, where the highly visible public housing project stood as an embarrassing metaphor for government's failings in both spheres. In the meantime, changes were brewing in the city and across the country that would forever change the fate of Columbia Point.

Kevin White Remembers

As for taking Corcoran for an ice cream, I did the same thing with Jim Rouse [the developer who rehabilitated Faneuil Hall and Quincy Market]. I don't know if it was nerves or to keep them off balance. I always liked Joe Corcoran. He didn't have the same national reputation as Rouse, but he had the same disposition. He wanted to produce a pretty good product—and I don't mean "pretty good" in a limiting sense, but caring about the project beyond the bottom line. And Faneuil Hall and Columbia Point became signature projects for both those developers.

—Kevin White, former mayor of Boston and now a professor and chairman of the Institute of Political Communications at Boston University, 1998

King's Lynne, 1998: A Mixed-Income Community Comes of Age

When the Columbia Point task force visited King's Lynne in 1978, the community was only two years old. Today, King's Lynne affords an interesting picture of what a mixed-income community looks like after twenty years.

King's Lynne is 100 percent occupied, with a true mixture of incomes—one-third low-income, one-third moderate-income, and one-third market-rate families. Each of those income levels is mixed racially—black, Hispanic, Asian, and white. All of the buildings, in all of the areas of the community, have a mix of all three income levels.

King's Lynne is one of the nicest places to live in the city of Lynn; the people who live there are proud of their community. It is not a "project"; the people who live there are not "project people." Nor is it a luxury community, with token low-income families scattered here and there, clearly identified and recognizable but tolerated by those paying market rents. As Eleanor Wessell explains, King's Lynne is a mixed-income community, one in which the preconceptions of both outsiders and residents are more than likely to be wrong:

> The only way they would possibly know [who is low-income] is if a neighbor told them. There are no differences between any of the units. People might say, "Oh, look, that guy's got a Cadillac. He's got to be a market." Nine chances out of ten he's a low. In some instances, people assume that if you're black, you're low. And that in fact is not anywhere the truth. Because we have black doctors and we have black lawyers and black school principals.
>
> And then there's those people who are moderate who don't understand the concept of mixed-income and they think they're paying top dollar. They complain, "I saw so-and-so next door to me who keeps their window open during the winter and they're wasting the heat and I'm paying big money and they're black so of course they're low." I spend a lot of time enjoying saying, "I'm sorry, but they're market and you're being subsidized."
>
> We are very good about that. We had a woman move in some years ago, and the minute she found out there were blacks and welfare people here, she was unhappy. We just broke her lease. Gave her her security deposit back and said see you later. Because if you are not willing to live in a community that is a community, then we don't want you. If you're not happy, we don't want you.
>
> A lot of our elderly people prefer the townhouses. A big family is not necessarily a low-income family. I have a black family, a mother with seven children. She's a market tenant. Now if you drove by and saw the kids out playing you would ordinarily say, "Ah, a low-income family." That's not true. And I would have said it too before King's Lynne. But that's what happens. Some people have large families no matter how much or how little money they have.
>
> We do nothing here that doesn't serve all three income groups. We brought in a family planning clinic. Our understanding was it would have a sliding fee scale. Well, it didn't, so we asked them to leave. Because with a sliding fee scale then anybody could go. It's very important. For one thing, the lows won't come if it only serves the lows, because that earmarks them low. Nothing comes into this community unless it can serve all three groups.

Eleanor Wessell debunks the patronizing notion that mixing incomes is a good idea because market-rate families are a "good influence" on low-income families. She should know: she has approved the eviction of as many market-rate as low-income residents. She also sets the record straight on the importance of support services for low-income residents. Yes, it was important to teach them how to open a checking account. Yes, it was important to teach them how to use a garbage disposal. Wessell herself had never had one. According to her, the key is to let the tenants design their own programs, based on what they need and why:

If I had to say who we have evicted over the years, it's been about equal across the board. That was not true when I first started. I thought sure it would be—but we spent a lot of time with our tenants. We did banking with our tenants so they would understand how you get a checking account. We made deals with banks so they got free checking accounts. We had the teachers come in to show them how to sew and make curtains and all of that stuff.

We did a lot of work. I had Joe put in a whole kitchen for me down in my office so that we could show them how to use the dishwasher, how to use the garbage disposal. These were things we didn't have. How to care for a rug. So there was a lot of work spent in teaching the America Park tenants so that when they went into their new apartments they knew what they were getting. I didn't know about that, either. I'd never had those things.

Twenty years later, Eleanor Wessell is still at the helm in her capacity as "resident representative" at King's Lynne. She is tireless in seeing to it that her community runs well, watching over residents in all three income groups—what she calls "my markets," "my mods," and "my lows." And she still calls it as she sees it:

I've heard people say, "Oh, you know, those market people have brought up the standard of the low-income people." That is not true. That is no way true. I have as much problems with my markets and my mods as I ever did with the lows. Don't get me wrong; I have problems. But the low-income people are—in most cases, not all—so happy to live here that they're not going to step on anybody's toes. The markets who are paying big money could care less because they're paying their money. And the mods are generally a mixture of the two.

Eleanor Wessell is still active on behalf of residents at King's Lynne. *Courtesy of Eleanor Wessell.*

18 The Court Takes Over

Three years before Corcoran, Mullins, and Jennison's initial meeting with the tenant leaders at Columbia Point, tenant activists across the city of Boston had taken a step that would ultimately change the fate of all of Boston's public housing projects. By the mid-1970s the tenants in such projects were concerned not so much about maintenance, or the screening of new tenants, or the enforcement of rules, as they were about basic safety. Tenants had become prisoners held captive in extremely dangerous conditions. Their efforts to get the attention of the housing authority—not to mention any purposeful action—were utterly futile. Then Boston's public housing tenants tried a new strategy: they sued the landlord.

On February 7, 1975, Armando Perez, a tenant at the Mission Hill project, and eight other public housing tenants filed a class action suit against the Boston Housing Authority, alleging that conditions in the city's projects violated the state sanitary

code. In the language of the court, the plaintiffs in *Armando Perez et al. v Boston Housing Authority*, represented by the Boston Legal Assistance Project, were "seeking to vindicate their statutory rights to decent, safe, and sanitary housing."

The next month, on March 28, Boston Housing Court's chief judge, Paul G. Garrity, ruled in favor of Perez, declaring that the majority of the BHA's twenty thousand units in fifty-seven housing projects were "not decent, nor are they safe, nor are they in compliance with the provisions of the state sanitary code." The BHA was operating housing that was in violation of the law, Garrity ruled, and the tenants were entitled to a remedy. The judge appointed a "master," Robert B. Whittlesey, to oversee the BHA's efforts to bring the living conditions at the projects across the city up to the provisions of the state code.

Bringing the issue of public housing before the court was another turning point in the history of Columbia Point. The BHA was the landlord for fifty-five thousand people, housing them in atrocious conditions. From the tenants' point of view, there seemed to be no way to hold the agency accountable. Accountable to whom? If the BHA didn't take care of the project, didn't live up to its responsibilities, what were the tenants to do? They had been abandoned by the city—left amid crime and neglect with no place to turn.

An article in the *Boston Phoenix* on November 6, 1979, provides a snapshot of Columbia Point at the time:

> In the early 1970s, the Boston Housing Authority stopped providing services to Columbia Point. Garbage was not picked up, windows were not repaired, toilets leaked for three months before they were fixed. Tenants nearly froze in the winter; pipes burst and apartments flooded. People began to leave. Squatters moved into some vacated units, prostitutes into others, and addicts and pushers turned still other apartments into shooting galleries.
>
> Today, Columbia Point is something like a ghost town. Despite a severe housing shortage and a long waiting list for public housing, the BHA has been using its rehabilitation money to board up most of the 1504 units at Columbia Point. Only about 350 families and 75 elderly remain where more than 5,000 people once lived. Weak but mean dogs roam the grounds. Small children use sticks to push chips of wood across puddles. Bundled up against the weather even when the sun is shining, the elderly sit on benches and politely, eagerly, greet passersby. Ragweed fills the cracks in the cement. The wind whipping around the high-rises creates the dreaded "canyon effect" that planners write Ph.D. theses on. You cannot walk far down a street without seeing a flattened, dried-out rat carcass. They are Columbia Point's version of the bear rug.

The "housing judge," Paul Garrity. *Courtesy of Paul Garrity.*

Ten months after the *Perez* case was filed, the court stepped in. After years of frustration and futility, it was as if someone was finally breaking down the door to rescue a long-abused child. Finally, someone would hold the Boston Housing Authority accountable. Finally, someone would require the housing authority to comply with the law. Fortunately, that someone was a scrappy, tenacious, outspoken judge. Judge Paul Garrity was the state "housing judge"—not to be confused with Arthur Garrity, the federal "busing judge" who ordered the Boston public school system into receivership and oversaw the court-ordered busing that ripped the city apart in pursuit of racial desegregation of the schools. Beginning with his ruling in March 1975, Paul Garrity handed down a series of increasingly tough and stringent rulings designed to compel the BHA to do its job.

On December 2, 1975, Judge Garrity issued a court order giving the BHA six weeks to make Columbia Point and Mission Hill fit for human habitation. The order established a timeline for BHA action, including deadlines for filing plans for repairing apartments and relocating tenants; for securing vacant apartments; for evicting or legalizing the status of squatters; and for providing effective security. The BHA failed to comply with the timetable outlined in the court order. Although it was in sympathy with the tenants and the goals of their lawsuit, the BHA argued, it did not have the resources to make the changes required by Judge Garrity. The BHA, by its own admission, was failing to address the mounting problems of Boston's public housing. But the reason, the housing authority insisted, wasn't incompetent leadership; it was that the BHA did not have enough money to do what was needed. Brendan Gerraghty, chief of the BHA's division of planning and modernization, told the *Boston Ledger* in a July 1979 article, "The needs we have in those developments, by HUD's own standards, are enormous. It would cost $150 million to put those projects in shape, and I'm getting $3.5 million a year to deal with that. The way we are trying to handle the older public housing is obsolete. And on top of that, the national commitment to public housing stinks."

In July 1976 Bob Whittlesey, the court-appointed master, issued a fifteen-hundred-page report specifying nearly one hundred recommendations for changes at the BHA, ranging from better screening of prospective tenants to more effective eviction of rule-breaking tenants. The report goes on to criticize the political patronage rampant for years at the housing authority, charging that "politics is so much a part of doing business at the BHA that its insidious effects are frequently not recognized."

A month later, public housing tenants again went into Judge Garrity's court, this time charging the BHA with "gross mismanagement, incompetence, and the waste of funds and property," and filed a motion to put the BHA into court receivership. A group of tenants held a press conference at Columbia Point immediately following their court appearance. Their spokesman, Leon Rock, explained the action: "Columbia Point has deteriorated so much that the majority of tenants have moved out. We see it as a conspiracy on the part of the BHA, UMass, and the JFK Library. We feel hopeless and helpless. The BHA is corrupt and unworkable. We're sure Columbia Point will close down unless the BHA goes into receivership." On June 1, 1977, Judge Garrity turned up the pressure, issuing a comprehensive consent decree specifying what the BHA was obliged to do to bring it into compliance with its statutory obligations. Once again, however, the BHA failed to make significant improvements.

While the judge was bringing legal pressure to bear on the BHA, the Columbia Point tenants were still working to reverse the worsening conditions at the project. In 1978, $10 million became available through HUD's Urban Initiatives Program for improvements at Columbia Point. The program required that a group of tenants be formally elected by the community to work with the BHA to ensure that the funds were being used in the best interests of the community. Hence, the Columbia Point Community Task Force was incorporated to work with the Boston Housing Authority and the Boston Redevelopment Authority to oversee the spending. The task force had little faith that the grant would make a difference, and with good reason. Columbia Point tenant Ruby Jaundoo, one of the first members elected to the task force, recalls the tenants' frustration with the earlier 1975 modernization efforts—what she calls "taking crumbs"—when Columbia Point needed so much more:

"Modernization" at Columbia Point, mid-1970s. *Courtesy of Corcoran, Mullins, Jennison.*

We started to fix up some of the units [in 1975]. By the time, I think maybe 250 families were still here. We had boarded up one side of the development because they basically said there was no money to rehab the buildings. We started doing some modernization, but we knew it wasn't enough to do a good job. So after we spent a couple of million dollars we said, "Hey, until we get enough money to do a decent job, we won't do any more."

They did what I call a cosmetic job. They pulled out the old kitchen cabinets and put in wooden cabinets. They put a little facade on the front of the building. I think they might have put on some doors. They made cosmetic changes, but the interior still looked the same. As you walked up the staircase, you didn't see any difference in the building, and you still had the housing authority that's going to manage this.

So you took a look at what you were trying to do and you realized this was sort of like handing out crumbs to someone. So rather than taking the crumbs, we stopped and we didn't do any more.

Like the Columbia Point tenants, Judge Garrity ran out of patience. On July 25, 1979, after more than four years of litigation, Garrity took the ultimate step: he put the Boston Housing Authority in receivership of the court. "If the BHA were a private landlord," Garrity declared, "it surely would have been driven out of business long ago or its board jailed or most likely both." Ironically—shamefully—the very fact that the housing authority was a public agency allowed it to get away with doing such a bad job for so long.

Garrity's ruling is a blistering critique of the BHA board—four of whose five members were appointed by Mayor Kevin H. White: "The [BHA] board's incompetence and indifference to [its] obligations had directly and substantially contributed not only to the BHA's failure to implement important provisions of the consent decree but also the unprecedented deterioration of the BHA's development and the widespread violations of the sanitary code. Throughout the four-year history of this case, the board has shown itself to be capable of nothing more than gross mismanagement. The unabated mis- and nonfeasance of the board necessitates the extraordinary action of appointing a receiver." The report cites the public housing tenants' "uncontradicted testimony" about "the shocking physical decay and social disintegration existing in the developments": "The history of this case and the repeated efforts by the [Plaintiff Class of] Tenants over the years in seeking and in following up every remedy short of receivership in order to obtain safe, sanitary and decent housing as mandated by law requires that they be permitted the only remedy which has not yet been attempted."

In short, Garrity was arguing, he had been pushed to the wall. Taking control of public housing out of the hands of the BHA was an extreme step—one he was forced to take after all other options had been exhausted. It meant that the Boston Housing Authority had failed utterly in carrying out its public mission; that no amount of exhortation by the court had been successful in coercing the BHA to do its job; and that the only recourse was for the court to intervene and take the housing authority out of the hands of the political officials who had been appointed to oversee it.

Judge Garrity, in a November 1981 interview with the *Boston Globe*'s Robert Turner, pulled no punches: "As the people who lived in the BHA housing became black and poorer, who really gave a shit about them? The political system didn't care. It's the same old story in Boston: race and poverty, and you're down the tubes." Nearly twenty years later, Judge Garrity's feelings about the way the BHA did its job have barely cooled: "They were the gang that couldn't shoot straight. And there was always the suggestion that the people who were in charge were political appointments. . . . They couldn't move from A to B to C to D. They'd go from A to Z and it took them eight times as long. It's not that they were evil. What's the phrase, 'the banality of evil'? These people weren't even banal; they were just grossly incompetent."

Putting the housing authority in receivership meant that it would no longer control the city's public housing projects or the BHA's $55 million budget. Those powers would revert to the judge and the person he appointed to be receiver. Garrity was reluctant to take the step—"The Court understands and realizes that receivership is an extraordinary remedy," his ruling states, "and amounts to a significant intervention into the affairs of what is traditionally considered the province of another body of government"—and emphasized that receivership would last "no longer than is absolutely necessary to achieve the result to which the tenants are entitled by law."

Not surprisingly, the issue of putting the BHA into receivership was a political hot potato in Boston. Just a few months earlier, in January 1979, Mayor Kevin White had gone on record supporting the BHA against the court, saying in his State of the City speech that "by intervening in the daily operations of the BHA, the courts have done far more to hurt tenants than to help them." By June the mayor was singing a different tune, supporting Garrity's position, stating "it is clear that the BHA is in very serious trouble."

Some noted that the impending mayoral election in the fall of 1979 may have had something to do with the mayor's change of heart. Kevin White had good reason to support the BHA: he had appointed four of its five board members. However, Judge Garrity's decision lifted the political burden of fixing what was wrong from the BHA, just four months before the mayoral election. Kevin White was easily reelected in November.

Beyond immediate political considerations, many people committed to public housing were wary of the ramifications of Garrity's decision. Housing advocates feared that the *Perez* case might be used as proof of the failure of public housing—and provide a rationale for abandoning the program altogether. Robert Whittlesey, who acted as the court-appointed master from 1975 to 1979 in the *Perez* case, explained in a 1980 article in the *Journal of Housing*: "The *Perez* case should not be seen as an indictment of the public housing program itself. Rather it was and is an effort to save critically needed housing in which almost 10 percent of the people of Boston live. Adequate funding was a factor, but sound public management was the key issue. Following years of political abuse, the BHA failed because of a want of effective leadership at the top and from the political neglect of those at the local, state, and federal level who could have made it otherwise."

19 Receivership

On February 5, 1980, Judge Garrity named Lewis H. "Harry" Spence, the thirty-three-year-old former executive director of the Somerville Housing Authority and the Cambridge Housing Authority, as the receiver of the Boston Housing Authority. At seven o'clock the next morning, Spence walked into the offices of the BHA on the fifth floor of the 53 State Street building and, amid the packing boxes of the outgoing BHA board members, began his new job of overseeing housing for about fifty thousand tenants—some 10 percent of the population of Boston—with an annual budget of $55 million. For the first time in its forty-year history, public housing in Boston was no longer controlled by the Boston Housing Authority.

There was a lot to be done. Harry Spence recalls the dimensions of the crisis in public housing in Boston when he inherited it in 1980:

Over 30 percent of the apartments in the system were vacant and the vacancy rate was accelerating. There was a sense of the entire asset rapidly being threatened with disappearing, because the speed with which units were emptying out and not being reoccupied was going up all the time. Projects that were 40 and 50 percent vacant were wildly out of control. Vacancies scattered all through the developments were havens for criminal activity. At projects like Franklin Field where there were thirteen apartments in one building, where it was widely known that a building operated as a drug supermarket, the position of the police—never formally, but always informally—was, "As long as it stays in the project, we don't care." So crime and violence flourished in the projects.

Add the fact that it was 1980 and the explosive violence around busing had led to a kind of prairie fire effect. You had huge racial tensions occurring in all of East Boston where fire bombings of black families' [apartments] had occurred and there was a constant threat of racial violence for the few remaining black families. At Hyde Park, a group of kids between seventeen and twenty would target a black family in the development and harass them until they left. Then they'd pick another family to harass until they left. And so on.

There was a sense of racial violence all over the city and meanwhile a rapidly accelerating collapse of the large developments in particular, Columbia Point being far and away the most accelerated, where about 80 percent of the units were vacant. Mission Main, Mission Extension, Orchard Park, Franklin Field, Bromley Heath, and Commonwealth were all just absolutely out of control. Rent collections were disastrous; we pretended to collect the rent and they pretended to pay it. The authority had a significant deficit. So it was, as I think everyone agreed at that point, the worst public housing authority in the country.

While the vacancy rate in the projects was high and getting higher, the waiting list for public housing had some ten thousand names on it. Why didn't the BHA fill the empty units, easing some of the pressure on the waiting list and reversing the abandonment of the projects? Spence explains how the process of abandonment began and then accelerated out of control:

> The vacancy rate was a result of the incapacity of the authority to turn vacancies around quickly. The authority would be slow to repair vacancies to get them prepared for new people to move in. In the meantime, a vacancy would be vandalized, and once it was vandalized obviously the cost of preparing it greatly increased. And then once you had large numbers of vandalized apartments, the authority didn't have the manpower or the capacity to repair them.
>
> The large number of vacancies began to create a kind of no-man's-land situation. You'd have an entry with maybe less than 50 percent of the units occupied. It would begin to be terrifying for the families who remained. Because kids would take over the vacant apartments, especially at night. Smoke dope, get drunk, smash stuff. And very quickly the whole hallway would empty out. So this was really spreading like an accelerating cancer. Because once it begins to take off, then the terror of the remaining residents increases. A kind of exodus from the project begins to occur—an accelerating momentum of abandonment.

The first order of business when Harry Spence took over receivership of the BHA was what he called "the stabilization program"—stopping the attrition of units in the city's largest developments before they were lost for good. As Spence saw it, the primary challenge was reclaiming lost territory: "The territory had been completely taken over; most of the projects were under the control of youth gangs and criminal elements. Essentially, the project manager operated at the sufferance of those gangs and the residents lived there at the sufferance of those gangs. . . . these were totally out-of-control communities."

The program to regain control of the projects had three major objectives: first of all, to secure the vacant buildings; second, to

Lewis H. "Harry" Spence, court-appointed receiver, Boston Housing Authority, 1984. *Courtesy of the* Boston Globe.

reestablish 100 percent occupancy in the most stable buildings; and third, to pursue funding to reclaim and gradually rehabilitate those buildings. Spence describes the almost military process of reclaiming the projects:

> We believed we had to prove we could take the territory back from criminal elements in the community. In order to do that, we had to be able to secure vacant buildings, which the housing authority had never been able to do. It would secure a building and it would be broken into; pipes would be broken, copper would be stolen.
>
> So we set about developing elaborate plans for welding and bolting every single entrance—including the cellar windows, doors, and all windows below the third floor—so that we could secure vacant buildings. At the same time we consolidated vacancies. We tried to regain control of half-occupied buildings by consolidating all the occupants in the most stable parts of the development. Our goal was to draw a line where we would eventually say we will not surrender any more units to vacancy beyond this point.

The abandonment of the projects was the natural result, in Spence's opinion, of what he saw as "institutional abandonment." While Mayor Kevin White's explanation was that public housing was a failed program, Spence saw it differently:

> Our explanation was that the city had walked away from the projects and any responsibility for them. The police had walked away. The housing authority effectively had walked away. These projects and the people who lived in them had been abandoned by the institutions responsible for their protection and their safety. And once the public forces of order and safety walked away, private institutions similarly began to flee. Social service agencies were more and more at risk and were leaving. The surrounding neighborhoods began to be affected in many instances. So residents just felt they'd been completely abandoned by the city.

Spence decided that a preemptive move was necessary to halt the abandonment, physical as well as institutional, of Columbia Point. He informed the city that unless it undertook an immediate, good-faith redevelopment effort, he would begin "reoccupying" the project—moving residents into Columbia Point from the waiting list. "We were opposed to the continuing triaging of the population because of the refusal to provide them with fundamental services for health and safety," Spence explains. "It was not only humanly vicious, but grossly illegal and the worst possible public policy." Although he believed that reoccupation of Columbia Point would be a terrible mistake, he was prepared to carry out the threat in order to "halt the charade" of pretending to plan while letting the project implode.

On February 21, 1979, a year before Spence was named receiver, three key players had taken the first definitive step in the planning for the new Columbia Point: the Boston Housing Authority, the Boston Redevelopment Authority, and the Columbia Point Community Task Force signed the "Columbia Point Redevelopment Agreement." After months of meetings, first convened in 1978 to determine how the $10 million from the federal Urban Initiatives Program would be spent, the three parties agreed that Columbia Point required nothing less than complete redevelopment. Inspired by the principles that had been tested at King's Lynne, they drafted a document that provided the basic foundation for all future efforts at Columbia Point. Its key elements included the following:

- All existing Columbia Point residents would be guaranteed housing on the peninsula at a cost not to exceed 25 percent of their incomes.
- The housing would be planned to accommodate a mixture of resident incomes.
- The Columbia Point Community Task Force, representing project residents, would participate jointly with the Boston Redevelopment Authority and the Boston Housing Authority in the redevelopment, construction, and management of all new and rehabilitated housing on the peninsula, including the developer selection process.
- Columbia Point residents would be eligible for job training and job opportunities associated with the redevelopment project.

The community envisioned in the agreement would be different. Columbia Point wouldn't be "project" housing that only the poor would tolerate. The Point wouldn't be a no-man's-land—prisoner of war camp, then city dump, then project—where only the poor would live. It would be a place where people who could choose would choose to live. There would be no difference between units for residents of different incomes. Low-income housing wouldn't mean low-quality housing. And the low-income units would be mixed in with units for moderate- and market-rate tenants. Low-income residents would not be isolated in the "low-income" area of the community. They would live side by side with people paying higher rents. In fact, with absolutely no outward indications of who was paying what level of rent, it was entirely possible that no one would know, ask, or even care who was "low-income" and who wasn't.

The redevelopment agreement specified that current residents of Columbia Point would have a subsidized unit in the new development. Every tenant recognized by the BHA would have a right to a unit, acknowledged and legally agreed to by the BHA and the BRA—and those rights could not be eroded as time went by.

The redevelopment agreement put a stake in the ground. This is the kind of community we envision, it declared, and these are the guarantees we make to the current residents of Columbia Point. The commitment to redevelop Columbia Point as a mixed-income community was something entirely new for Boston. "We're trying to make the BRA and the BHA aware that any facility located here must be suitable for *anyone*," Terry Mair, president of the tenants' task force, told the *Boston Phoenix* in November 1979. "You can put someone making less than $10,000 a year next to someone making $50,000. We're saying that anyone who needs housing should be able to live here regardless of color or income."

The vision of a mixed-income community instantly drew skeptics from all sides, including those who most wanted to see it come true. The article in the *Phoenix* quoting a sampling of voices shows what the mixed-income proponents were up against:

> The wife of a builder in Braintree: "There's a reason why people are on welfare. They are hard-core unemployable. They don't have the social skills to keep a place clean. They'll dump garbage everywhere. Give them a nice place and they'll just ruin it for everybody."

> A certified public accountant: "There will be resentment on both sides. The poor will be surrounded by stores where they can't buy anything. How are white kids who have everything they want going to get along with poor black kids? I'd resent a woman who stays home all day with her kids because she's on welfare while I'm out working."

> A black UMass field officer: "The mix would work if the minorities were working-class poor. But putting somebody on welfare next to somebody who is pulling eight hours a day isn't going to work."

Regardless of the skeptics, the Columbia Point tenants were determined. Terry Mair explains what it meant to the residents of Columbia Point to be involved in planning for the redevelopment of the project:

Columbia Point residents' newsletter, 1981. *Courtesy of Esther Santos.*

[The BHA and the BRA] thought the task force would be a token, a rubber stamp. They didn't expect the kind of involvement they got. The name of the game in the ghetto is survival, and that's what we are fighting for. We've got nothing more to lose.

When I first started going to meetings, conversations went on as if I wasn't there. It hurts to be in a room and they're talking about your future as if you weren't there. The problem is, I'm black, a woman, and a mother living in public housing. But being low-income doesn't mean being dumb. We were smart enough to hire consultants to teach us what we didn't know. We've learned the techniques and strategies. The BRA and BHA kept saying, "You can't be housing developers; you haven't got any experience." We kept telling them that the community is not interested in being planned for; the community is interested in planning.

In the context of the history of the project, the redevelopment agreement was a watershed document, Columbia Point's Declaration of Independence, laying the groundwork for full tenant participation in the redevelopment process. Finally, the right people were

Terry L. Mair signed the Columbia Point Redevelopment Agreement for the Columbia Point Community Task Force, Kevin P. Feeley signed for the Boston Housing Authority, and Robert J. Ryan signed for the Boston Redevelopment Authority, February 21, 1979. *Courtesy of the Harbor Point Community Task Force.*

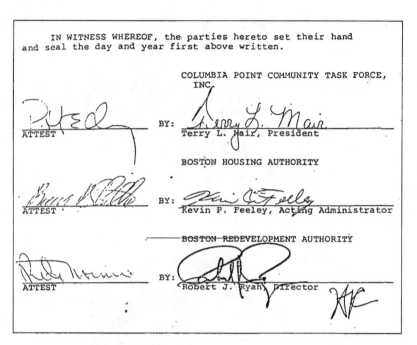

at the table: the tenant task force, the BRA, and the BHA. None of the earlier plans for the project—the many that never came to fruition—had combined the three groups. Instead, the BHA focused on plans to rehabilitate the housing project, the BRA focused on development of the land surrounding the project—and the tenants were left out of the process entirely. This time, the three would work together on all phases of planning.

The document's promises aren't extravagant—nothing more than a decent place to live. But those promises, which would later be witnessed and guaranteed by the court, in the person of the court-appointed receiver, were new to Boston's public housing tenants. The promises were the end of a long, hard road that no one knew but the tenants themselves. Some tenants were skeptical even of these "guaranteed" promises—as they should have been, given their experience. But their skepticism was matched by a determination born of that same experience. As Terry Mair put it, "We've got nothing more to lose."

20 Shotgun Marriage

Ironically, it took the election of conservative Republican Ronald Reagan in 1980 to breathe new life into the plans for redeveloping the public housing project at Columbia Point. The administration was voted in under the rallying cry of "let's reduce government." At the time, Columbia Point was costing the government money; the feds were only too grateful to anyone who offered to help solve the public housing problem—and to take it off its hands. Sensing that the new political environment might be favorable to its plan, Corcoran, Mullins, Jennison dusted off their three-year-old proposal for redeveloping Columbia Point. Knowing that their first step had to be local, CMJ approached Boston Housing Authority receiver Harry Spence.

Like other public housing advocates, Spence had philosophical objections to converting public housing to private, mixed-income housing. Low-income housing, they argued, was desperately needed, and there was no inherent reason why a low-income, high-rise project shouldn't work. After all, they argued, Columbia Point had worked well enough in the 1950s and early 1960s—until the BHA stopped maintaining the project, screening applicants, and enforcing the rules. Spence feared

that CMJ's proposal to sell a federal public housing project to a private developer for the first time in history might establish a bad precedent, one that would allow the government to retreat from its commitment—in his view, its fundamental responsibility—to provide public housing to those who needed it. Columbia Point originally provided fifteen hundred units of low-income housing; CMJ's proposal was for a community of twelve hundred units, only four hundred of them low-income. While Joe Corcoran saw this as a net gain of four hundred

dred livable low-income units, Spence and other public housing advocates saw it as a net loss of eleven hundred urgently needed low-income units.

Harry Spence articulated these reservations in a speech entitled "The Plight of Public Housing," delivered on April 23, 1980:

The so-called mixed-income approach is not, in truth, a *solution* to the problem of public housing; it is largely an *elimination* of the problem of public housing. It begins by withdrawing from 75 percent of the task—for the redevelopment plan usually reduces to one-fourth of their original number the units available for low-income occupancy. The mixed-income alternative is roughly 25 percent more sophisticated than the argument of those who say to me, "Tear it all down and get rid of those people." The private, mixed-income model may be appropriate in certain unusual and specific circumstances. But let us not seek false comfort in illusions that we are solving the problems of the poor by displacing them.

Spence met with Joe Corcoran in 1981 to discuss CMJ's 1978 proposal for Columbia Point. At the time, though, Spence preferred to keep public housing public; he persisted in believing that, given enough money and support, it could be viable. Accordingly, he rejected CMJ's proposal, inviting the company instead to submit a bid for modernization at Columbia Point. CMJ didn't want any part of it. "Do that and you'll have another disaster," Joe Corcoran argued. "You'll have to come back in ten years and pour all that money back into it again, because structurally the BHA doesn't have the ability to manage it. Public housing authorities have demonstrated in virtually every city in America that they cannot manage family housing. It's a bad idea to put all low-income families with all their social problems all together in one place. You just repeat the mistake."

Undaunted by Spence's rejection, Joe Corcoran took his proposal directly to the regional office of the U.S. Department of Housing and Urban Development (HUD). The new regional director, James DiPrete, a Republican appointee, was intrigued with the idea of redeveloping Columbia Point as a private, mixed-income community. After touring King's Lynne and talking to the tenants there, DiPrete, the former mayor of Cranston, Rhode Island, was sold on the concept. He invited Joe Corcoran and Joe Mullins to come to Washington with the Columbia Point tenant leaders Ruby Jaundoo and Roger Taylor to present the proposal to his superiors at HUD. At this point CMJ also enlisted the help of Washington lawyer and former Massachusetts senator Edward Brooke to press for redevelopment of the public housing project. Reagan administration officials embraced the concept. They recognized that this was an opportunity to demonstrate that private enterprise could provide housing for the poor while reducing federal expenditures and the government's role. As Joe Corcoran sums up HUD's response, "They liked the plan, probably for the wrong reasons, but they liked it."

When Harry Spence heard that CMJ had taken its proposal to Washington after he had turned it down, he felt that the developers had done an "end run" around the BHA. Joe Corcoran explains: "I had no intention of letting Harry Spence kill a plan that could give the city and the residents a jewel instead of a desperate ghetto." And Corcoran knew that HUD would be the banker for any further investment in Columbia Point, whether by the BHA or a private developer.

When HUD indicated that it would not make money available to the BHA for Columbia Point if it were to be used only for modernization, Spence reluctantly had to face the fact that a private, mixed-income complex was the only solution. The next challenge, as he saw it, was to make a case for privatization and converting Columbia Point to mixed-income without at the same time appearing to condemn all of the other low-income, high-rise projects in the city:

This sign on Mount Vernon Street warned drivers not to venture too close to Columbia Point in the early 1980s. *Courtesy of Bob Kuehn.*

> We said, look, every other development in this city exists in some kind of a neighborhood context. Columbia Point was established as an exile community, with no relationship to any existing neighborhood or community. You cannot sustain a pure public housing development in that measure of isolation. . . .
>
> The housing advocates were saying that because we were giving up Columbia Point, we were giving up on the whole public housing program. We argued that in fact those other high-rise developments were salvageable because they had some neighborhood context. And that neighborhood context provided some hope for saving them as public housing developments with some significant changes.

Finally, the process of privatization and revitalization at Columbia Point was under way.

On September 12, 1982, a formal document, *Columbia Point Peninsula Request for Developer Proposals*, was issued by the BHA and the BRA, "in partnership with" the Columbia Point Community Task Force. The selection of developers, as part of the entire redevelopment process, was to be jointly run by the three parties. The BRA was given the task of overseeing the process for selecting a developer. The agency issued a request for proposals that required submissions by February 1983. The only proposal submitted by the deadline was CMJ's, proposing a legal joint venture with the Columbia Point Community Task Force. As Joe Corcoran observes dryly, "Nobody else wanted any part of it." CMJ was elated. Harry Spence, however, was not. Declaring the process flawed because there were no other proposals, he complained vehemently to BRA

Robert J. Ryan, director of
the Boston Redevelopment
Authority, 1984. *Courtesy
of the* Boston Globe.

director Robert J. Ryan, and Ryan decided to extend the deadline for another three months. Spence backed up his insistence on additional proposals with a declaration that the BHA, which held title to the land, would refuse to convey it if CMJ's was the only proposal.

Ryan recalls how complex the issues were. All of the players had their own concerns and their own constituents to answer to. The federal government had never sold a public housing project before. The Boston Housing Authority had to answer to a Superior Court judge. The Boston Redevelopment Authority had jurisdiction over some of the questions involving Columbia Point, but not all. Ryan explains: "All of those things were out there. We told Joe [Corcoran] we were going to put all this into the mix. Even HUD said, 'Look, we're not going to designate this on a sole source basis to one developer and off you go and do it, because there may be a whole host of people who want to get involved in this.' Getting HUD to the point were they felt comfortable that this was not going to tear apart some existing policy within the federal structure was an issue, too."

By the spring of 1983 two more development teams came forward and submitted proposals. In June the task force published an impressive *Summary of Proposals* for the residents of Columbia Point, including a clear time line of the entire redevelopment process and a detailed explanation and comparison of the three different plans, with respect to design, finance, phasing of construction, plans for relocation of existing tenants, management, the role of the task force, and employment.

The three proposals are markedly different. CMJ's design, by the Boston architectural firm of Goody, Clancy & Associates, was organized around a broad central mall leading from the entrance directly to the water. The mall formed the "main street" and central gathering place for the development, with a variety of housing arranged on a rectangular grid of streets, all with views of downtown Boston in one direction and the water in the other. In the second, from Columbia Associates, Boston architect Sy Mintz proposed a dramatic redesign of the site, with a series of new waterways that would literally bring water and water views into the community. In addition, Mintz's plan called for raising the site in several places, creating a hilly, modulated landscape instead of the totally flat one at Columbia Point. The third proposal, from Housing Innovations, suggested a design dominated by two elements: four 35-story tower complexes and a central green parallel to Mount Vernon Street, including a "town center" area of shops and community buildings near the main entrance.

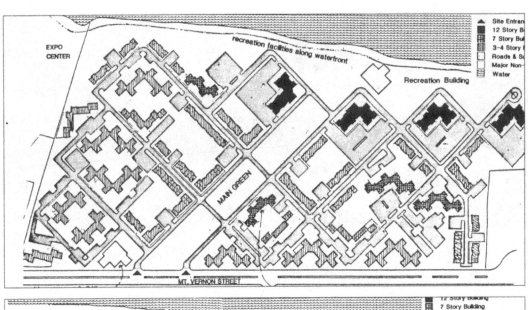

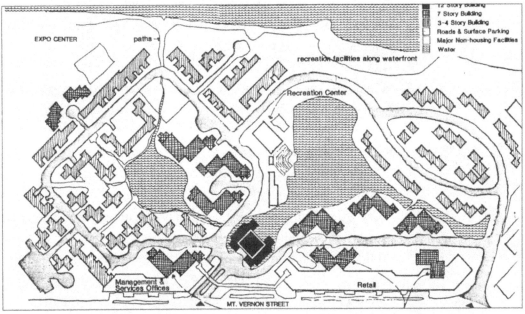

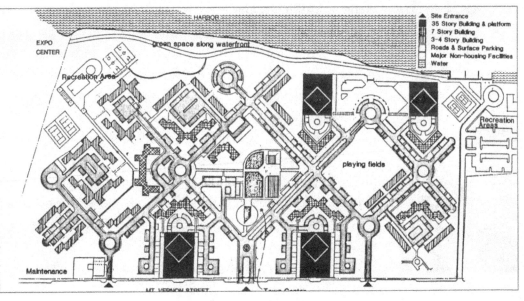

The Columbia Point Community Task Force's summary of the three proposals to redevelop the housing project submitted by Corcoran, Mullins, Jennison; Columbia Associates; and Housing Innovations. *Courtesy of Corcoran, Mullins, Jennison.*

Members of the Columbia
Associates development
team included (left to
right) Edward McCor-
mack, John Cruz, and Bob
Kuehn, in photos taken in
1976, 1983, and 1994,
respectively. *Courtesy of
the* Boston Globe.

Mayor Kevin White, 1979.
Courtesy of the Boston
Globe.

Columbia Associates was a partnership initiated by Sy Mintz. It included Bob Kuehn, a Boston developer; Ed Fish, who owned Peabody Construction Company; former attorney general Edward McCormack, a well-connected real estate lawyer and Kevin White confidant; Thomas Finnerty, the law partner of Senate president William Bulger; John Cruz, a minority contractor; and the National Housing Partnership (NHP), a private, for-profit corporation chartered by Congress with the goal of building low- and moderate-income housing. By 1982 NHP was the largest owner of multifamily housing in the country.

After the Housing Innovations proposal, with its high-rise towers, failed to make the first cut, a major political storm began to break around the two remaining proposals. Both developers left in the competition had formidable support. While the Columbia Associates team had the strong backing of Harry Spence and the BHA, the Corcoran, Mullins, Jennison team had the explicit backing of the tenant task force. The selection process was headed for a standoff.

Harry Spence charged that CMJ was playing unfairly because the partners had begun meeting with the Columbia Point tenants well before the request for proposals was issued. In addition, Spence believed that CMJ had the support of the mayor and, through the mayor, the BRA. "We actually believed the thing was wired by the BRA for Corcoran, Mullins, Jennison from the start," he says. Chronically skeptical of Mayor White's commitment to housing, Spence threw his support behind Columbia Associates, believing that NHP had the deep pockets that would be needed to see the project to completion. Spence recalls: "The residents supported CMJ. We took the position with the support of the court that we thought that was nice but not determinative. They were a small number of people—this was an enormous project. And frankly, we felt they'd been wined and dined by CMJ rather successfully."

What Harry Spence dismisses as "wining and dining," Joe Corcoran characterizes as establishing a relationship with the tenants, explaining their vision of what could become of Columbia Point, and encouraging the tenants to educate themselves in every aspect of redevelopment precisely so their opinions could not be dismissed by the experts and politicians as "nice but not determinative." In fact, Corcoran makes no secret of having cultivated a relationship with the tenants at Columbia Point—"Guilty," he says—or that the relationship was a positive factor in the tenants' choice.

As Eleanor White, deputy director of the Massachusetts Housing Finance Agency at the time, observes, "Joe Corcoran was smart enough to have made incursions at Columbia Point—that is the only way to describe it—and to have befriended the tenants. It was a brilliant stroke. He was really ahead of his time in that." What's more, CMJ's was the only proposal to include partnership between the developers and the tenants. According to White, "It was probably the first time that a private developer wanted to share that much power with a tenant group."

Ruby Jaundoo, one of the most influential voices on the task force, explains how she viewed the two proposals. The members of the Columbia Associates team "were very adamant about the fact that they were in the housing business," she says. "They run the housing, and the tenants live in it." But the tenants were determined to be partners in redeveloping Columbia Point. "We had already gone that route," Jaundoo explains. "We were living in a housing development and that's all we did. We just lived there. We had no say in what went on. Having an equal say in what goes on here . . . was the key to selecting CMJ, and then their track record."

Spence's charge against CMJ was a matter of some controversy—one that played out prominently in the pages of the *Boston Globe*. On August 13, 1983, a *Globe* article entitled "Rebuilding of Columbia Point Threatened by Dispute over Developer" reported that the BHA, the BRA, and the tenant task force "appear headed toward a bitter confrontation and quite possibly a deadlock." In the article, Harry Spence charged that David Connelly, a social worker who at the time was working to provide social services at King's Lynne, where CMJ was the developer, had been meeting with the Columbia Point tenants and "coaching" them to choose the CMJ pro-

David Connelly, a social worker at CMJ's King's Lynne redevelopment in 1983, in a 1997 photo. *Courtesy of Corcoran, Mullins, Jennison.*

posal—in violation of an agreement among the developers that none of them would approach any of the three parties involved in selecting a developer during the process of requests for proposals.

Although Connelly was indeed under contract with CMJ to provide social services at King's Lynne at the time, his work with the Columbia Point tenants was as an independent contractor on the BHA payroll. Connelly insists that Spence's charges are entirely false. "I told [the tenants] they ought to fight for partnership, that it was important that they forced whoever they chose to go into a partnership with them," Connelly explains, "whether they chose CMJ or NHP or Ed Fish or whoever." What about the fact that CMJ's was the only proposal that included tenant partnership? Connelly says that the tenants could have gotten some kind of a partnership from any one of the developers: "They were in a much stronger position of power than they knew they were."

According to the *Boston Globe*, Joe Corcoran was furious at Spence's charges:

> Corcoran says the reason his proposal got the nod from tenants is, first, that they judged it superior, and second, that he had been discussing with tenants the possible redevelopment of Columbia Point for 15 years and that they know his commitment to the place. He accuses Spence of being self-righteous and something of a conspiracy theorist. "Harry does not have a monopoly on integrity," he declares.

Another element in the drama was the long-standing antagonism between Harry Spence and Mayor Kevin White. "We had an irresistible force meeting an immovable object," Spence explains. "The judge and I weren't going to move, and the mayor wasn't going to move." It's a good thing that such an important effort wasn't derailed by this "high noon" scenario; far more important issues were at stake than whether the receiver or the mayor would be the first to blink.

Fortunately, the political pressure to find a solution to Columbia Point superseded the clash of egos. All of the players—Harry Spence, the mayor, HUD—were united in feeling the heat. As Harry Spence explains: "We believed it was terribly important to get Columbia Point not only off of the back of the public housing program in Boston—because it stood like a kind of endless indictment of the public housing program in Boston. But in those days it was constantly cited nationally—along with projects like Pruitt-Igoe in St. Louis and the Robert Taylor Homes in Chicago—as an example of what a disaster public housing is. So we wanted to move forward."

Meanwhile, the task force, fearing that the BHA and the BRA were going to choose Columbia Associates as the developer, took its case to the streets. "We got ourselves together," Esther Santos recalls, "went to the JFK building [where HUD's regional office was located], put up our signs and made some noise." The task force argued that the redevelopment agreement and subsequent memorandum of understanding, which was drawn up for the developer selection process, had made it clear that all three parties—the BHA, the BRA, and the task force—had to agree on the developer. The tenants weren't about to let the city's public officials break another promise. Esther Santos explains their indignation and their determination to make the BRA and the BHA stick to their word: "Are you saying to us that our thoughts, our work, everything means nothing, that once they choose the developer we're going to sit back and say nothing? Not after we've fought for fifteen years before the whole thing came together. We said, 'Absolutely no, we will have a say.' We wanted to be a part of what was going on from beginning to end, so we took it to the mayor."

Developer Arthur Winn, 1984. *Courtesy of the Boston Globe.*

To break the logjam, the mayor suggested a joint venture and appointed Boston developer Arthur Winn, well respected by both sides, to serve as mediator. Before being called in, Winn recalls watching at a distance "what looked like a pretty sophisticated battle between two groups." The Columbia Associates group was so strong, Winn explains, that "it could not be ignored by virtue of the quality of the partners, even if one wished to politically." Likewise, Corcoran, Mullins, Jennison could not be ignored—not because of political clout, but because they had taken what Winn describes as "a softer approach" in forging an alliance with the Columbia Point tenants as they had done at King's Lynne. In short, Winn says, it was like the nuclear deterrent: both sides had the power of mutual annihilation. "Both forces could have blown up the deal and both understood it," Winn recalls. "It took them about a New York minute to recognize everyone had a gun. So if anyone pulled their gun, there was no deal."

A rendering from CMJ's proposal. *Courtesy of Corcoran, Mullins, Jennison.*

Winn maintains that Mayor Kevin White did not favor CMJ over Columbia Associates during the mediation: "Kevin was never shy, and I don't recall Kevin, who could have communicated in many ways in those days, saying anything. [He] was amazingly neutralized either by the power of both teams or by the merits of the situation or by the stars. But, in fact, he never directed me. . . . Kevin was uncharacteristically hands off."

BRA's Ryan Objects to Spence's Unilateral Decision

August 10, 1983

Mr. Lewis H. Spence
Receiver/Administrator
Boston Housing Authority
52 Chauncy Street
Boston, Massachusetts 02111

Dear Harry:

Your letter stating your preference among Columbia Point redevelopers, delivered yesterday, has caused me serious concern. It represents a departure from the process which you and I, together with the Columbia Point Community Task Force, have agreed to conduct.

That process, agreed to nearly a year ago, calls for the three parties to reach common agreement on the selection of a developer through joint consultation. Contrary to your letter, no such consultation involving the tenants has taken place.

Based on our agreement to seek consensus, and their confidence that you and I, together with the tenants, would reach shared decisions in good faith, three distinguished development teams chose to participate in the selection process. In reliance on our commitment, they expended considerable sums in responding to the extensive and costly requirements we imposed on them.

The process we have conducted has been lengthy and thorough. At each point along the way we have taken elaborate steps to see that we were working in concert and that no unilateral actions were taken.

As recently as last week, in the concluding interviews with the two developer finalists, you and I publicly agreed to meet together with tenant representatives, and through discussion seek a common opinion on the preferred developer. We agreed that it is essential to conclude these discussions this week in order to retain HUD funding and honor our joint commitment to the developers to do so. I am also aware that you intend to go on vacation next week. I am informed that the tenants' Task Force prepared for these discussions by concluding their review in a meeting conducted at Columbia Point on Monday night.

It is therefore startling to me that, without consulting the tenants or myself, you delivered your "firm conclusion" in writing on Tuesday. You should understand that I can respect your preference for the Columbia Associates team. They are an impressive organization and have responded well to the challenge of Columbia Point. Many of your observations about them have merit.

I may not share completely your opinions regarding Columbia Associates. As you know, the independent development analyst we jointly retained, Minot, De Blois, and Maddison, has concluded that the CMJ proposal is stronger financially and contains substantially less risk. I certainly do not feel comfortable with your characterization of the attitudes of CMJ. In fact, I asked to speak to you and the Task Force President directly on this issue last week.

My concern however is not with the quality of your opinions on the two developers. It is these opinions which you and I agreed to meet and share. There is considerable room for honest differences among us in evaluating these two outstanding proposals. What is critical at this juncture is that our respective points of view be explained and agreement sought through the cooperative process at which we have worked so hard during the past year.

By flatly declaring your conclusion and placing it in the public domain, a wholly unnecessary level of conflict has been created.

**Boston
Redevelopment
Authority**

Robert J. Ryan, Director   August 10, 1983

Mr. Lewis H. Spence
Receiver/Administrator
Boston Housing Authority
52 Chauncy Street
Boston, Massachusetts 02111

Dear Mr. Spence:

Your letter stating your preference among Columbia Point
redevelopers, delivered yesterday, has caused me serious concern.
It represents a departure from the process which you and I, together
with the Columbia Point Community Task Force, have agreed to conduct.

That process, agreed to nearly a year ago, calls for the three
parties to reach common agreement on the selection of a developer
through joint consultation. Contrary to your letter, no such consultation involving the tenants has taken place.

Based on our agreement to seek consensus, and their confidence
that you and I, together with the tenants, would reach shared decisions
in good faith, three distinguished development teams chose to participate in the selection process. In reliance on our commitment,
they expended considerable sums in responding to the extensive and
costly requirements we imposed on them.

The process we have conducted has been lengthy and thorough.
At each point along the way we have taken elaborate steps to see
that we were working in concert and that no unilateral actions
were taken.

As recently as last week, in the concluding interviews with
the two developer finalists, you and I publicly agreed to meet,
together with tenant representatives, and through discussion seek
a common opinion on the preferred developer. We agreed that it is
essential to conclude these discussions this week in order to retain
HUD funding and honor our joint commitment to the developers to
do so. I am also aware that you intend to go on vacation next week.
I am informed that the tenants' Task Force prepared for these discussions by concluding their review in a meeting conducted at
Columbia Point on Monday night.

1 City Hall Square
Boston, Massachusetts 02201
(617) 722-4300

The interests of the Columbia Point tenants
compel us to seek a decision, so that this
troubled project can finally be integrated into a
mixed income community of decent, safe
housing. By working together up to this point,
we have achieved a level of progress which had
not been accomplished by our predecessors
over the last ten years. We have received two
very worthwhile proposals. It behooves us to
return to our commitment to hear from the
tenants, who are directly affected, and through
discussion to reach a shared conclusion. If each
party reaffirms its willingness to return to the
decision making process to which we committed ourselves, I remain available to conclude
the work we set out to accomplish.

Sincerely,

Robert J. Ryan
Director

cc: Judge Garrity
    Roger Taylor, Columbia Point Community
    Task Force

Bob Ryan says there might have been some confusion about
White's support for the CMJ proposal; it was the BRA staff, not the
mayor, who favored it. Ryan recalls:

The BRA staff came out with a recommendation [for CMJ's proposal],
not because of Kevin White and not because of me. Just because Joe
Corcoran did a good job of putting it together, he should get the designation. And Harry [Spence] had his people on the other side. And
that's when we had to work out an agreement ourselves. Had a cup of
coffee. We've got a lot of people in the room. We've got a very good
project and a lot of good resources. People have been in this game a
long time. They know how to do this thing. This pie is big enough for
everyone. So then along comes Arthur Winn as Madeleine Albright, if
you will.

Winn spent the month of October 1983 attempting to put together a solution that would allow everyone to lead with their
strengths. Ed Fish's strength, on the Columbia Associates side, was
construction. Yet CMJ, as Winn saw it, was a company of "pure developers" who needed to have control over the project, including
construction. CMJ had insisted on two things: that the tenants remain co-general partners with a 10 percent financial stake in the
project; and that CMJ be designated the managing general partner.
CMJ also wanted its private management company to manage the
new mixed-income complex. The company believed that management control was essential to the ongoing viability of the new community.

Winn recognized that redeveloping Columbia Point was more
than a real estate deal to Joe Corcoran: "This was a place he identified with personally as a Boston boy, and he wasn't going to lose."
The deadlock was broken, according to Winn, when Ed Fish "took
a step back and allowed the deal to proceed in the only way it could
from Joe Corcoran's point of view." In the end, Fish agreed to let
CMJ take primary responsibility for the construction of the project.
According to Winn, Fish's accepting a limited partnership was the
key to resolving the deadlock, for which Fish deserves a tremendous
amount of credit. As for his own role, Winn insists, "I had done
nothing on the negotiation except provide a vehicle for this cathar-
sis to play itself out without blowing up."

In the end, the mayor officiated as a sort of justice of the peace in
a "shotgun marriage" between the two developers. In November
1983 Winn announced that the development team would be called
Peninsula Partners, a limited partnership consisting of CMJ, Bob

Kuehn, the National Housing Partnership, Peabody Construction Company, Cruz Construction Company, and the Columbia Point Community Task Force. NHP, unwilling to participate in a project that they didn't control, withdrew within the first six months.

As Joe Mullins explains, this marriage of both teams was cumbersome from the start: "There was a joke in town at one point: 'Anybody who is not involved in Columbia Point, please stand up.' . . . I liken it to Noah's Ark. There were two of everything. We had two architects, two sets of engineers, two sets of contractors, two sets of developers, and mini partners all around. It was a nightmare. But that was it: both teams, take it or leave it."

According to Joe Corcoran, the only way around this cumbersome partnership was to name a managing partner, regardless of the financial split. To CMJ, it was critical to be able to put its stamp on the project. In the end, Peninsula Partners agreed.

At the time, the estimated cost of the development was $150 to $200 million. By the time construction was completed, in 1990, that figure would exceed $250 million, which included $50 million in reserves. Funding for the project came from a variety of federal, state, and private sources. The Massachusetts Housing Finance Agency, under the leadership of executive director Marvin Siflinger, made a $151 million, 9.5 percent tax-exempt mortgage commitment. The federal government provided $21 million — $9 million remaining from HUD's 1978 Urban Initiatives grant and a $12 million Urban Development Action Grant. Seventy-five million dollars of private equity investment and $3 million from a Massachusetts Chapter 884 grant completed the financing.

CMJ had always envisioned the ideal mixed-income community as comprising equal proportions of low-income, moderate-income, and market-rate residents. This was the formula at King's Lynne, where mixed-income worked extremely well. When the planning for subsidized units at the new community that would be known as Harbor Point was put in place, however, there was no financial mechanism available for moderate-income subsidies.

By the time the development team was finally chosen, the first of many crises occurred: the federal Section 8 money, the key to subsidizing the 400 low-income units, had run out. The Section 8 program, developed by HUD during the Nixon administration, allowed low-income tenants to pay 25 percent of their income for rent, with HUD reimbursing the property owner for the difference. Howard

Cohen, a private attorney representing the BHA, came up with an ingenious solution. He knew that the BHA had set aside Section 8 money for 350 low-income public housing units at Franklin Field. So Cohen worked out a swap whereby Franklin Field would give Harbor Point its 350 Section 8 units, and Franklin Field would ask for modernization money that was still available for public housing but not for the privately owned Harbor Point. The remaining 50 units of low-income housing units at Harbor Point would receive a state rent subsidy under Chapter 707. The final decision on the "swap" was up to Harry Spence. He approved it, implementing Cohen's plan and clearing the way for the redevelopment to go forward. Once the deal had been struck, Harry Spence and the BHA put their full support behind getting the job done.

Ultimately, the political imperative to do something about Columbia Point was greater than the ideological and philosophical differences among the major players. At last a development team was in place and the financing cobbled together. The way was clear for Corcoran, Mullins, Jennison and the Columbia Point Community Task Force to begin in earnest what they had first envisioned five years earlier: working together as equal partners to create a new community.

Sign points the way to
Harbor Point, 1999.
Maggie Turner.

21 Designing the New Community

Once the development team was determined, it seemed to many that the biggest obstacle had been overcome. CMJ, however, having lived through the redevelopment of King's Lynne, was only too aware that the work was just beginning. Columbia Point residents were full of skepticism and cynicism: they thought the developers were only in it to make a killing. As soon as they closed the deal, they were going to kick the poor people out and convert the place into high-priced waterfront condominiums. The Columbia Point Commu-

nity Task Force had been co-opted by the developers and had sold out their community. Mixed-income would never work. Since when would anybody who could afford to pay market rents choose to live next to poor people?

It was possible, of course, that the simplest version of the story was also the truest: the developers meant what they said, and the task force was fiercely determined to turn their community around. Even with the best of intentions on both sides, building a strong partnership between the developer and the task force would be difficult enough. Joe Mullins describes the unusual chemistry of the partnership:

> We were asking the tenants to trust us at a time when they had no reason to trust anybody. . . . Here was a guy from Dorchester, Joe Corcoran, and a guy from South Boston, Joe Mullins. Those two communities surrounded Columbia Point but had never wanted anything to do with it. And here you had people from those communities coming in there trying to help them solve the problem and really giving them the best opportunity they've ever had in their lives. It was kind of a powerful thing.
>
> [The task force] fought like heck for their development. They put so much into it. They put more into it than we did, really. Because they were there for the worst of times. And they're still there today living it. It was very hard work.

Growing up in South Boston, Joe Mullins remembers the Quonset huts of Camp McKay out on the peninsula and the dumps beyond; the troop trains

Left to right: Joe Corcoran, Joe Mullins, and Gary Jennison. *Courtesy of Corcoran, Mullins, Jennison.*

bringing Italian prisoners of war into First Street; Italian families bringing meals out to the prisoners on the peninsula. He also remembers the families who were lucky enough to move into public housing right after the war. "I knew some families who moved out to Columbia Point from South Boston," he recalls. "When they moved in it was really sort of a sought-after prize. Everyone was thrilled with the idea they were moving into something new like that." In fact, among the kids in his grammar school, living in public housing was something of a status symbol. "Some of the girls who lived in the project looked down on the girls who came from the neighborhoods," Mullins recalls, "because they had central heat and modern kitchens and modern apartments. I don't remember the boys doing that, but I remember the girls who lived in public housing thinking they were kind of above everybody else."

Joe Corcoran, too, grew up in "mixed-income housing" long before the term was invented. He sees mixed-income housing as a key part of the American dream. In fact, it's the story of his own life:

When I was born in 1936, the youngest of eight children, my father had been out of work for three years. I remember being quite shocked when I learned this in later years. I had always pictured my father as working—which he was, but he wasn't getting a paycheck.

Our neighborhood was mixed, economically and ethnically. The Bradfords were two gentle, elderly, kindly Yankee brothers who lived in separate homes on Jerome Street, living on their inherited and invested wealth. When Mr. Bradford finished his Sunday paper, he would leave the funnies in his porch window, which was a signal to my sisters that they could come and take the paper home. Sunday papers cost fifteen cents, a luxury that he knew our family couldn't afford.

In my parents' opinion, the really fortunate families in our neighborhood were the civil service employees—the policemen, the firemen, the postmen. Mr. Ryan on Sawyer Avenue was a pumper with Engine 17 on Meetinghouse Hill. He had eight children—four of them became Jesuit priests. Since my father, an Irish immigrant, only had a sixth-grade education, he didn't qualify to take the civil service exams.

Mr. Bonoveri on Cushing Avenue was an Italian immigrant contractor. We could tell he did well, because he owned his large single-family home. Directly across the street from us was the Wong family, who ran the Asia Restaurant on Stoughton Street.

Uphams Corner was a mixed-income neighborhood long before we ever made up the word, and we never considered ourselves poor or inferior. As a teenager, I can remember waiting for a rapid transit car at Park Station going back to Andrew Square toward Dorchester, and watching the white kids on the other side of the tracks going west to affluent communities like Arlington or Belmont, and genuinely feeling sorry for them because they didn't live in Dorchester.

In many respects, Corcoran, Mullins, and Jennison were completely different from their tenant partners, but in one respect they were the same: none of them grew up with money. Joe Corcoran and Joe Mullins, from Dorchester and South Boston, went to college on the G.I. Bill. Gary Jennison, from Hungry Hill in Springfield, got to college by winning several scholarships, including one from the Council of Jewish Women in that city. The partners spoke the same language and didn't pull any punches with each other. Discussions were open and disagreements were aired frankly.

In 1984 CMJ took over management of Columbia Point under contract with the Boston Housing Authority. The interim management period enabled CMJ to find out exactly what the existing conditions were at the Point, to analyze the problems they were up against, and to identify and deal with as many of the "bad apples" as possible—just as they had done at King's Lynne. Columbia Point had 350 remaining families, some of whom had multiple problems. CMJ received special funding from HUD during this time to deal with the problems, especially getting rid of drug dealing and attendant

Help Comes from the Archbishop

Opposition to the plans for redeveloping Columbia Point surfaced early and came from many sources, among them the Affordable Housing Coalition, the Massachusetts Tenants Organization, and Project Care and Concern, a food bank run by two nuns, Sister Joyce McMullen and Sister Jean Stanton. Opponents argued that the loss of low-income units—from fifteen hundred in Columbia Point to only four hundred in the new community—set a dangerous precedent when low-income housing was sorely needed. This threatened essential Urban Development Action Grant (UDAG) funding applications that required city, state, and federal endorsements.

Sister Joyce McMullen and Sister Jean Stanton, members of the Notre Dame order, had operated a food bank at Columbia Point since 1973. They suspected that the developers secretly intended to displace the public housing tenants and told Columbia Point residents so. Joe Mullins recalls that the development team was summoned to a meeting with Archbishop (now Cardinal) Bernard Law at the instigation of Father George Carrigg, pastor of St. Christopher's Church. Mullins, Marty Jones, Roger Taylor, and Ruby Jaundoo went to see Archbishop Law to address the rumors and answer the charges. Mullins explains:

> The Catholic nuns worked at Columbia Point; they were giving free bread, cheese, and advice to people living out there. Well, they were out there really spreading the word that we were going to kick all the poor people out.
>
> We were summoned to Lake Street, and the archbishop was very stern. He wanted to know, "What are you doing? I understand you're kicking all those poor people out." So, after he went on for a while, it was Ruby and Roger who carried the day by convincing him that they, the residents, were very much in favor of the plan. They thought their best chance for turning Columbia Point around into a new community in which they would have better housing, opportunities for their children, jobs and all the rest of it, would be within the partnership.
>
> We then went on to tell him that, without the federal funding, the development would be a dead deal. By the end of the meeting the archbishop turned around and said, "How can I help?" He'd gone from being a skeptic to an ally. So we said, "Why don't you write a letter to the president?" And he said, "Of the United States?" We said yes. He then responded, "Well, I guess you can't go higher than that."
>
> President Reagan ultimately called Archbishop Law, by the way. We were looking for an Urban Development Action Grant of $12 million and we were in competition with everybody else in the country. And the fellow in Washington said that he was told at the time the decision was made to hold up announcing all the awards around the country until the president had a chance to call the archbishop to let him know it had been approved.
>
> Ruby carried the day, because it's one thing for a developer to talk to someone like Archbishop Law and tell him what we think is best. But it's something else for a tenant advocate who's been living there in deplorable conditions to speak up and say, "This is the best thing that's ever happened to us. We think you should support us." It was very powerful. I thought she did a great job. Ruby's a wonderful person. Not many words, but she is a very strong woman, very compelling, very influential.

crime. CMJ also brought in a social service program to work with the families, conduct job training, and establish the basic infrastructure for the new community.

The Columbia Point Community Task Force had been working with Antonio DiMambro, a Boston architect and planner who had worked successfully with tenants in Cambridge public housing. His role began with assisting the task force in the selection of a developer—explaining to them what each one of the three developers' teams was proposing—and continued throughout the design process. DiMambro emphasizes that he worked for the tenants. "It was very important for them to feel comfortable," he explains, "that they could ask questions to someone that wasn't a representative of the official architect, that wasn't a representative of the developer, that wasn't a representative of BHA. I was their own representative."

DiMambro's charge was to explain what the proposals and architects' renderings meant, "in simple English," and to bring the tenants' concerns back to the negotiating table. The process, he says, was an educational one for all parties involved: the tenants had to learn to understand the developers' and architects' perspective, but equally important, the professionals had to learn from the tenants. DiMambro summarizes the tenants' major concerns:

Joe Corcoran and Joan Goody both grew up in mixed-income neighborhoods: Corcoran in Dorchester's Uphams Corner, pictured here, where triple-deckers prevail, and Goody in Brooklyn, New York. *Courtesy of the* Boston Globe.

First of all, they negotiated a guarantee that the people who lived at Columbia Point were not going to be displaced from the project. That a certain number of units were going to kept in perpetuity for low-income residents. That if people who lived there had a higher income over time, they were not going to be pushed out; they could remain there but pay proportionately more rent.

The second thing that they were concerned about is they did not want to be second-tier citizens. That was important to them in the actual location of families within the development. They didn't want to be in a corner of the development while the wealthy people would be in another corner. So in the relocation plan a lot of attention was paid to mixing the incomes.

The third thing that they were very concerned about was the actual design of the units. Because they felt that the old units were not designed for them. And in fact the old public housing was designed as a transitional housing stock to help people in the first two or three years of their lives together, married or whatever, and then move on. The reality is that this housing remained the only option for many residents. Even if they had seven kids, they were still living in an apartment that was designed only for four. So to make sure there was a variety of housing options was very critical.

For example, everybody concurred that large families should not have housing that required an elevator because there was a correlation between elevator buildings and vandals in the stairs. So we felt that adding townhouses, with direct entrances and exits from the street, would be a much better solution. That the backyard for kids was also a very important thing. That parking should be visible from the apartment. For many of these families, the car was the only possession. And so they didn't want to have a big parking area; they wanted to have small parking lots close by the housing. They had preferences regarding certain types of windows. . . . It was a wonderful thing. Very often architects don't think about that.

Many of the tenants' design preferences, DiMambro came to understand, were driven more by concerns about security and functionality than by aesthetics: "At the beginning the tenants did not want to have a waterfront park. I couldn't understand that. And it took some time because clearly I felt that it would be an asset for them. In the end it became very clear they were scared because in the old community the worst part of the site was in the back of the project by the water. And they felt that if we were to do a park here that's where the drug dealers would go. That's where the bad things would happen."

CMJ's architect, Joan Goody, listened carefully to the tenants and DiMambro, and over several months of meetings developed and refined a design that was responsive to what she was hearing. Joan Goody and Joe Corcoran agreed that the first thing they had to do was destroy the image of the old Columbia Point and create a new image. What was the image of the old Columbia Point? Thirty almost-identical buildings of drab yellow brick. A flat, constant roof line—what architects call a "table-top." Disorienting, mazelike streets. The waterfront—the site's most attractive natural feature—completely blocked by massive buildings.

Goody and Corcoran both wanted a neighborhood with some of the same qualities they remembered from the mixed-income neighborhoods in which they had grown up: connected street patterns as opposed to private, exclusive cul-de-sacs; for townhouses, parking at

Architect's rendering of
Harbor Point facades.
*Courtesy of Goody &
Clancy*

the front curb; individual front doors with porches or stoops facing the street; private backyards. In short, spaces where neighbors mixed casually, with lots of activity on the sidewalks and streets—to encourage "eyes on the street," neighborliness, and community.

Goody's design starts with a completely new street pattern—a simple, straightforward grid system. Ingeniously arranged at a forty-five-degree angle to the water's edge, every street looks either out to the sea or toward downtown Boston, so that "the minute you drive down a street," she explains, "you have the sense there's something wonderful beyond." The "freedom" of such a system, according to Goody, is essentially American:

> Ninety-five percent of the United States is laid out on a simple grid system because it gives you access. It makes things clear. Many people have even written great papers about the fact that the grid system is very American. It's very open-ended. It gives you a sense of freedom to go in any direction in the town. Freedom to expand. As opposed to the cul-de-sac, which is very dead-ended and very exclusionary. The suburban cul-de-sac definitely says, "Either you belong here or don't drive in here." So this wasn't cul-de-sac world. . . . Anybody can find their way around. A stranger comes to town and can find his way around. In a strange way, it's welcoming.

Fortuitously, the new street pattern also allowed Goody to save almost a third of the existing buildings, with minimal disruption of the underground utilities—water, gas, and sewer—that were expensively laid on the peninsula's unstable subsoil.

Columbia Point had always been isolated, not just physically and socially, but also architecturally. The architecture of Columbia Point didn't say "Boston" or "New England"—all it said was "housing project." Its character wasn't associated with the traditions of the city; it was the character of poverty. The design for Harbor Point connects it to Boston and to New England, Goody explains, in a way that Columbia Point never had been:

> You don't create in the abstract. Every new community should be seen in the context of the surrounding city and the surrounding neighborhoods. You don't build in Boston the way you would in San Antonio or Charleston. So we studied the neighborhoods of Boston. And we wanted to emulate what is desirable middle-class housing in Boston. To attract the market-rate people but also because that's what the low-income tenants want. They want to live like everybody else. And Commonwealth Avenue [in Boston's Back Bay] of course was one of the ideals. So we actually used the dimensions of Commonwealth Avenue here. And we tried to make the buildings that lined it all be five stories or four stories.

We looked at little townhouses in this area and we tried to make them look like normal New England townhouses. And we painted them all slightly different colors, with a kind of pale blue and ochre that are characteristic of New England. We tried to use only materials and colors that were local. And we incorporated the little details to make them look as much like an old street as possible.

Ten of the old buildings—three seven-story and seven three-story buildings—were renovated using such details as pitched roofs, entrance canopies, bay windows, and brick stain. Families would live in the ground-floor units; in the three-story buildings, large units had private entry doors with direct access to front and rear yards. The rehabilitation assignment was given to Sy Mintz, the architect from the Columbia Associates team. His style of introducing large cornices and imposing bay windows contrasted with Joan Goody's more traditional style for the new buildings. The contrast in architectural styles turned out to be fortuitous, giving Harbor Point an eclectic feeling that the place wasn't built all at the same time.

While the design for Harbor Point was taking shape, so was the partnership that would guide the new community. Betty Quarles, an active member of the task force for more than twenty years, recalls her own skepticism in the beginning. Housing for poor people, especially black poor people, she says, was always supposed to be punitive. It was never supposed to be as nice as the housing people pay for:

Ruby would probably say the same thing that she says all the time: "What is it? Black folks are not supposed to be cool in the summer? They're not supposed to have a nice place to live? What are black folks supposed to have? Nothing?" We have air conditioning. We have wall-to-wall carpeting. We have a dishwasher. The way they were talking about us, it was like we're not supposed to have this. When we lived in Columbia Point we didn't have it, so why should we have it now?

You would say, "Why would these guys want to come up here and do all this for these people?" But as time went along, you learned to trust. And they didn't try to talk over us. If you didn't understand when they'd be saying something, you'd ask them to slow down, and they would repeat it in our language, so that we would know what they were talking about.

We would sit there until we hammered it out. If not, we'd start all over again. People don't realize what the people on the [task force] did for them when they did this place, and the long hours that you spent. I said, "God, my kids might not know who I am." They were older, but you'd leave home at nine o'clock, and you say, "I'll be home maybe five or six," and you didn't get home till ten. There was always some-

Examining the plans for
Harbor Point. Left to right:
Esther Santos, Ruby
Jaundoo, Roger Taylor.
Courtesy of Corcoran,
Mullins, Jennison.

body there; my older daughters were there to fix food for my youngest
daughter. . . . But it took a lot out of you. People just don't know.

Esther Santos, another tenant leader, describes the partnership
between the task force and CMJ:

They sat back and listened to us. They told us up front that they were
not there to tell us what to do and what not to do. They were very interested in us learning not so much the dos and the don'ts, but not to
bang our head against the wall and not get anywhere. The decisions
we made were our decisions because we got information we needed.
Not one time in my involvement did they ever come and say, this is
the way you should do it. Or this is not the way you should do it. And
that was unusual.

And they were not pushy. I'll say it anytime, anywhere, they did not
say to anyone, "This is the way it should be. You should do this. You
should do that." They gave you the kind of information you needed to
evaluate the whole situation.

But according to Ruby Jaundoo, this doesn't mean the partnership was always easy:

It's not that we always agree. Sometimes we try to pull each other back,
you know, shake our coattails and say, "Hey, wait a minute, you're going a little bit too fast. You did not get permission from us to do X, Y,
and Z."

We had exactly a match to everything that they had. We had our
own architect. We explained to our architect what we wanted, if we
saw things that they were putting together that we didn't necessarily
care for. We would iron these things out, and we all would come to
some sort of compromise.

While the task force members were working to build a partnership with the developers, they also worked to convince their neighbors that redevelopment was real. The task force understood the tenants' skepticism—they had been skeptical themselves at first—and worked hard to build credibility. One of the most effective ways to do so, they discovered, was for residents to see plans for the new community actually taking shape. One of the things that helped the Columbia Point families to understand the new community was the model apartment. An exhibit in the community building included the windows, the cabinets—actual physical evidence of what would be in the new units.

Walking through the model unit helped residents believe that the new community was something real. Residents could learn how to use and how to maintain the garbage disposal, the dishwasher, the wall-to-wall carpeting. "It wasn't just one-way communication," Dave Connelly explains. "We held a lot of sessions where we would ask people what they thought things should be like. What they wanted in their new community." Residents, for example, told the architects that the windows in the model unit weren't right; they wanted windows they could pull out and clean from the inside. The windows were changed.

"Going through the process step by step," Ruby Jaundoo recalls, "it started to become a reality. But the feeling in the pit of your stomach doesn't go away until the place is all done and everything's put in its proper place."

Many people in the community weren't interested in what was happening to Columbia Point, Esther Santos explains. Some were skeptical, but others simply didn't want change: "Even though flyers go out, even though you have community meetings and you don't go. You're not aware of what's going on. So what are you going to do? A lot of people didn't want change. They wanted to continue doing what they were doing. And they were doing wrong things. They didn't want redevelopment."

Etta Johnson, who later became president of the task force, had been living at Columbia Point since 1967, but had kept mostly to herself. When she began hearing rumors that Columbia Point was going to be done over and the people who were living there were going to be kicked out, she decided to go to the task force meetings and see for herself:

I was hearing all kinds of rumors. In 1985 the task force was doing a survey, and they came into my house and asked a lot of general ques-

Roger Taylor, executive director of the Columbia Point Community Task Force, 1978. *Courtesy of Corcoran, Mullins, Jennison.*

Columbia Point Resident Survey: Excerpts

In 1985, Housing Opportunities Unlimited (HOU) conducted a survey of the 350 Columbia Point families to plan for their relocation to Harbor Point. No wonder residents like Etta Johnson were so amazed when the HOU representatives came around and conducted the survey. After living in the project for years, to be asked what you wanted, and to be offered such an appealing range of options, must have been astonishing.

Hi. My name is _____. I'm with the Resident Services Staff of the Columbia Point Task Force and other members of the Columbia Point Partnership. (We had an appointment to tell you about plans for the Point and get some information from you about your needs.) The Partnership is the developer for the renewal out here at the Point. My main job is to develop better tenant services for all the residents here, but we're helping out with the relocation plans, too, so that we can make sure as many people as possible stay here. . . .

Let me start by showing you the Memorandum of Understanding. This will explain your rights as a resident of Columbia Point, and will tell you about the agreement between the new owner and the residents. . . .

(After asking for the names of all of the people who live in the apartment:)

Is there anybody else in the household we haven't listed yet? I understand you may be worried about identifying people who aren't on the lease. But we need to know how large the household is in order to make sure the new unit you get is the right size. And the new management is going to be very strict about who's on the lease. So now may be a good time to get everything straight. So, does anybody else live here in the household?

Temporary Relocation

We are going to try very hard to make sure that everybody can stay on the site throughout the renovations. Our experience is that people who stay on-site find it easier to keep involved and help make decisions about the future of the development. So our first priority is to keep everybody on-site if at all possible. . . . There will be some noise and some construction dust and dirt. And it will go on for some time. If you think those things would bother you, and you really feel like the best thing for your family is to move off the site until the work is complete, we'll try to help you do that. . . .

By the way, there will be no pets permitted in the new Columbia Point, except for Seeing Eye and Hearing Ear Dogs. So you'll need to work on a plan for finding another home for your pets, if you have any, within the next few months.

New Home

We don't know if we'll be able to have exactly the apartment for everybody that they want, but so we'll have an idea about preferences as we tell the architects what to plan for, could you answer a few questions about general preferences of your family. We won't hold you to your choice. This is really just an opinion poll.

If you had a choice, would you like your apartment to be located:

__ near the water
__ near Mount Vernon Street
__ somewhere in between
__ near community facilities such as the clubhouse/pool

If you had a choice, would you like to live in:

__ a new townhouse
__ a new high-rise building
__ a new/rehab mid-rise building

Would you like to have a small private yard associated with your apartment?

tions about, would you like a waterfront apartment, would you like a
townhouse, what size do you need, and all this stuff.

I chose I wanted a waterfront apartment. At that time I needed a
two-bedroom because my oldest son would probably be soon leaving
and I only needed two bedrooms for myself and my other two sons.
But then the nuns [Sister Joyce McMullen and Sister Jean Stanton of
Project Care and Concern, who ran a food bank on the Columbia
Point peninsula] started all these rumors about no, you think you're going to get a waterfront apartment. You think they're going to move you
over there. I'm hearing this from a nun, a sister, who does religious education. She told me I was a damn fool if I thought that I was going to
get a waterfront apartment.

From the outside, it is hard to understand why the Columbia
Point tenants were so skeptical. Why weren't they excited about the
plans to completely redevelop the community? Why weren't they
flocking to meetings to help with the planning? What may look like
stubborn pessimism to outsiders was to insiders just common sense.
Promises like these had been made and broken over the years. It was
easy to play on these deep-seated fears; the rumors were far easier to
believe than the promises of the developers and the task force. Etta
Johnson recalls the effect of the nuns' warnings:

Etta Johnson, 1998. *Roger
Farrington.*

> She just said, "You won't get it." I think she was harming the residents
> more, making them afraid that you were going to get kicked out and
> not get what you want. You're not going to be there, after all that. So I
> figured I better start going to the task force meetings and find out my-
> self what's going on. Because if I'm going to have to move, I'll do it
> now.
>
> And I come to find out that Sister Joyce and all the other people
> who were spreading these rumors really didn't know what they were
> talking about. So I went back to some of the people who told me those
> things and said, "You need to go to the meetings because what you're
> telling me and what I'm hearing are two different things."

Gradually Johnson came to understand that this time the talk of
turning the project around was for real:

> I was processing the meetings. They were going to do it over. All the
> residents there would have a guarantee that they would be able to stay
> there if they wanted. They had us sign a piece of paper when we did
> the survey, and that contract said, you're guaranteed a unit. That piece
> of paper did mean something.
>
> I believed that they would give me a hand and all this stuff. The
> only thing I didn't believe is are you going to do it over. Because in the

past, like three times they said they're going to do Columbia Point over, and you would see a couple of little changes in the building, and all of a sudden they're out of money. They'd do the short buildings in the front, but not the tall buildings in the middle and the back. They never touched those. So it all sounded good, but my question was, When are they going to start knocking buildings down? In 1986, when they started the demolition, I knew it definitely was going to happen; until then, I was skeptical the whole while.

. . . And I did get my waterfront apartment. I got my waterfront town-house. And she told me that I was a fool for thinking that I was going to get it.

22 The Wrecking Ball

In 1986, just as plans were progressing rapidly for Harbor Point, Congress changed the tax law and threatened to stop the project dead in its tracks. The 1986 tax bill changed real estate forever and, according to some analysts, was a major factor in the real estate depression of the early 1990s.

Marty Jones, vice president of CMJ at the time, explains the rationale for tax reform at the federal level: "Congress believed that people were investing in real estate that didn't make economic sense. In 1986 there were all kinds of what people called 'see-through' office buildings—huge office buildings that were built and nobody was in them. They provided tax benefits, whether or not they were occupied. . . . The classic real estate investors were doctors and lawyers. The dentist in Iowa would invest in an office building in Boston and get tax losses. That's what really stuck in everybody's craw."

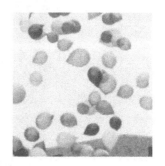

By 1986, millions of dollars' worth of buildings were standing, not because of any need for them, but because the tax code provided incentives to investors. The tax reform proposal eliminated those incentives. Although subsidized housing was one of

a few types of real estate that emerged with ongoing tax incentives, the type and structure of the incentives were completely changed and became targeted to corporations, not individuals.

The financing of Harbor Point depended, as did all subsidized housing projects at the time, on private investors' receiving a variety of tax advantages—all of which would be virtually wiped out by the new law. Harbor Point's financing plan was based on a $151 million loan from the Massachusetts Housing Finance Agency, a $9 million Urban Initiatives Grant, a $12 million federal UDAG loan, a $3 million state grant, and $75 million in private investment. Fifty million dollars of that private investment—about a quarter of the total financing—was projected to be from individuals. So the new tax law effectively killed the project.

During the three years of planning, from 1983 to 1986, CMJ had sunk time, effort, and $5 million of its own hard money into the project, then borrowing an ad-

"Two workers erect chain link fencing in projects near demolition site," Columbia Point, 1986. Boston Herald.

ditional $7 million from the bank. These up-front costs on the project were exceptionally high. Political pressures had necessitated changes in design. As a former dump, the site required extensive engineering studies and test borings. The project was also subject to formal review by three government agencies—the BRA, the BHA, and the MHFA—each with its own parameters and guidelines. Out of the blue, three years and $12 million into the deal, the tax law hit.

Congress was allowing a few exceptions to the new tax bill, grandfathering in projects like Harbor Point that had been planned on the financial assumptions of existing tax code. In order to be eligible for "transitional rules" that would allow the tax credits, however, these projects needed approval from the House Ways and Means Committee and the Senate Finance Committee. CMJ worked with Representative Brian Donnelly, an influential Dorchester Democrat and member of the Ways and Means Committee, who was able to get Harbor Point approved for transitional rules by the committee, which was headed at the time by Representative Dan Rostenkowski of Illinois.

The Senate, however, was a different story. The chair of the Senate Finance Committee was Bob Packwood, a Republican who was the author of the tax reform bill. He had instructed his staff to strictly limit the number of projects approved for transition rules. Joe Corcoran contacted the staff of senators Ted Kennedy and John Kerry to alert them to the situation. Senator Kennedy recalls:

I strongly supported the fundamental purpose of the 1986 tax reform legislation, which was to close tax loopholes that benefited wealthy corporations and wealthy individuals, and use the savings to reduce tax rates for everyone. One of the loopholes being closed was a widely used tax shelter for real estate. I favored closing the loophole, and was very surprised to learn that the tax shelter was at the heart of the financing arrangement being used for the Columbia Point project.

We obviously had to try to work out a reasonable compromise. The city and private developers had committed significant resources to turning the troubled housing complex into the success story it is today. To squander the opportunity to redevelop this area of Boston that my brother loved so much would have been a tragedy, particularly for the hundreds of low-income tenants who lived there. . . .

[Senator Packwood] was skeptical at first about what I was proposing. But I explained the need to redevelop Columbia Point, how the project had been in the works for nearly a decade, and would be crippled if the bill changed the law and pulled the rug out from under us.

Ted Kennedy on Columbia Point

Almost from the beginning, the project began to deteriorate. I remember visiting it during Jack's Senate campaign in 1958 and later in my own campaigns for the Senate. Jack especially loved the view of the ocean from Columbia Point.

Year after year, the residents were promised that rehabilitation would occur, that development would take place, that a new day was just around the corner. Sadly, these promises were broken as often as they were made. Despite other development in the area, including the new campus for UMass, the planned construction of the Massachusetts Archives and Jack's presidential library, the housing project stayed isolated and kept on deteriorating.

Jack had wanted his library to be in Cambridge as part of Harvard. But the plans to build the library there didn't work out, so our family chose Columbia Point because it was close to the water and had breathtaking views of the Boston skyline. Jack loved the sea and sailing and the city, and Columbia Point symbolized all of these favorite things of his.

—Senator Edward M. Kennedy, 1998

At first, the best that Kennedy could get was only minor relief— far less than was needed to proceed. The redevelopment of Columbia Point had reached yet another impasse: Packwood had gone as far as he would go, but it wasn't far enough to secure the private investment the project required. When Senator Kennedy personally delivered this news, Joe Corcoran candidly told Kennedy the deal was dead. Eddie Martin, the former HUD regional director who was now working for Kennedy, called Corcoran back and told him he was an "ingrate" for not thanking Kennedy for his efforts. Joe Corcoran had a question for Eddie Martin in reply: "Would you have preferred that I misled Kennedy and let him think what he did was enough, when I knew it wasn't?"

Then Kennedy's staff invited CMJ to come to Washington. "Kennedy told me in no uncertain terms," Corcoran explains, "that we would receive the additional tax credits because he was committed to this project." Nevertheless, the meetings between the CMJ team and Packwood's staff were discouraging and divisive. Corcoran recalls: "Packwood's staff were young ideologues who strenuously resisted the concept of tax credits because they were costing the Treasury millions of dollars. I countered sharply, saying that the Columbia Point project had cost the federal government more [than the tax credits] over the past ten years, that the government was a disgraceful landlord housing citizens in horrid conditions, and that we were about to take the project off their hands, eliminating the deficits and giving new hope to the folks living in the project."

While the two sides wrangled, Ted Kennedy crafted a political, not an ideological, solution. He cut a deal with Packwood: if Packwood would approve the transition rules for Harbor Point, Kennedy would work in return to pass the 1986 tax bill intact, helping Packwood fight back amendments that would weaken it. Kennedy even agreed to vote against the Individual Retirement Account amendment—a very popular one that the Democratic party was supporting.

On the day of the vote, June 24, 1986, Kennedy called Corcoran to let him know that they had been successful. Kennedy joked that he had waited for Senator Howard Metzenbaum—who had been a gadfly on all transition rules—to leave the Senate chamber for the men's room. By the time he returned, Kennedy had presented the language to the Senate and gotten voice vote approval, with no debate for the one-time tax credit that allowed the developers the opportunity to replace the equity they had planned to raise with the old tax shelter. The CMJ team stayed on to watch Kennedy fight

Marty Jones at the Harbor Point dedication, 1987. *Courtesy of Corcoran, Mullins, Jennison.*

Upper right: Esther Santos speaks at the Harbor Point dedication ceremony. Left to right: Father George Carrigg of St. Christopher's, Marvin Siflinger, executive director of the Massachusetts Housing Finance Agency, Senator William Bulger, Congressman Joseph Moakley, Senator John Kerry, Joe Corcoran, and Senator Ted Kennedy. *Courtesy of Corcoran, Mullins, Jennison.*

Lower right: Columbia Point Community Task Force at the Harbor Point dedication ceremony. Left to right: Linda Wade, Etta Johnson, Martha Little, Betty Quarles, Ruby Jaundoo, Joyce Crump, Roger Taylor. *Courtesy of Corcoran, Mullins, Jennison.*

back amendments with Packwood; he had delivered on his promise to CMJ and delivered on his promise to Packwood. Once again, the project was back on track.

On January 24, 1987, a bitter cold Saturday, more than four hundred people gathered at Columbia Point for a long-awaited moment: the first swing of the wrecking ball and the "christening" of the new community as Harbor Point. The festivities that day form a bookend to a similar if smaller gathering at the same spot on a hot July day some thirty-three years earlier, when Boston's Mayor John Hynes presided over the groundbreaking ceremony for Columbia Point on the barren mud flats of Dorchester Bay.

Members of the Columbia Point Community Task Force, residents, the development team, housing officials, and dignitaries—Senator Ted Kennedy, Senator John Kerry, Congressman Joe Moakley, Governor Mike Dukakis, Senator Bill Bulger, BRA director Steve Coyle, MHFA executive director Marvin Siflinger—took their places in St. Christopher's Church, just across Mount Vernon Street from the housing project. There the Concord Baptist choir sang gospel songs before the congregation.

CMJ vice president Marty Jones opened the ceremony by declaring that Columbia Point, long a symbol of failure and neglect, was now "a symbol not of problems, but of solutions. It's now a symbol not of dreams, but of real accomplishments." Extending a greeting to all of the gathered officials "from all levels of state, local and federal government—bankers, lawyers, investors, contractors, architects," Marty passed over them for the moment to call first on a resident of Columbia Point—task force president Esther Santos.

Santos in turn began by introducing the members of the task force—each of them resplendent in a blue satin sash—and asking them to stand. They were applauded warmly. The many people who worked to make Harbor Point a reality followed. Senator Kennedy declared that, despite the raw weather outside, "that cold will not be felt in the future for hundreds of families because of their commitment and their work over the years":

> I think today is a day of victory for the perseverance, the continued efforts of the tenants within this community. They've been working for twenty-three years. They've been tireless in speaking to those of us in the Congress and the Senate, and the local officials, and their perseverance is going to mean a better quality of life, not just for themselves but for future generations. . . .

Balloons are released with the swing of the wrecking ball at the Harbor Point dedication ceremonies, 1987. *Boston Housing Authority.*

"The Harbor Point Experiment"

The balloons released by a wrecker's ball last weekend at Columbia Point signaled the start of a social experiment more far-reaching than that undertaken by the construction of the housing project there 33 years ago.

The 1,500-unit, low-income, public-housing project is being partially demolished—and totally renovated—to make way for a 1,283-unit mixed-income, privately financed development. The old project had long ago deteriorated into a shunned urban wasteland, a symbol of the failure of the public housing policies of a generation ago.

The new development—with a new name, Harbor Point—is no less visionary than Columbia Point was. But care and sensitivity are needed to ensure that it does not turn sour as Columbia Point did. The new vision is that people with a wide range of incomes can live together in a small, architecturally cohesive community, sharing such amenities as a clubhouse and recreational facilities. . . .

Many of the current tenants have been involved in the planning for the new community. They already sense the subtle pressures of the future, when their families are surrounded by the trappings of a style of living that their new neighbors take for granted, but which they do not expect to share.

Corcoran, a social dreamer as well as a hard-headed developer, is conscious of these concerns. Training sessions and counseling programs will be held for the Columbia Point tenants who are to become Harbor Point residents. The aim will be to help the low-income families understand that they will be "welcoming" the newcomers into their community. . . .

The newcomers will enjoy a handsome view and a proximity to Boston. They must also realize that a social conscience and a neighborly understanding will be demanded of them when they move to Harbor Point. They must harbor no expectations that their arrival will be allowed to displace their low-income neighbors.

—*Boston Globe* editorial, January 28, 1987

I've been glad to be a foot soldier in the march that all of us have undertaken to try and see today a celebration of success, because that is what today really is: it is a celebration of hope.

After a benediction by Father George Carrigg, the pastor of St. Christopher's, the crowd filed out into the cold afternoon and crossed Mount Vernon Street into the project for the groundbreaking—more accurately, demolition—ceremony. Standing before an abandoned building, Governor Dukakis called for a drum roll, and a huge crane swung a wrecking ball, knocking out a section of one of the buildings and sending its bricks flying. All at once, a thousand multicolored balloons were released over the project while hundreds watched and cheered. The crowd then headed for the community building, the scene of many meetings over the years, for warmth and a reception complete with music, dancing, and a big cake inscribed "Harbor Point 1987."

For many Columbia Point residents that day, the new community became a reality at last. For them, the first swing of the wrecking ball was more than a ceremonial formality. "Those cranes have brought more life to this place than I've seen in years," one resident exclaimed at the event. "It's something that has been coming for a long time," said Miriam Manning, longtime resident and head of the project's day care center. "At one point, I felt it was never going to come true. So today really made a change in my life." Task force member Joyce Crump concurred: "It's just a miracle, that's all I can say, it's just a miracle. I believe it's going to happen. I got that true belief that it's going to happen."

Part 4
Harbor Point, 1988–2000

23 The Blitz

In September 1984 Corcoran, Mullins, Jennison took over management of Columbia Point, acting as agent for the Boston Housing Authority with full power to enforce the lease. CMJ welcomed the opportunity to manage the project during the two-year interim before construction began on Harbor Point. As the company had done at King's Lynne, taking over interim management enabled it to clean up the worst problems at Columbia Point and to begin laying the groundwork for the new community—an effort CMJ called "The Blitz."

At the time CMJ took over responsibility for managing Columbia Point, the community had almost completely disintegrated. Eleven hundred apartments were vacant; only 356 families remained. Squatters had moved into many of the vacant units, even though heat and electricity were turned off. Stairwells were dark, strewn with garbage, broken glass, and discarded hypodermic needles. Drug dealers operated with impunity, knowing that the Boston police would not come into the project. Stray dogs roamed the project in packs.

Dave Connelly, the director of Housing Opportunities Unlimited (HOU), the social service provider at Harbor Point, explains the attitude of the police toward the project. The police "were decent people, but in their minds they had written the place off," he says. "They just wanted to contain it. It was like the mentality that created the Combat Zone [Boston's red-light district]. There are certain activities that were allowed to go on in the Combat Zone—like certain activities that were allowed to go on at the Point—that you wouldn't allow elsewhere." The Boston Housing Authority, too, had written off Columbia Point. "If it was Old Colony, one of the projects where firemen's mothers lived," Connelly says, "they would never allow that to go on."

Even while external order had broken down at Columbia Point, some residents were still managing to raise their families within their apartments. Ruby Jaundoo, a community leader and longtime resident, emphasizes that, even in its worst days, Columbia Point was a caring community: "People think because Columbia

Above: Redevelopment of Columbia Point, 1987. *Courtesy of the* Boston Globe.

Right: Groundbreaking for the new health center at Harbor Point, 1987: Mayor Ray Flynn (second from left), Ruby Jaundoo, Roger Taylor, Joyce Crump, Esther Santos, Betty Quarles, Representative Jimmy Brett, Joe Corcoran, and Representative Paul White. *Courtesy of Corcoran, Mullins, Jennison.*

Demolition at Columbia
Point, 1987. Boston
Herald.

Point was Columbia Point—and you can define that any way you
want—that people didn't necessarily care about where they lived.
That wasn't true. People did care about where they lived. People
cared about each other. It was a community of people that was always there to support one another." By 1985, however, the remaining residents were virtual prisoners in their own homes, keeping
their children in day and night; terrified of having a fire in the apart-

"Mattie Hall, a resident of
Columbia Point since 1971,
has a bird's-eye view of the
demolition work taking
place opposite her
apartment," 1986. *Courtesy
of the* Boston Globe.

ment or a child who was sick, because help would not come into
the project. In the end, as former task force president Roger Taylor
sums it up, "It was just a matter of, you exist on your own or you
don't exist at all."

"The Blitz" was CMJ's effort to rehabilitate and maintain the existing buildings at Columbia Point—a physical demonstration of
what effective, caring management could provide. The Blitz was
meant to show tenants that their rent payment would provide real
services—graffiti would be removed; plumbing and heat would be
supplied—a level of management attention Columbia Point hadn't
seen since its earliest days. Management began by consolidating the
356 remaining families scattered throughout the project into the

buildings at the northern end of the site. The only other building that was left occupied was the elderly building at the opposite end of the site. Marty Jones, vice president of CMJ at the time, was responsible for overseeing new construction and the relocation of the Columbia Point residents. She explains the special pains that were taken to accommodate the needs of the elderly:

> They did not want to move twice. [The original building that housed most of the elderly] was sort of their little enclave, so we agreed to let them stay there. Talk about living in the middle of a war zone. The first building we created was the new elderly building. It was the right place for it to be in the long run, but it was the wrong place to be from a construction phasing point of view because it was right in the middle of the site. So the elderly lived through years and years of construction all around them, both in the old building and then in the new building. It was a little island.

Once the Columbia Point families were consolidated, the interim management team, headed by Paul Whitley, began a massive clean-up effort, hiring forty Columbia Point residents to help. Dan Murray, vice president of CMJ's management company at the time, recalls the conditions at that juncture. "They would knock out the lights in the hallways in the old Columbia Point buildings," he says. "You would be scared because there were these alcoves, and you wouldn't know who the hell was in there. In the old days, some of the residents would knock out walls. If they had a four-bedroom apartment and they knew that there was nobody living next door, they would knock out the walls and make it a seven-bedroom." Ironically, Murray says, the prevalence of guns at the project was a deterrent to break-ins. "That's because the [apartments] had steel doors and you figured they might have guns on the other side," Murray says. "You wouldn't go breaking in or you might get shot right there."

One of the first orders of business was to inspect and secure every vacant unit in the project. Wendell Yee, CMJ's regional property manager, oversaw the effort. Yee had worked on turning around two other CMJ developments, King's Lynne and Quaker Meadows, both in Lynn. Starting in the winter of 1985, Yee headed a team that inspected every single vacant unit at Columbia Point. The metal doors on the vacant units had been "tack welded" shut by the Boston Housing Authority. Using flashlights because the electricity had been turned off, Yee's team broke the weld on each unit. Yee vividly recalls their grim search. Even though they didn't find people in the units, they found plenty of evidence that people were liv-

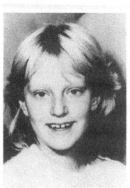

"Looking for Sarah Pryor. Exterior of 119 Monticello building searched by police and door welded shut," 1986. Boston Herald.

Sarah Pryor, whose body was mistakenly rumored to have been dumped at Columbia Point. *Courtesy of the* Boston Globe.

ing there and, according to Yee, "would probably be back that evening": "Some of those units had been broken into and were being used by squatters. You could see the drug paraphernalia and mattresses and candles on the floor. We came across some units that had animal skeletal remains; they had just boarded [the animals] up in there. It was a pretty sad situation."

Shortly after the inspection job was completed, Sarah Pryor, a young white girl from the affluent suburb of Wayland, disappeared and a nationwide search ensued. The Boston police received an anonymous tip that Pryor's remains could be found in one of the vacant units at Columbia Point. Based on the tip, Yee's team reopened and re-searched every one of the units that they had just welded shut. A week-long search by a team of forty investigators came up empty. More than a decade later, in 1997, Sarah Pryor's remains were discovered in a wooded area not far from her home. It is telling, however, that the public was all too ready to believe that Columbia Point was the scene of the crime, and that a comprehensive search was undertaken on the basis of a single anonymous phone call. "To so many folks it made perfect sense," Miles Byrne, now manager of Harbor Point, observes ruefully. "And quite frankly, even those of us who worked there at the time were thinking, please don't find her here."

Building a new community at the Point wasn't just a physical challenge: transforming the barren, prisonlike wasteland into a beautiful new waterfront community. It was also a social challenge: restoring order to a place where the basic rules of civilized community had been ignored and unenforced for years. When CMJ took over management of Columbia Point, the first step was for the partnership between the development team and the task force to hold a series of community meetings to develop a management plan, and then to have it approved by the BHA. CMJ and the task force were not inventing a new set of rules. They were simply enforcing the housing authority's existing rules—making sure the community was aware of those rules and aware they would be enforced in a thorough and consistent manner. Wendell Yee recalls the earliest days of laying the foundation for the new community: "It was not an easy task to go in and say, 'The rules are changing.' It was transitioning people from no rules to a set of standards that they had to live by in order to be able to move into the new community. Some of the families realized that they were not going to be able to live within those parameters and they moved out voluntarily. . . . As the agent for the housing authority, we went in there and we enforced the rules and the lease—something the housing authority never did."

Once the vacant units were searched and sealed, CMJ management turned to the most difficult and urgent problem at the project: drugs. For years, drug dealing took place in the open, on any street corner of Columbia Point. Turning around the drug situation would require the absolute commitment of the residents and management. The remaining residents had had enough; the tenant task force voted overwhelmingly for a policy of zero tolerance of drugs. CMJ, too, was willing to do whatever it took to get rid of the drug dealers.

It was clear to CMJ that the Boston police force had neither the determination nor the resources to root out the drug dealers at Columbia Point. Prior to CMJ's taking over, the BHA had employed a security force that was considered a joke by the residents. Because the problems were too severe to continue with a traditional security company, the tenant-developer partnership decided to establish its own security force, called Old Harbor Protective Services. They brought in Edward Connolly, the seventy-one-year-old former deputy superintendent of the Boston police, to run it. Connolly was a policeman of the old school, a street cop, who insisted that his security officers have police powers and be allowed to carry guns. At the same time, he promised that his officers would be trained never to draw or use their weapons unless their own lives were threatened.

Although the task force was determined to put an end to drug dealing and crime in their community, at the same time they were wary of bringing into the project an armed security force led by a hard-driving ex-cop. Ruby Jaundoo interrogated Connolly and expressed her concerns about overzealous guards turning Harbor Point into a police state. Connolly reassured her that, although he had been shot three times himself, he had never shot anyone in his fifty-year tour of duty. However, he didn't want his officers to be at a disadvantage in the existing situation at the project.

The Boston Police Department, aware of the monumental challenge of restoring law and order at Columbia Point and stymied in its own efforts to do so, readily agreed to "deputize" the private security force with the powers of arrest and the right to carry arms. Eddie Connolly had excellent rapport with the Boston Police Department and was able to summon them to Harbor Point on a moment's notice. After years of turning their backs on Columbia Point, the Boston police were finally rebuilding their connection to the Point.

CMJ management also spent a lot of time building connections with the Boston Police Department, especially focusing on the drug problem at the Point. Abandoned cars needed to be towed out. Fights with knives and guns had to be stopped. Dan Murray recalls

"Betty Williams,
Columbia Point resident,"
1986. Boston Herald.

that on the very first weekend the new security force was on duty, a young man at Columbia Point started a fight with one of the guards. A crowd quickly developed, and the man's girlfriend pulled a knife on the security guard. "He proceeded to tell her as she went towards him with the knife," Murray says, "that he would kill her if she took another step. At which time she dropped the knife." The Boston police arrived and dispersed the crowd, arrested the man, and initiated eviction proceedings against the girlfriend. "It was a test," Murray says. "It was the first weekend. We had to win."

With the task force 100 percent in support, management's strict enforcement of the policy against drugs, and the ability of private security to use force to break up drug dealing, positive inroads were being made. According to Murray, one of the major players in the drug activity at Columbia Point was Toby Johnson, known on the street as "Blood"—the ringleader of the "Detroit" gang and one of the major drug dealers on the East Coast, who eventually was killed in a gunfight in Roxbury. Blood reportedly headed a $7-million-a-year operation that extended all the way from Massachusetts to the Carolinas. Although he didn't live at Columbia Point, the project was his territory. He and his lieutenants conducted a major drug operation out of the Point, receiving pure heroin, cutting it with quinine, recruiting kids under sixteen to carry the drugs and the money, and using taxicabs to deliver the merchandise.

When CMJ management made it clear that they wanted to put an end to drug activity at the Point, they were helped by tips from the community—where the drug activity was going on, when the big buys were going down. Some tips came from people who wanted to put an end to drugs at the project; others came from people involved in the drug activity who wanted to settle a score. The Drug Enforcement Administration would ask CMJ management to shut off the water to the buildings before raids, so that drugs could not be flushed down toilets. After several major busts, Dan Murray recalls, "people were doing things less openly." Guns, violence, and open drug deals began to dissipate.

Betty Quarles, a longtime member of the task force, recalls how teenagers at Columbia Point would be drawn into the drug scene in the early 1980s, hired to "hold" drugs—keep them in their apartments—for as much as five hundred dollars a day: "I could see some of the kids, especially if their parents were on welfare and they don't have much money. Their friend next door, his mother might have a job, and he might have the name-brand sneakers. But this kid doesn't have the name-brand sneakers, so he gets into holding drugs so that he could get some money. Sometimes the parents wouldn't even ask them, 'Where did you get this from?'" Quarles remembers what she told her own kids: "I said, there's only three things going to happen to you if you're out selling drugs. Either you're going to get shot, you're going to jail, or you're going to die." She didn't stop at warning her own kids; she found out who was in charge of the gang from Detroit and walked right up to him. "You don't know me. I'm Betty Quarles," she said:

Columbia Point resident Clark Jones, 1986. Boston Herald.

> "That's my kid. Leave him alone. . . . If I find out that he's selling drugs, he's going to be locked up, and you're going to be locked up with him. You want to do anything to me, do it now. Don't wait until I turn my back."
>
> And then he said to me, "You know what? You're the only parent that I know of out here that came and approached me about saying they think their kid is selling drugs." I said, "I don't want my children involved in it. That's not the life for them." And I just walked away from him. My son was standing right there.

When Quarles looks back on what she did, she says she wouldn't do it today. Why not? "Because kids now would kill you quicker than they would then."

In fact, most of the individuals whose names come up in the stories of drug dealing at Columbia Point are dead; the luckier ones are in jail. Dan Murray describes one boy, about fifteen years old, who carried drugs and money for Blood—and was later killed with him. "He was caught in a building with fifteen hundred dollars in his shoe," Murray says, "which he said he got from a paper route." It was a fate suffered by many of the young men at Columbia Point. "He was fifteen but he was bad," Murray says. "He was a bad kid that you knew was never going to make it. After a while, Dave [Connelly, director of HOU, which provided social services at Harbor Point] realized there are some kids you're never going to save. Those are the hard core—and they don't have to be thirty; they can be fifteen. They have gone the fast-money route. As I said, he had fifteen hundred dollars cash in his shoe. And he ended up dead."

Once the word got out that drugs were not going to be tolerated, once enough busts had taken place, once the major dealers found that it was too difficult to operate out of the former housing project—a process that took several years—the flagrant, open drug activity at the Point had been cleaned up.

While the security force was cracking down on drugs and violence at Columbia Point, Housing Opportunities Unlimited was working with the Columbia Point residents. HOU offered residents many kinds of support. They referred people with drug habits to rehab programs and worked with management to hold their units and get care for their children while they were in treatment; found jobs; helped neighbors settle disputes in constructive ways; and developed programs for kids with special needs. If residents played their stereos at full blast at 2 A.M., they would receive a letter from management. At first, residents were shocked; for years, no one had enforced rules of any kind. Soon, however, the community began to understand that things were going to change.

Getting rid of the drug dealing didn't end the drug problem. Many tenants struggled with drug addiction. "We suggested forming a residents-at-risk committee," Wendell Yee explains. "A panel of four or five residents would meet with a resident at risk and say, 'Look, you've got to clean up your act. We're here to support you. But if you don't clean up your act you're going to go.' And I think hearing it from your own peers has a much greater impact than hearing it from management, who would automatically say, 'Clean up your act or we're going to evict you.' A lot of them entered treatment programs. Some were successful, some weren't."

Dave Connelly began by looking for the natural leadership in the community. "The sort of heart of Columbia Point at that time was the Hassett day care center," he says, "so I used to go there in the mornings first thing and have my coffee." Residents coming into the day care center would be surprised to see a white man, Connelly recalls, and would assume he must be either "a cop or an insurance man." But in his view, finding community leaders was

More demolition at
Columbia Point, 1986.
Courtesy of the Boston
Globe.

critical. No matter how much help was coming in from the outside,
no matter how much money was being invested by the developers,
Connelly explains, "the only permanent change that will ever happen is if the people living there change their own community."

Even though Columbia Point had deteriorated on the outside,
Connelly discovered that many people in the project were still managing to do an excellent job of raising their families:

> There was a real core of Columbia Point residents who were committed
> to their families, committed to raising them right, committed to school-
> ing as an ideal. What we had to do was spread that core out. And get
> that core to begin to set the goals for the other people here. What hap-
> pens in a project like this is that good families control their own house-
> hold. In other words, when they come in the door, they close the door
> and that's their household. When they go out into the hallway, that isn't
> theirs; it belongs to the project. We were hoping to get the family that
> was doing a good job of controlling their own household to begin to
> think about controlling the whole Columbia Point environment.

One of the key issues that had to be addressed as part of restoring
and enforcing the rules was the payment of rent. For years, many
Columbia Point families had not been paying rent. In a number of
cases, the apartments were in such bad condition that tenants were
not legally required to pay the rent. According to Wendell Yee, the
fact that some families owed as much as eight thousand to ten thousand dollars in back rent was a clear indication that the housing authority was not enforcing rent collection. As they had at King's
Lynne, where rent arrearages had also been a problem, management began by working with the families to understand and address
the problem. "HOU became very successful working with families,"
Wendell Yee explains: "They started workshops on budgeting—establishing what your priorities are. If you don't have a roof over your
head, what else is there? The roof over your head, the food in your
belly and your children's, have to be a priority in life."

At first, the BHA expected CMJ to enforce its policy requiring
eviction of all residents with arrearages that they couldn't pay off
within twelve months. "When we started going through the rent list
and found out that a lot of the people here had an arrearage," Ruby
Jaundoo recalls, the BHA wanted CMJ "to start sending these people fourteen-day notices to quit [initiating the eviction process]."
Jaundoo was well aware that when the BHA stopped enforcing the
collection of rents, many tenants stopped paying. But she did not believe that eviction was the solution: "The task force put their foot

down and said, 'No, you're part of that process of people being back on their rents, because you haven't enforced the collection of rents.' We let people know they're supposed to pay their rent. But if no one is enforcing the rules, we get lax on some of the things that we do." Jaundoo argued at first that all arrearages should be written off. Besides feeling it would be unfair to punish people for ignoring a rule no one was enforcing, she also questioned why tenants should be required to pay rent for substandard housing. But as she began to realize that the fairness issue cut both ways, she had to, as she put it, "rethink" her position: "What about the others? There were 30-some odd people out of 350 who weren't paying their rent. What about the other 320 who had been paying their rent on time and living under the same conditions? I paid up mine every month; why should you get away with owing two thousand dollars? So we had to make a compromise."

The compromise reached by the tenant-developer partnership was for each of the families in arrears to work out a repayment plan. First of all, HOU "recertified" each resident, making sure that the rent they were currently paying was appropriate based on their income. Residents would then agree to stay current with their rent while gradually paying off their arrearage each month, depending upon what their budget would allow. Eventually, management collected 95 percent of the arrearages. The repayment program came with both a carrot and a stick: residents who failed to keep up with their payment schedules were in danger of losing their rehousing guarantee. On the other hand, those who were up to date with their rent received a five-hundred-dollar credit.

"The Blitz" was a success. Restoring and enforcing the rules at Columbia Point was sometimes a matter of pure force — as in Eddie Connolly's armed security force's rooting out the drug dealers — and sometimes a matter of careful compromise — as in HOU's face-to-face settling of arrearages. In a matter of just two years, however, terror and violence had been largely eliminated at the Point, and a strong foundation was laid for the new community.

24 Goodboy

For years, Columbia Point had been a dumping ground for stray dogs and cats. People would simply drive out to the project, open the door and let out the dog or cat, and drive away, leaving the problem for Columbia Point to deal with. In addition, many tenants kept dangerous dogs—German shepherds and Dobermans—for "protection." By the time CMJ took over management of the project, not only were the packs of dogs a problem outside, but they would also roam up and down the stairwells, easily entering buildings whose doors were broken and hanging off.

Many animals were abused and neglected; the stray dogs had become a menace to the community. "I was afraid to come out of my unit to go to work in the morning," Ruby Jaundoo recalls. "There was a big parking lot in back of where I lived and the parking lot would be full of stray dogs. And I was petrified. I would have to wait until someone came along to move the dogs along. That was how terrible it was. I think everyone on the task force had experienced something similar, with animals just roaming the site."

In all of its developments, CMJ always had a strict no-pets policy. Wendell Yee,

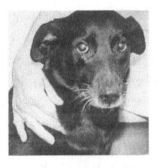

site manager at King's Lynne, recalls the magnitude of the pet problem CMJ inherited there: "When we took over King's Lynne there were about 126 units occupied, and there were probably three hundred dogs running around the site. So we put a no-pets policy into effect. . . . We called the animal control office to pick up some of the stray dogs, and they refused to do it. They were just swamped; they didn't have the capacity to take any more animals."

As with the crackdown on drugs, the first step at Columbia Point was getting the community to agree to the no-pets rule; the task force endorsed it unanimously. Although Congress had passed a law in 1983 permitting elderly and disabled public housing residents to keep pets, Harbor Point was not bound by this law because it was private housing. In fact, the housing authority had a no-pets rule, and the lease explicitly forbade pets; but the rule had never been enforced.

Sister Joyce McMullen of
Project Care and
Concern. *Courtesy of
Corcoran, Mullins,
Jennison.*

The tenant-developer partnership set a date by which each family
was required to find a new home for its pets. If the residents didn't
make arrangements by the deadline, HOU would take remaining
pets to the Animal Rescue League.

It was difficult for families who had become attached to their pets
to give them up, but most recognized that keeping pets, especially
with so many people in such a relatively small area, wasn't a good
idea for the animals or for the new community, especially if things
were to improve. The residents recognized, however reluctantly,
that pets had to go.

The no-pets rule would trigger a major media event that would
force Harbor Point—and the tenant task force—into the public
spotlight. Before the storm was over, the task force would stand up
to the developer, insisting on taking a much harder line on pets than
CMJ. They would stand up to the media and feel the full heat of
public indignation. They would stand up to the mayor and refuse to
buckle under political pressure. The case of an Afghan hound
named Goodboy and his ninety-one-year-old owner would be a watershed event for the task force, in which they stood together as owners and protectors of their new community.

Throughout the development of Harbor Point, the position of the
task force was never an easy one. On the one hand, in their dealings
with the developers, they constantly advocated for the low-income residents of the community. On the other hand, they had to answer to
the accusations of many Columbia Point residents and dispel the rumors that seemed to be in constant circulation. "It wasn't an easy sell,"
Ruby Jaundoo recalls. She had heard it all: "You're selling the community out." "Maybe you'll be left here, but we'll be gone." "You're in
the developer's pocket." "You're getting some sort of kickback."
"You're going to be protected, but what about me?" Jaundoo even recalls one resident, who later became a member of the task force,
claiming that the developers were going to build a brick wall and put
the poor people on one side and the rich people on the other.

In addition, the task force had to contend with various "tenant advocate" groups—in particular, the Massachusetts Tenants Organization (MTO) and the nuns of Project Care and Concern—feeding
the rumor mill inside the Point and enlisting outside media support
with their constant warnings that the developers wanted to "kick out
the poor people."

The task force was used to taking heat from the residents and

"The Dog Was a Prophet"

Alice Stacy. All this 91-year-old wisp of a woman asked for was the right to share her life with the closest friend she had on the planet—a stray Afghan hound she called Goodboy. Back on a 98-degree day in June when a developer named Joe Corcoran tossed Alice out of her home for the past 25 years in Columbia Point, the dog finally stopped trembling . . . and died.

To this day, Alice believes the dog was a prophet. He trembled enough for both of them, because Alice never did. After one night in exile from the Point, Alice was then welcomed back by Joe Corcoran's hypocrites as if she were Cleopatra. She was granted a brand-new apartment—provided she stays there alone.

—Peter Gelzinis, "Recalling the Year's Heroes," *Boston Herald*, December 22, 1988

standing up to the developers. Now a frail ninety-one-year-old woman was about to put them in a very hot public spotlight. Alice Stacy had been living at Columbia Point for twenty-five years. When CMJ took over interim management, Stacy was one of only three white households left in the project. She was living on the fifth floor of the building for the elderly with her Afghan hound, Goodboy, and her black-and-white cat, Mischief. For years, Stacy had been unable to take Goodboy out of the building. Instead, he had been urinating and defecating in Stacy's apartment and the hallway.

The task force announced the new policy to the community: all pets had to go. CMJ offered to relocate any tenants who wanted to keep their pets, even promising that those tenants could come back if they didn't have pets sometime in the future.

The newly rehabilitated elderly building, 40 Westwind Court, with a large furnished lobby, a landscaped courtyard, and a convenience store and restaurant, was one of the first buildings to be completed at Harbor Point. The elderly residents had selected their own apartments and were excited about moving into the completely renovated building. When Alice Stacy missed the no-pets deadline, insisting on moving Goodboy and Mischief in with her, the other elderly residents exploded. The idea of bringing the Goodboy problem into the brand-new building had them up in arms.

CMJ had anticipated that the Goodboy issue had all the ingredients of a public relations disaster. In fact, the Massachusetts Tenants

"91-year-old returned to Columbia Point apartment." "Alice Stacy, 91, sits in her apartment bedroom as things are moved in by movers in the background," 1988. *Courtesy of the* Boston Globe.

Organization had already alerted the Society for the Prevention of Cruelty to Animals to the no-pets policy being implemented at Harbor Point. In an attempt to head off a showdown, CMJ suggested a compromise: a grandfather clause in the lease that would allow only the elderly residents to keep any existing pets, but would not allow any new pets. The task force refused to compromise, however. Many of them were mothers of young children who themselves had recently gone through the ordeal of having to give up the beloved family pet.

CMJ suggested moving Stacy into the one ground-floor unit in the elderly building—intended for the building maintenance man—and fencing in an area outside for Goodboy. Again, the task force would have none of it. They took a much tougher position on the pet issue than CMJ was willing to settle for.

Then the media got wind of the story. An editorial in the *Boston Globe* on February 27, 1988, headlined "A Peevish Pet Policy," began by congratulating CMJ for converting Columbia Point to "a handsome waterfront community." However, it proceeded to charge that CMJ's no-pets policy "threatens to shroud the opening [of Harbor Point] in controversy and, worse, an air of mean-spiritedness." Charging that the developers "refuse to explain the reasons for the no-pets decision," the editorial quoted Alice Stacy saying of her beloved pets, "They're all I've got."

"She is right," the editorial declared, "as anyone who has ever worked with or cared about an elderly person knows. Pets provide a needed companionship and relieve loneliness." Portraying CMJ as cold and calculating, taking away all a poor, ninety-one-year-old woman had left in life, the editorial called upon CMJ to "do the right thing for its elderly tenants."

Meanwhile, the Massachusetts Tenants Organization and the MSPCA were calling for CMJ to change its policy on pets and evictions. Both organizations were adept at garnering media attention: the MTO dramatized its position with candlelight marches by tenants.

Picking up the scent, the media took off on the chase. Photos of Stacy and Goodboy made the front page of the tabloid *Boston Herald*. Editorials excoriated the developers. For months, Stacy and Goodboy were regulars on the evening news. Meanwhile, Dave Connelly of HOU was busy trying to find an apartment off-site that would be acceptable to Stacy. She turned down the first three private apartments he found for her, insisting on BHA elderly housing. The BHA, however, well aware of the situation, wanted nothing to do with her. Finally, Connelly found her a new apartment in the nearby Lower Mills section of Dorchester and persuaded the BHA manager there to accept her.

While the press was having a field day tearing into the "heartless developers" who were forcing a ninety-one-year-old woman to part with her only companion, the residents of Columbia Point, especially the elderly who lived in the building with Goodboy, saw things differently. "They were fed up," according to Ruby Jaundoo. "Everyone on the task force was united behind enforcing that rule." The media never mentioned or showed the condition of Stacy's apartment. The story they were interested in was the one about the feisty old lady being evicted by the cold-hearted landlord; they didn't want that story to be ruined by the reality of the situation. But the residents of the project had lived in a community without rules and regulations, and they were determined that their new community would not suffer the same fate. For them, Goodboy was a test case.

"The dog was like a big pony," task force member Etta Johnson explains. "She was a small skinny lady whose dog is—what's the nice word?—defecating all over the unit. She couldn't even take the dog outside." The other residents had no sympathy for Stacy. "We had to get rid of our dog," Johnson says. "So why is this lady having all this fuss with hers? We could take care of our dog. So why all of a sudden is there all this fuss, when she can't even take care of hers?"

For Ruby Jaundoo, the pet issue wasn't about one woman and her dog; it was about sanitation and how that one dog affected the health and well-being of the broader community. "I personally don't feel that I want to take away a companion from an older person," Jaundoo explains. "But when that companion becomes more than that person can take care of, then it becomes another issue. It becomes an issue of sanitation." Indeed, the "sanitation" issue had

Harbor Point Community Task Force Press Conference: Alice Stacy, Goodboy, and the No-pets Policy

When the redevelopment of Columbia Point was initiated in 1984, the Columbia Point Task Force, elected by the residents of Columbia Point, voted unanimously to ask the new managers, CMJ management, to enforce the lease. . . .

We have called this press conference today to set the record straight for the benefit of our own residents and the community at large. Here are the facts:

1. A no-pets policy is not against any law of the Federal or state government.
2. Columbia Point is now family public housing, and the existing public housing lease provides that:
3. Those families that do have pets are in violation of their leases.
4. The new development, Harbor Point, will continue with a no-pets policy, and that policy is legal and in the best interests of the vast majority of residents.
5. The Tenant Task Force is a full, legal, and equal partner with the private developer, and the no-pets policy and other policies carried out by management are the policies of the Partnership. . . .

The Task Force policy will not change. At long last we feel we have control of our destiny and we resent and infer intrusion by outsiders who do not live here.

—Press Release, Harbor Point Community Task Force, April 1988

The Goodboy Legislation

Following all of the publicity around the Goodboy incident, an ordinance was approved by the Boston City Council and signed by the mayor, allowing elderly and handicapped tenants to keep pets in both private and public housing, as long as they obey the rules about animal control and care. The ordinance prohibits any housing development from evicting such tenants for keeping pets.

In June 1989, on the one-year anniversary of Goodboy's death, the state legislature passed a bill allowing elderly in state-financed housing to own pets—known as the "Goodboy legislation" in memory of Stacy's dog.

Ten years later, the broader issue of pets in public housing was still unresolved: on June 23, 1998, a "legislative alert" from the New England Affordable Housing Management Association warned of a pending bill that included a provision allowing pet ownership in all federally assisted housing.

reached emergency proportions. Wendell Yee was in charge of the team of people who had to go in and clean Alice Stacy's apartment: "You went into that unit and literally had to get ice scrapers to clean the dog feces off the floor. It was that thick. The woman was not able to go out. It was a pretty sad situation. And it was not an easy thing to do but you had to do it. . . . This had been going on maybe a year or so. Literally, the people went in there with face masks and ice scrapers to get the stuff off."

Ice scrapers notwithstanding, the task force by this time was in the middle of a media storm. They stepped forward into the spotlight, holding a press conference to declare publicly, in no uncertain terms, that they were the representatives of the Harbor Point community, and the community had decided that a no-pets policy was in its best interests. The press conference was a perfect example of what Joe Corcoran had always seen as the real value of making the tenants full partners in a redevelopment project: it was one thing for the "heartless developer" to say "no pets," but another thing altogether for the residents to stand up and say, this is what we want for our community.

The drama came to a climax on moving day, June 15, 1988, in ninety-eight-degree heat. Stacy had finally agreed to move into the apartment in Lower Mills, rather than be separated from her dog. HOU had moved Stacy's belongings the day before, and on Wednesday, with all the local television stations on hand, they loaded up Stacy and Goodboy and headed for Lower Mills. When the van pulled up in front of Stacy's new apartment, with the TV cameras rolling, Goodboy took a tentative few steps out of the van, made a couple of loud gasps, and keeled over—dead. Just in time for the evening news.

Stacy ordered the van to turn around and take her directly back to Harbor Point. In her new apartment in 40 Westwind Court, she was as feisty as ever, and still talking to the press. "They are a heartless people," the *Herald* reports her saying, "and I am damned mad at them. . . . I like it here, but it's going to take me a long time to get over it all. You know I had a premonition it was going to happen— and then they took him away on a stretcher."

Goodboy's death—on live TV—kicked the story into even higher gear. The talk shows picked up the story. CMJ's receptionist of ten years, repeatedly reduced to tears by the calls that were jamming the switchboard, announced she was taking early retirement. Mayor Ray Flynn called an emergency meeting at City Hall to ask CMJ and the task force to change their policy, saying that no other issue in his entire term in office had generated as many phone calls.

Meanwhile, another elderly resident, Cotelia Thomas, was taking up Stacy's cause and refusing to give up her dog. Again, CMJ was ready to compromise with a grandfather clause. And again, the task force held the hard line. CMJ suggested a face-saving compromise, in which Cotelia Thomas got a letter from a veterinarian recommending that her black Labrador retriever not be moved. Reluctantly, the task force agreed, and Thomas and her pet were moved into a ground-floor unit in a building at a remote end of the site. After two years Thomas's dog died; but both she and Stacy lived at Harbor Point until they moved out into nursing homes and died.

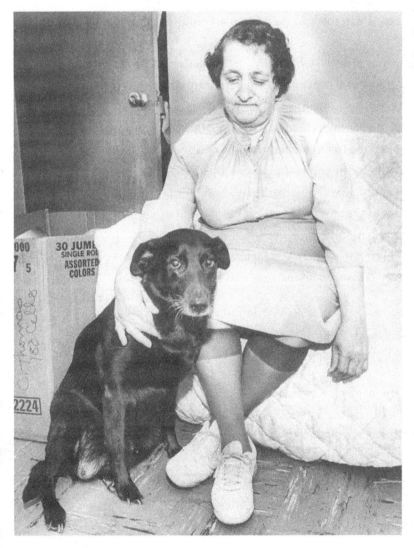

"Mrs. Cotelia Thomas, of Columbia Point, with her pet dog, Princess," 1988. Boston Herald.

25 Renting and Recession

To make Harbor Point work, CMJ had to fill 883 units with market-rate renters. The challenge was a significant one: how do you get people who are able to pay market rents to choose an apartment at the site of one of the most notorious public housing projects in the nation? The future of Harbor Point depended on CMJ's ability to make good on its promise that it could attract these tenants. The company developed a careful and detailed marketing strategy to make sure it was successful.

The first element of the marketing strategy, which CMJ had also used at King's

Lynne, was to physically separate the old community from the new. Harbor Point was built in phases. The first phase of construction was at the south end of the site, while the 350 Columbia Point families were living in, and in some cases relocated to, the buildings at the north end of the site. Marty Jones, CMJ vice president at the time, explains that the relocation phase went smoothly, thanks to the work of Housing Opportunities Unlimited, meeting individually with every family to explain their rights and give them the written, legally binding rehousing guarantee; and thanks to the task force, explaining to the residents how the relocation process would work:

> The residents were sophisticated enough to understand—and the resident leadership was able to sell to the residents—that some of them were still going to be living in some of these God-awful buildings for years while new, high-income people moved into the new development. The reason for that was that we didn't want to load up the first section of the site with all low-income people. It had to be a proportionate mix, and they really understood that. You needed to do it slowly and spread people out over the entire site. . . . The fact that that was fairly easily accepted by the community is very interesting. People were willing to do that because they really understood the concept.

The plan was to bring prospective renters into Harbor Point using the more scenic road around the university, rather than coming right down Mount Vernon

Aerial photo of Harbor Point, 1992. *Landslides.*

The mall at Harbor Point was modeled on the Commonwealth Avenue Mall, 1991. *Courtesy of Corcoran, Mullins, Jennison.*

Massachusetts Archives becomes another of Harbor Point's institutional neighbors. *Courtesy of Peter Vanderwarker.*

"State Archives Will Soon Have a New Harbor Home"

At a cost of $19 million, the taxpayers of Massachusetts have erected a building at the edge of Boston Harbor that will serve as the state's attic, the government's filing cabinet and a vast memory palace for the commonwealth.

The Massachusetts Archives, Museum and State Records Center, enclosing 102,000 square feet on a 4½-acre site at Columbia Point in Boston, is to be opened by Gov. Dukakis on Nov. 19 and be available to the public a week later.

The museum section, featuring displays on the "People, Places and Politics" of Massachusetts, will open first. The archives and records center should be ready by early December.

"I would say we have what will be the best archival facility in the nation—it's state of the art," Secretary of State Michael J. Connolly said last week.

For decades, the state has been storing its official papers and treasures in a crowded, musty basement section of the State House on Beacon Hill, a convenient spot for tourists but an inappropriate place to sort, preserve and display the state's vast holdings. . . .

The state constitution says, "The records of the commonwealth shall be kept in the office of the secretary," and Connolly is proud of the new building, with its high-technology security, climate control and firefighting systems.

He's also proud that the construction was completed on time—in 36 months—and on budget.

The gleaming glass and stone building will soon house and display some of the oldest and most valuable documents and artifacts in American history . . . the original versions of the Massachusetts Constitution, the 1628 Charter of Massachusetts, the diaries of Plymouth Colony Governor William Bradford, Indian treaties and the papers of such patriots as Sam Adams, John Adams and John Hancock.

The collection also includes birth and death records, lists of immigrants arriving at the Port of Boston, muster rolls from the Revolutionary and Civil wars, and the "Eastern Lands Papers," which describe the history of Maine before it separated from Massachusetts in 1820.

—*Boston Globe*, November 10, 1985

Street past the still-to-be-redeveloped areas of the former housing project. Many years previously, the University of Massachusetts had put a Cyclone fence along the Mount Vernon Street side of its property to protect itself from the problems at Columbia Point. CMJ sought and received permission from the chancellor's office to reopen the access to Mount Vernon Street. Prospective renters were then able to approach Harbor Point by driving along the water past UMass Boston, the Kennedy Library, and the new Massachusetts Archives, Museum and State Records Center, which had opened in 1985, and enter the community from the south.

"From a marketing perspective," Joe Corcoran explains, "the approach was all-important":

> When people came to the site, the first thing they saw was this new building, the ocean, this great routing along the University of Massachusetts and the water. And they came right into the development. So at the outset they saw the full potential of the site. . . . We did the same thing up in Lynn: we marketed the top of the site first and moved all the original folks into buildings down at the bottom of the hill, and then we finished off the top of the hill overlooking the city.

Bringing prospects to Harbor Point via the university road wasn't misleading, Corcoran insists. "That isn't to say that we didn't tell them what it was all about. We just wanted to give them the impression of what it was going to be like. And we were putting our best foot forward." Doing so, he explains, is critical to the success of any development, market-rate or mixed-income: people need to be able to picture what the site will ultimately look like. CMJ, Corcoran explains, was simply applying the same principles of marketing a market-rate development to marketing a mixed-income community.

Corcoran is a realist, a pragmatist, when it comes to the challenge of making a mixed-income development work: if you can't attract the market-rate tenants, you can't have a mixed-income community. "We use good marketing techniques to make mixed-income development successful," Corcoran explains. "We make no bones about it—we bring that dimension to all of the developments we get into. We can get the market to live there so it can be a mixed-income development. Some assisted-housing developers can't do that because they don't have any market sense."

Corcoran believes that developing and implementing a careful marketing strategy is rare in the world of subsidized housing. "People think, it's going to be all subsidized and we don't care," he says. What about the accusation that such an approach conceals part of the real identity of the community? "True," Corcoran says. "Because

April Mercedes Hernandez, second from left, and the Harbor Point Leasing Office staff. *Courtesy of Corcoran, Mullins, Jennison.*

otherwise you wouldn't be able to fill the place up with market-rate people. It's a tough enough situation in any event, given the nature of the place. You want to really show it at its best."

April Mercedes Hernandez was in charge of leasing the market-rate apartments at Harbor Point—"showing it at its best." Before coming to Harbor Point, she had worked on leasing the Greenhouse, a new luxury apartment community located on Huntington Avenue near Boston's Symphony Hall. There she faced a challenge similar to that at Harbor Point: convincing renters that the Greenhouse was part of classic Back Bay rather than the less established fringes of the South End. But the challenge at Harbor Point would be even greater. "Everyone in the industry thought I was crazy to want to do it," Hernandez recalls:

> It was an incredible challenge just based on the number of units—883 market-rate apartments—not to mention the stigma attached to the property when it was Columbia Point. Everyone said no one's ever going to want to pay market-rate rent out there. You just can't do that sort of thing. That made me want to do it even more. . . .
>
> I had grown up living across the street from public housing and I was a city girl. A lot of this was about race, about mixing people together. Many people felt you just couldn't do this in Boston. But I believed that you could do it and that's how it should be.

When the first new buildings at Harbor Point were ready for leasing in the summer of 1988, market rents were one thousand dollars per month for a two-bedroom apartment and eight hundred dollars for a one-bedroom. Only a few buildings were completed: one building with about one hundred units, a smaller building of twenty units, and a few townhouse apartments. The rest of the site was still under construction, and most of the development's most attractive

---

Harbor Point Demographics: 1998 Household Profile

Total Market Households	863
Minority	359
Total Subsidy Households	398
Minority	328
Total Households	1,261
Total Minority Households	687

Resident Profile

Total Market Residents	1,658
Minority	763
Total Subsidy Residents	1,263
Minority	1,078
Total Residents	2,921
Total Minority Residents	1,841

Average Household Size

Market	1.9 persons
Subsidy	3.2 persons

Income Profile

Median Market Individual Income	$33,000
Median Market Household Income	$49,000
Median Subsidy Individual Income	$7,000
Median Subsidy Household Income	$10,000

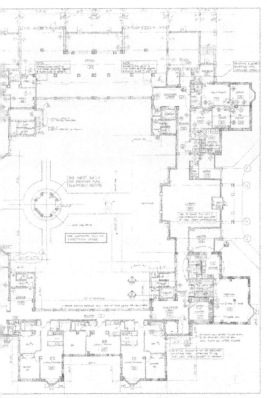

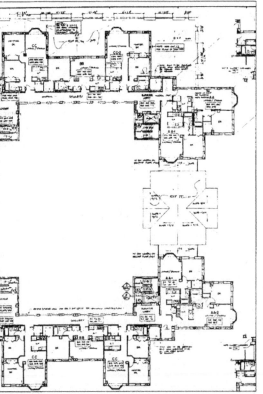

Harbor Point architectural
plans. *Courtesy of
Corcoran, Mullins,
Jennison.*

amenities—the clubhouse, the fitness center, the pool, the water-front park—existed only on paper. Hernandez, however, was un-daunted. "Marketing is perception," she says. "It's what you create. It all depends on the way you look at things."

Hernandez decided not to put directions to Harbor Point in the advertisements that ran in the *Boston Globe*. At the time leasing began, Harbor Point was receiving a lot of negative publicity in the Boston newspapers for the evictions of some of the most notorious Columbia Point tenants. "I felt that if people saw directions in the ad," she explains, "they wouldn't even make the phone call. We would have lost out on a lot of people we didn't even know about." Instead, the ad was listed alphabetically under "Boston waterfront."

Once the calls began coming in, Hernandez and her team continued to "create the perception":

We didn't say, "We're in Dorchester at the site of the old Columbia Point." Right away we're going to lose people. You aren't even going to have a chance to let people know what it's like. It doesn't have anything to do with tricking people. It's just being able to give people an opportunity to learn more about it. So when they ask where it is, you say, "Gee, where are you calling from?" If you have somebody calling from Boston, the way you answer is probably going to be quite a bit different than if you have somebody calling from out of town or out of the country.

So you say, "Are you familiar with the Boston area? We're just a hop, skip, and a jump from downtown Boston. Very convenient. We're a brand-new, $200-million ocean-front community right next door to the JFK Library and the Mass Archives. It's like Cape Cod in Boston. We're on fifty beautiful acres of waterfront property. So come out of the city a few minutes. We're right on the Red Line. We'll give you a whole lot more for your money than you'll get downtown. You won't have to deal with the absentee landlord. You won't have to deal with the old brownstones. You won't have to deal with not being able to find a parking space. We give you all of that here and more—for less rent."

Hernandez and her team were successful in getting people to come out and take a look. Most people were struck by Harbor Point's dramatic waterfront location and the many advantages of renting there. Typically, the leasing office did very well "closing" customers—getting the deposit—but problems would arise once the customers went back home. "They'd talk to their friends, family, and co-workers," Hernandez recalls, "and they'd say, 'What, are you crazy? You can't rent up there.'"

If they didn't know the area and their co-workers did, they would say, "Oh, that's really bad out there. You really don't want to live out there."

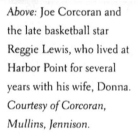

Above: Joe Corcoran and
the late basketball star
Reggie Lewis, who lived at
Harbor Point for several
years with his wife, Donna.
*Courtesy of Corcoran,
Mullins, Jennison.*

Above, right: Participants
in a summer basketball
camp run by Reggie Lewis
at the new development.
*Courtesy of Corcoran,
Mullins, Jennison.*

So we ended up with a huge cancellation rate—you'd lose six out of ten
between cancels and declines, when you're used to losing one out of ten.

In the beginning, that was hard to deal with. It was kind of a shame:
you could sense people wanted to rent here, but there was so much
negativity. You just see if you can overcome the objections. It's not
right for everyone.

As Hernandez saw it, her job was to create the perception, put the
new development in its best light, help people visualize what the final
product would be like, and even try to overcome the objections. Then
she had to step back and let the customers make their own decisions.

Hernandez drew on the relationships that she had developed with
the real estate brokers from the Newbury Street area when she was
leasing apartments in the Greenhouse. Initially, the downtown brokers were reluctant to take the time to take prospective renters out
to Harbor Point. To attract them, the leasing office developed a brokers' program whereby they were paid a full month's rent in commission by CMJ.

Although the leasing office anticipated that the market for Harbor
Point would come from people living on the South Shore, it turned
out that these prospects were more likely to be aware of Columbia
Point's history and therefore less likely to want to live at Harbor
Point. Instead, the people most interested in Harbor Point turned
out to be the young urban professionals and graduate students who
saw in the community a variety of advantages over comparable

Above: The entrance at Harbor Point, 1991. *Courtesy of Corcoran, Mullins, Jennison.*

Below: The children's pool at Harbor Point. *Courtesy of Corcoran, Mullins, Jennison.*

Harbor Point Occupancy Rates

Construction of all 1,283 units at Harbor Point, including the renovation of existing buildings and completion of new ones, was finished in 1990. Residents moved in as the apartments became ready. Occupancy rates at the apartment complex increased as Boston's rental real estate market tightened.

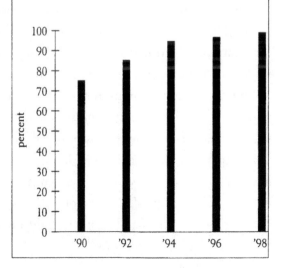

apartments in downtown Boston, Brighton, or the Back Bay—lower rents, new buildings, and on-site parking.

While Hernandez and her team were "creating the perception," they also explained to prospective renters that Harbor Point was a mixed-income community—one-third of the apartments would be occupied by families whose rents were subsidized. "We didn't make a big deal out of it because it shouldn't be a big deal," Hernandez explains. "We certainly told people that it was mixed-income. But if we make a huge topic out of it, people are going to think, 'What are they doing this for? Is something wrong?' [On the other hand,] we didn't want anybody moving in there if it wasn't for them. So part of the procedure was to bring the client into your office and have a conversation with them. Find out what was important to them in their new home and so forth. And then tell them a little bit about Harbor Point as far as it being a mixed-income community with all different kinds of people living there."

Some people were immediately turned off. "We had people who said, 'Oh, I don't want to live with subsidized people,'" Hernandez recalls. "We had plenty of people like that. They didn't want anything to do with it. Some people had a real problem with paying one thousand dollars a month next door to somebody who was only paying one hundred dollars a month." Joe Corcoran estimates that Harbor Point lost about 20 percent of the market to people who walked away because it was a mixed-income community—an expected, and acceptable, loss. "That's their choice," Hernandez says. "The last thing I want is someone living at our development who doesn't want to be there."

According to reports in the media, some market-rate tenants claimed that they were not told in advance that one-third of the apartments at Harbor Point were subsidized. An article entitled "Harboring No Illusions," by Debra Rosenberg in the August 25, 1989, edition of the *Boston Phoenix*, while generally optimistic about the "housing experiment" at Harbor Point, reports that one year after leasing began, some market-rate tenants didn't know that theirs was a mixed-income community until they read about it in the paper. Others were reportedly confused about the mechanism for subsidizing low-income families, assuming that their higher rents were directly paying for their neighbors' lower rents. At the same time, the article reports, the Massachusetts Tenants Organization was claiming that the developers' ultimate objective was to kick out the four hundred low-income families and turn the development into an all-market-rate, luxury waterfront development. Harbor Point, like Columbia Point before it, was never at a loss for rumors.

Above: A new roofline at Harbor Point helped change the former public housing project's image. *Courtesy of Corcoran, Mullins, Jennison.*

Right: A classified newspaper advertisment for Harbor Point. Rents had to be lowered when the bottom dropped out of Boston real estate in the late 1980s. *Courtesy of Corcoran, Mullins, Jennison.*

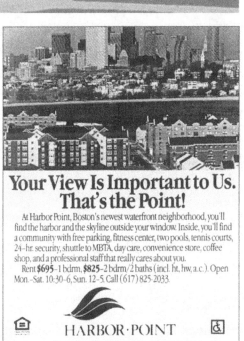

Your View Is Important to Us. That's the Point!

At Harbor Point, Boston's newest waterfront neighborhood, you'll find the harbor and the skyline outside your window. Inside, you'll find a community with free parking, fitness center, two pools, tennis courts, 24-hr. security, shuttle to MBTA, day care, convenience store, coffee shop, and a professional staff that really cares about you.

Rent **$695**-1 bdrm, **$825**-2 bdrm/2 baths (incl. ht, hw, a.c.). Open Mon.-Sat. 10:30-6, Sun. 12-5. Call (617) 825-2033.

HARBOR·POINT

Professionally managed by CMJ Mgmt. Co.   Financed by MHFA
Rental furniture available from Putnam. Units available on open occupancy basis.

In 1989, just one year after leasing began at Harbor Point, the real estate market in Boston began to crash. Soon, the major recession that was hitting the entire New England market began to take its toll on Harbor Point. After an exceptionally strong start, with some ninety apartments rented in the first month, new rentals fell to only a few each month. As vacancy rates began rising all over the city, landlords began lowering their rents. In order to continue to present Harbor Point as being a good deal compared to Boston rents, the leasing office had to lower rents even further.

In order to attract the market, many landlords began paying the brokers' fees; Harbor Point's program of paying brokers a full month's commission was no longer exceptional. Moreover, when existing leases came up for renewal, instead of increasing rents or keeping them the same, they had to drop them—otherwise, people who had been living at Harbor Point would be paying more than people just walking in the door. In 1990 Harbor Point began offering a free month's rent as an incentive to attract new tenants.

Between 1988 and 1992 rents throughout the city dropped by 20 percent. Harbor Point's financial plan, based on full occupancy and steadily increasing rents, was in trouble.

The recession caused even more serious problems for Harbor Point's investors—yet another threat to the financial stability of the development. Harbor Point had received its first, and worst, financial blow in 1986, when federal tax reform threatened to scuttle the entire project. At Harbor Point this meant a major change in the investment strategy. Even though Senator Ted Kennedy's efforts to qualify Harbor Point for "transition rules" in the 1986 tax reform legislation were successful, the tax incentives now took the form of tax credits that were attractive to corporate, not individual, investors. Among Harbor Point's major new corporate investors were Massachusetts savings banks. Thriving in the late 1980s, they were flush with cash to invest and eager to take advantage of the tax credits to offset their earnings. They began investing in Harbor Point in 1986, signing agreements committing them to invest a certain amount each year for several years, and receive tax credits in return.

Then in 1990 the recession hit. As borrowers defaulted on their loans and federal regulators were requiring increased reserves, savings banks were suddenly in deep trouble, starting to go bankrupt and in turn defaulting on their payments. Moreover, because the savings banks were no longer making a profit, they had no use for the tax credits that only a few years earlier had been so attractive.

A year after opening, Harbor Point was caught in the financial crisis that was sweeping the real estate industry. The new community's

The Harbor Point fitness center. *Courtesy of Corcoran, Mullins, Jennison.*

The new townhouses at Harbor Point. *Courtesy of Corcoran, Mullins, Jennison.*

savings bank investors were defaulting on their payments, and in the meantime, the economic recession in Boston and across the country was depressing rents. Fully 70 percent of the revenues at Harbor Point were projected to come from market rents. Not only were those rents now below what had been projected, but as many as half of the market-rate units were standing empty.

In 1991, caught in the double bind of defaulting investors and a revenue shortfall, CMJ undertook a major restructuring of the financing of Harbor Point. Many of the original investors, no longer in a position to take advantage of the tax credit and unable to continue to invest on schedule, simply wanted to get out of the deal. Some had already defaulted on their investment obligations. In place of the struggling savings banks, CMJ sought an investor with the capital to invest in Harbor Point who could benefit from the tax credits.

They found their investor in the Chevron Corporation. Chevron purchased the interests of the defaulting partners and made a total investment of $34 million, creating a cash reserve large enough to tide Harbor Point over until the recession ended and rents rebounded. In fact, CMJ, by selling the tax credits to Chevron for a higher price than the original investors had paid, ended up with capital reserves of $50 million.

While CMJ was arranging for the financial security of Harbor Point, the leasing office responded to the recession by becoming more creative—visiting corporations, schools, and hospitals, offering housing to employees, running open houses—not only beating the bushes but continually finding new ways to beat them. Although the recession was a serious setback, the worst real estate recession since the 1930s, the infusion of capital from Chevron meant that Harbor Point was now set to weather the storm.

26 Moving into Harbor Point

Starting in 1988, the community on the peninsula was once again a place where people wanted to live—something it hadn't been for decades. Dave Hanifin, a white law school graduate in his twenties, and April Young, a black graduate student also in her twenties, were among the first market-rate residents to move into the new community.

Dave Hanifin moved into Harbor Point in July 1989, just one year after leasing of the first completed buildings began. He had just graduated from Boston University Law School and had been living in student housing in Allston. His room-

mate was aware of Harbor Point because his law firm had been doing legal work for CMJ. Hanifin recalls their first visit to Harbor Point: "I remember going to the leasing office and into the very beautifully decorated model apartment. They were very clear about the fact that it was mixed-income, and they showed us a spanking brand-new apartment that no one had ever lived in before. It had a parking garage underneath the building. And the entire complex was scheduled to have some really wonderful amenities—a health club and swimming pool and tennis courts and all kinds of things that were very appealing to somebody coming right out of school and starting out professionally."

Hanifin was sold; he moved in and loved his new apartment. He hadn't sought out Harbor Point because he wanted to live in a mixed-income community, yet he wasn't put off by the idea. Having grown up and gone to college in upstate New York, he had never heard of Columbia Point. Shortly after he moved in, however, watching a video about the redevelopment of the housing project had a

profound effect on him. "I still have a vivid memory to this day of a point in the video where they were showing the old dilapidated buildings," he recalls. "There were some mattresses stacked up. Kids were jumping onto the mattresses, and that was the only playground they had at that point. That image still stays with me to this day. And then seeing now the tot lots and playgrounds that were built into [Harbor Point]. It's a vast improvement for kids. Just thinking

"Before" and "After"
cornerstones from
Cityscapes by Robert
Campbell and Peter
Vanderwarker, 1992.
"Before," *courtesy of
Corcoran, Mullins,
Jennison;* "After," *Peter
Vanderwarker.*

about what the kids faced previously and opportunities that are
there for them now."

Hanifin's first formal involvement with the community was as a
building captain, the representative from each building—"almost
like a resident advisor in a dormitory," he says—who acts as a liai-
son between the residents of that building and management. Becoming a building captain required getting a certain number of sig-
natures, which helped Hanifin meet both old and new residents in
his building, as well as meeting all of the other building captains.
The issues that came up mostly had to do with maintenance, Hanifin explains: "Instead of walking their trash down to the trash
chute, some residents would just put it out in the hallway at
night—with the intention, I think, of taking care of it the next
morning. Then other residents in that hallway would complain
about the odor or about the unsightliness of it. It would run the
gamut. It could be noise complaints—somebody who's playing
their stereo too loud at inappropriate times. It could be people who
had laundry on their balcony."

Hanifin worked with the other building captains to identify things
the community needed and make sure they got them. He recalls that
the exterior lights were a big issue. "People felt safe when the lights
were working," he says, "and not when the lights were out." At one
point, the Harbor Point Community Task Force, which had changed
its name officially in 1986 when the legal documents creating the
partnership were signed, felt that management wasn't being responsive to the issue of broken exterior lights. The task force suggested that
the building captains bring the issue directly to the attention of the developers. "I can remember going out at one point at night," Hanifin
says, "and making a list of all the lights that were out. I remember
bringing this entire list to Gary Jennison and saying, 'These lights
have been out. Here's the exact location. These are the dates. They've
been out since X, Y, and Z. Let's see what we can do about it.' That
got it fixed. And I think it made everybody feel better. Sometimes it
took some real prodding. But there was also a sense of accomplishment when they did get fixed, knowing that was something that the
tenants were really concerned about and we were able to fix it."

When he was elected to the task force, Hanifin became even
more involved in identifying and resolving the issues that came up
in the community. Most issues, he says, didn't break down along
lines of market-rate versus low-income residents. "For the most
part," he says, "it was an issue of respect for everybody. When you
put a large number of people into a relatively confined area, people

Midrise buildings and
townhouses create a
diversity of housing types.
*Courtesy of Corcoran,
Mullins, Jennison.*

Racial Mix of Harbor Point Residents, 1999

White	1,104	37.0 percent
African American	992	33.2 percent
Asian	458	15.3 percent
Hispanic	336	11.2 percent
Native American	97	3.2 percent

need to respect other people's right to quiet and the ability to sleep and the ability to enjoy their tenancy."

But some issues did break down along low-income/market-rate lines. One issue of particular importance to market-rate tenants, Hanifin recalls, was whether to continue the shuttle bus service that ran from Harbor Point to the nearest T station—UMass/JFK, as the old Columbia stop was now called. He remembers market-rate tenants coming to the task force to complain about the shuttle service being curtailed: "There came to be more market-rate tenant outrage over that—people feeling like they had moved in with the notion

Harbor Point building captains. *Courtesy of Corcoran, Mullins, Jennison.*

that [the shuttle] was always going to be there. I was on the task force at the time and it really boiled down to a financial issue: the deficits that the site was running at the time and how to address them." Even though Hanifin used the shuttle every day as part of his commute to his job at a law firm in downtown Boston, as a task force member he appreciated the cost to the community of running the shuttle and supported reducing the service. "I was very much in support of doing what we needed to do," he says, "despite the fact that it may have not been other market-rate tenants' wishes. I didn't see myself as being the representative of the market-rate tenants, because I had been elected by the community at large. I viewed myself as being the representative of all the tenants."

Hanifin recalls the task force taking "night owl" walks around the community to check on the site. "I can remember walking around with Esther [Santos]," he says. "I felt more comfortable because she was an older resident. It wasn't like, here's this white new guy coming in, trying to tell us what to do." Hanifin was particularly impressed with Esther Santos's way of talking to children in the course of these walks around the community. "I have a vivid memory of her approach to kids," he says:

> These were younger kids who you really wouldn't want to scream and yell at. Who were basically hanging on the branches of very young trees. They were doing what kids do, which is swing from branches they can hang on. I remember Esther going up to some kids and really trying to explain to them that these trees were new and that if we wanted trees to be here in the future we needed to respect them.
>
> She understood that they were maybe getting some enjoyment out of it, but tried to really explain to them why it wasn't a good idea to do

Left: Tennis at Harbor Point, 1995. *Courtesy of Corcoran, Mullins, Jennison.*

Below: Volleyball at Harbor Point. *Courtesy of Corcoran, Mullins, Jennison.*

April Young. *Courtesy of Corcoran, Mullins, Jennison.*

Dave Hanifin, 1998. *Roger Farrington.*

that. I just remember that being the right approach, in my mind—to try to make kids understand why they shouldn't do something, rather than just chastising them for doing something that they might not at first think there's anything wrong with.

Santos's gentle way of educating Harbor Point's children in the importance of preserving their young and growing community, with its easily broken branches, made a deep impression on Dave Hanifin. "I became a fan of Harbor Point and the people who lived there," he says. Although he moved out in 1994 when he married a woman who had always wanted to live in a Victorian house, he maintains close ties to the community.

He believes that although mixed-income housing helps, it doesn't address all of the problems of low-income people, especially with the recent cuts in the government safety net of welfare and family assistance. "I think it certainly does help to change people's attitudes when you change their surroundings," he says: "What was done at Harbor Point was to empower people to have some control over the site and to have some involvement in the management so that they really have a sense of ownership. But I also think that you really have to provide people who were previously dependent on public assistance with opportunities so that they can become economically independent and secure. . . . I don't think [mixed-income housing] can totally and dramatically change people's lives without giving them meaningful economic opportunities as well."

To that end, Hanifin is now on the board of a nonprofit organization called the Columbia Point Employee Ownership Project, whose goal is to provide training, education, and support to people who are interested in starting their own businesses. The fledgling Ownership Project's first such enterprise is a carpet-cleaning business currently operating at Harbor Point.

April Young moved into Harbor Point in December 1992, answering an ad in the *Boston Globe* for "luxury waterfront apartments." Having grown up in Miami, she liked the idea of living near the water and liked the fact that the development was brand-new. "That's where I come from," Young explains. "If it's old we knock it down and build a new one. We don't believe in restoring things." Living in Cambridge while pursuing her doctorate degree in anthropology at Harvard, Young felt isolated—her residential life tied to the university—and was looking for a sense of the wider Boston community. She knew nothing about Harbor Point's history or that, as a

The Schmidt family at Harbor Point. *Courtesy of Corcoran, Mullins, Jennison.*

mixed-income community, it was a national model for affordable housing.

Young vividly remembers her first impression of Harbor Point: "That day was tremendously cold. The wind off of the water was just coming down that mall. It was really chilling me. I stopped at the management office and then they told me that I had to actually walk down to the leasing office. If it hadn't been such a long walk back to the train station I think I might have gone away. But it was just so bitterly cold. It was beautiful. I remember feeling very inspired about the wide-open space. I had a good feeling about it."

At the time, Young was planning to do her doctoral research in Brazil on health-related issues. A few months after moving into Harbor Point, however, she learned that there were a health center and a youth center on the site. "It was kind of an anthropologist's dream," she says, "a little village, as it were." She decided to do her research at Harbor Point instead. As a way of getting inside the community, she decided to run for a seat on the task force and was elected the following spring.

Young has a unique perspective on Harbor Point. On the one hand, she looks at it with the objectivity of an anthropologist. On the other, she looks as it as a young, black, female, market-rate resident:

Harbor Point is a very complicated community, very complex. It's beautiful, sort of this remade thing. The process was very resident-focused and resident-driven, and that has dignified what has been constituted there. On the other hand, there is a whole tension between market-rate residents versus subsidized residents—not so much between residents themselves as around how the place is presented, how it is policed, what the terms of living there are.

Take, for instance, the use of space. Longer-term residents tend to be subsidized residents. The way that they use the space, the way that they inhabit the space, is going to be a little bit different than market-rate, two-year people who are passing through. Subsidized residents treat this more like a neighborhood, doing things out on the porches, in the streets, on the grass, as opposed to shorter-term residents whose domain is really just their units. They're only in the common spaces as they go and come from their units. That's a different way of using space. And if we decide that we're going to police and patrol things like noise, things like kids, things like "black presence"—this becomes problematic.

What Young finds "problematic" is the tension between the interests of marketability—making sure Harbor Point is "presentable" as a

Students at Harbor Point, 1999

More than 675 Harbor Point residents are enrolled in area colleges and universities in undergraduate and graduate programs. They include:

Bentley College	1
Berklee College of Music	31
Boston College	10
Boston University	126
Brandeis University	2
Emerson College	8
Emmanuel College	23
Harvard University	17
Massachusetts College of Art	5
Massachusetts College of Pharmacy	13
Massachusetts Institute of Technology	4
Mount Ida College Junior College	10
New England Conservatory of Music	10
New England School of Law	26
New England School of Optometry	4
Newbury College	8
Northeastern University	121
Quincy Junior College	5
Simmons College	3
Suffolk University	34
Tufts University	32
UMass Boston	148
Wentworth Institute of Technology	33
Wheelock College	1

place where market-rate renters would want to live—and the right of the people who live there to inhabit their neighborhood in a way that is comfortable. Young points, for example, to rental agents who say, "'I brought some people out there to look at the unit and these kids hanging on the corner scared them away.' Well," she says, "let's unpack that. These are kids who live in this neighborhood. Harbor Point, like any other urban area, has the problem of idle kids—finding places and things for kids to do. Imagine kids just standing there; because they're black children or Latino children, we visualize that as a threat. . . . What I'd like us to understand is that when we roll security through there and we 'broom' those kids, we are subjecting a certain group of people to a particular kind of jeopardy."

If black children are seen as a threat merely by virtue of their being black, Young suggests, maybe the solution isn't to "broom" them off the street corners, but rather to look at the attitude of the person who feels threatened. As a mixed-income community, Harbor Point has a responsibility to protect the interests of all its residents: "As for white folks' fear, I think it's an education process and we need to call it out. We don't abide it without comment. We certainly don't work through these things by pandering to them. At Harbor Point, like most communities, the incidence of random violent crime is very, very low. So we need to call it. We also have to be willing to stand our moral ground. If people aren't willing to challenge their own fear, don't live here."

Young feels that the residents' "self-determination" in planning their new community is the key to its success. In her view, resident involvement in general and the task force in particular have "dignified what the community has become":

I think you have a very empowered, just wonderfully sophisticated group of women [at Harbor Point] who are the core of that community, who are brilliant in their leadership. They're so fair and so democratic. They put up with stuff that I would never put up with, from any number of people. They're very interested and invested in the process and in fairness.

The fact that they are African American women, that they are "subsidized" residents of the community, has hindered acknowledgment of the gift that they bring to a housing initiative. And if we're talking about replicating Harbor Point, being a model for new approaches to affordable housing, we have to factor in their brilliance, their sophistication, their role in the process.

Harbor Point is justifiably a national model for affordable housing, in Young's view. Building a strong mixed-income community is

The Harbor Point Drum and Bugle Corps. *Courtesy of Corcoran, Mullins, Jennison.*

a long process, she says, insisting that residential involvement must be a key piece of that model:

In the HOPE VI program [the federal program to convert public housing projects into private, mixed-income housing, described in chapter 28], that perspective of resident-driven, resident-focused agenda around what's going to happen in the community is consistently missing. The HOPE VI program will go under if they do not change that. Communities will be physically revitalized, but you'll either have to police them very heavily and escalate the scale of the policing over time, or you'll have lots of damage and vandalism because people aren't invested in the community. You won't have that resident authority and those structures kind of built into the bricks and mortar of the place in the way that you do at Harbor Point.

April Young moved out of Harbor Point in December 1995, three years after moving in. At the time, she was having difficulty writing her doctoral dissertation, whose subject was Harbor Point; her professors and colleagues suggested that she was in effect attempting to

Harbor Point float in
Dorchester Day parade.
Courtesy of Corcoran,
Mullins, Jennison.

"write up in the field"—a notoriously difficult task for any anthropologist. When she moved to Boston's South End, she found it a striking contrast to Harbor Point. "Harbor Point felt to me like a community," she explains, "where I knew people, I knew the place, I was very tied to it. In the South End, everything was very anonymous. Some people have critiqued Harbor Point for being a place where real mixing doesn't happen between groups; but it's a much more congenial neighborhood environment than many other areas. That was kind of a shock."

April Young continues to have strong ties to Harbor Point, visiting more than once a week. Her involvement is on a personal level rather than an institutional one. "I learned so many lessons out there about what makes communities successful," she reflects. "It takes vision, brilliance, grace of leadership that really only comes from talented, inspired people. That can't be taught; it has to be inspired. Without the particular people involved, the nature of their commitment, the content of their history and experience of that place, their blood in the ground in the way that it is, it would be different. I wouldn't say it wouldn't work, but it would be different. For all of its limitations, there's a light that shines off of Harbor Point."

27 Running the New Community

For the members of the task force, seeing construction of Harbor Point completed and moving all of the former Columbia Point residents into their new units wasn't the end of the journey toward a new community. It was just the beginning. Task force member Esther Santos has been working tirelessly for her community for more than thirty years. "We worked from day one to reach consensus about redevelopment and then worked hard for ten years or so to get that done. We thought that was the hard part," she says, laughing. "This is the hard part."

Santos's determination to keep her brand-new community as clean and beauti-

ful as it was on the day it opened echoes the feelings of the people who felt privileged to move into the brand-new Columbia Point back in 1954. "To maintain Harbor Point as beautiful as day one when we moved in is really hard," she says. "Some children never had shrubbery, grass, flowers. Columbia Point didn't have any of those things. You have to teach the children you don't pull them up. You don't trample on them. As I told one child, 'No, no. Please don't walk on the flowers.' The mother sat right in the window and didn't say a word. She gave me a dirty look because I spoke to the child."

Making sure the community works is a constant job. "A lot of times one would think you'd have input in the very beginning, and after things are up and running, you go home, sit down, and be quiet," Ruby Jaundoo explains. "That's not what happened. You have to stay involved, and we stayed very much involved. I feel this way: if you don't continue to work at something that you helped create or build, it's not going to maintain itself. Someone has to maintain it. It's still an everyday struggle to keep it going."

The community may be relatively new, but the issues involved in making it work are the same as ever. "Those of us that are good housekeepers really try to keep our building clean and our apartments clean," Santos explains. "Then there are those that think, 'What the hell. They don't care, I don't either.'" The difference between Columbia Point and Harbor Point, Santos

says, is the way the community follows up on people who are not complying with the rules and regulations. "The difference is we have HOU that works with the residents," she says. Housing Opportunities Unlimited reminds residents of their responsibilities, gets them the help and support they need, and lets them know that if they don't change, they will have to leave.

Dave Connelly works with those residents, most of whom do get help and change. Even so, "there still are residents that hate everything that happens here," Connelly says. "These are people who we have helped get into drug programs. But when things get out of control in the family or their life, they look outside of themselves for blame. Not that they have to blame themselves, but they have to look inside themselves to fix it, the way we all do. They don't do that; they look outside. That group is small and getting smaller."

Some subsidized tenants reportedly resented the new rules imposed by management, including no washing or repairing cars, no sitting on the front stoop, and no loud noise between 11 P.M. and 8 A.M. They saw these rules as being overly restrictive of the subsidized residents and overly accommodating to the market-rate residents. Some even suspected that the rules were another way of driving out the low-income people. They had been used to living at Columbia Point in a certain way and now were being asked to live in another way.

Jeannette Rinaldi, right, Harbor Point resident, casts her vote in the Harbor Point Community Task Force election, while Thelma Peters of the Boston Housing Authority and Task Force Election Committee looks on, May 1989. *Courtesy of Corcoran, Mullins, Jennison.*

Fitness center director Don Fry outside the Harbor Point Clubhouse. *Courtesy of Corcoran, Mullins, Jennison.*

Dave Connelly suggests another perspective on the rules: not as issues dividing along lines of race or income, but as shared issues that need to be worked out among all of the members of the community: "If you go to the [predominantly white] D Street project, you'll see kids hanging out in the parking lot, playing music loud, and residents are calling and complaining about it. So I don't think it's a matter of race; I think it's a matter of civics, of being civil to your neighbor. . . . It was the same thing at King's Lynne, where the kids would be hanging out in a parking lot drinking beer and playing loud music, but they were almost all white."

According to Ruby Jaundoo, one of the toughest struggles the task force faces is dealing with families that have multiple problems, that are constantly violating the rules and regulations, and that look to the task force to bail them out:

> I've had a couple of residents who call on the phone and say, "You tell Ruby Jaundoo to get down to the court right now and tell this person to leave me alone." Like I'm supposed to come down there and make it all go away.
>
> When a person gets in trouble they would say to me, "Miss Jaundoo, you've been knowing me for thirty years." [And I say,] "That's right, I've been knowing you for thirty years, but that doesn't mean you can break the rules. You can read. You know the rules and regulations as well as I do." That's the most difficult part—when people get themselves in a position where they're in an eviction process and they try to throw that guilt thing on you.

People facing eviction often find any number of ways to shift the blame from themselves. According to Dan Murray, now president of CMJ Management Company, they claim that their kids never did anything wrong; that it's a case of mistaken identity; that it's racism; that the developers are only out to make their money. They charge that the task force plays favorites; that people who are their friends break just as many rules but don't get eviction notices. According to Wendell Yee, rumors about management attempting to throw out the low-income families are especially persistent at the sites where there are tenant-developer partnerships, and tenants who get into trouble go to the elected members of the task force and appeal to them as their longtime neighbors from back in the days of the housing project.

Interestingly, market-rate residents and subsidized residents have been evicted from Harbor Point in similar percentages in recent years. In 1998, for example, a total of thirty-four tenants were

Betty Quarles walking with security officers Lance Norwood (left) and Kevin Caniff (right). *Courtesy of Corcoran, Mullins, Jennison.*

evicted; twenty-five were market-rate and nine were subsidized. Those figures represent about 3 percent of the market-rate units and 2 percent of the subsidized units. Nonpayment of rent was the primary reason, and a range of offenses accounted for the remaining evictions.

Eviction, as far as Ruby Jaundoo is concerned, is a matter not of personal favors but of rules and regulations. Her commitment to the low-income residents of Harbor Point is profound, quiet, and unwavering. But she is also a believer in personal responsibility. "Although we work very hard at trying to help people maintain their tenancy—and I think every avenue is taken," she says, "the responsibility has to go back to you after one has done everything."

And then they will use these excuses and say, no task force member—and I guess they're talking about me too—is ever called in for a private conference [the first step in the eviction process]. And I say, if those task force members aren't breaking the rules and regulations, there's no need for them to come before the governing board. But if their kids are out there violating the rules, fighting other people, knocking people down and kicking them in the head and things like that . . . that's their responsibility, not mine.

For Jaundoo, the way you show respect for people—and the only way to make a community work—is by holding them responsible for their own actions. Her determination to protect the rights of the low-income residents is matched by her determination to hold them responsible for their own actions. "[Jaundoo] would always take the position of the tenant until every last defense was used up: 'How do you know that? What did he say? How did she know that?'" Joe Corcoran explains. "But at some point, she knew that the person was completely out of line and she couldn't do any more."

According to Harbor Point manager Miles Byrne,

> Ruby will say, "We have an obligation to these low-income folks. They were abandoned for years. If I'm the last person standing, I'm going to make [the developers] remember their commitments. You've got my name on Harbor Point property. But these people are my name . . . and these are the commitments I made to them when I signed my name."
>
> She may say that twice a year, she may say it eighty times a year. I tell you, it's invoked and it's right. . . . If it's a rent issue, she'll say, "Screw it. We'll work on it." But if it's a family that she sees is hurting the community and not making an effort to change, she says, "Get them out of here. I've worked too hard to make this a better property. You cannot hurt others."

Etta Johnson, president of the task force, says that residents constantly come to the task force asking for little things. "It's nothing big; it's small stuff," she says. Things like, "I know children aren't allowed inside the tennis courts when someone's playing tennis, but we'll be careful." Or "I know babies under a certain age or a certain height aren't allowed in the pool except at certain times, but we'll be careful." The rules are the rules, she tells them. "You weren't here in Columbia Point," Johnson reminds the newer residents. "You don't know what it was like. Rules are made to be enforced, and we're here to make sure they're being enforced. And we're not changing those rules just because you've got a son or a daughter who wants to break them. It don't work that way. . . . Because at Columbia Point, the BHA did not enforce the rules. You did what you want, when you want, and how you want. And there was nothing said."

In fact, the eviction policy of the Massachusetts Housing Finance Agency—the state agency that holds the mortgage on Harbor Point—is clear. Any resident subject to eviction for cause is entitled to a "private conference," a grievance hearing in which the resident has the opportunity to hear and answer the charges. At Harbor

Children of Harbor Point

About 650 of Harbor Point's current 3,000 residents are children under the age of eighteen. Most are from low-income families; nearly 12 percent are from market-rate families. Their average age is ten, and they are evenly divided between boys and girls. Here's what one fifteen-year-old boy and one seventeen-year-old girl had to say about life at Harbor Point in 1998.

The fifteen-year-old-boy is a student at South Boston High School.

Q: So how long have you lived here?

A: I've lived here for fourteen years.

Q: Do you have any memories of Columbia Point?

A: It was old and dirty.

Q: What did you do when you were little?

A: I used to go skipping rocks. Catching bees in a bottle. I would catch grasshoppers and put them in a bottle. Other kids used to flip on a mattress.

Q: What was it like to grow up here?

A: There used to be killings and stuff back in the old Point. Now there's stuff like basketball. I had to stay in because I was young. I couldn't go out like I can now.

Q: Your Mom made sure you came in. What about here? Does it seem safer now?

A: Yes.

Q: What do you do for fun?

A: Play cards and basketball.

Q: Did you choose to go to South Boston High School?

A: Yes, I chose to go to Southie.

Q: What's the racial situation at Southie?

A: There's no problem. I thought there would be more white people than black. But there's really more blacks than whites [at the high school].

Q: What do you want to be when you grow up?

A: I want to play basketball and work at a bank when I get older, when I finish college and stuff.

The seventeen-year-old girl is a graduate of a pilot high school in Boston who plans to attend a local community college and pursue her dream of a career in the theater.

Q: What do you remember about Columbia Point?

A: We had a lot more crime and a lot of people were getting shot. Like you'd hear gunshots over here almost every night. A lot more teens were getting arrested. People were dying. And cops were out here more often for arresting than they are now patrolling the area. They changed it around and they got Harbor Point and it was cool. I didn't like moving. Packing up my stuff.

Q: What do you remember of the transition time from Columbia Point to Harbor Point? Do you remember the construction?

A: It was a lot of noise. I hated it because every other day there was a new detour from getting off the school bus. You couldn't cut through that way anymore. You had to walk around. That's one of the reasons I hated moving. I was eight years old and I had to carry these boxes. I said, "I hate this. I don't want to do this

Children help plant new trees at Harbor Point, 1989. *Courtesy of Corcoran, Mullins, Jennison.*

The children's pool at
Harbor Point, 1990.
*Courtesy of Corcoran,
Mullins, Jennison.*

anymore." Moving from street to street to street. It was kind of terrible.

I remember the first week that we were finally getting settled in our new apartment and I looked out the window and they were demolishing our old building. I started remembering all the stuff that I'd left there and I wanted to go back.

The first few years of Harbor Point, there was much more activity than before because instead of letting the drug dealers and the gangsters stay here, they were kicking them out. I remember that being like a big thing for the first couple of years.

It was like getting rid of the bad people and moving around a lot. People moving around, learning new streets, learning new addresses. And so after that, I can't really recall a time that I didn't live at Harbor Point. Because after that you get used to it. You're like, okay, I live at Harbor Point. And you tell people to come and see you. Your friends, they're used to Columbia Point. So you have to give them directions. I didn't have any problem because a lot of people I still knew from Columbia Point were here.

And then they opened the pool in the summer and we all went swimming. Or riding bikes or going to play or watching the boys play basketball. Or you, like, had your friends come over on weekends and spend the night. It was basically the same. Just, like, a different name. And there was more room for new people to come in. Getting used to new people. But other than that it was the same.

Q: You don't have to go into details, but what's the drug scene here?

A: I wouldn't know. Even though I live out here I don't go around. If there are drugs, I haven't seen any. The worst I've seen is, like, someone smoking marijuana. But that's it. You don't see, like, people— when it was Columbia Point, people were shooting up crack in the alleys and all that other stuff. You don't see that. You don't see, like, prostitution out bold in the street. Prostitutes getting picked up by pimps. You don't see that anymore. The worst thing you could see a kid doing here is sitting at the bus stop smoking a cigarette or smoking a joint. And they're like, "Oh, my gosh, that's bad." But you don't care because you compare it to, like, the way it was.

Point, the grievance hearing is held before the governing board, which consists of two members from CMJ and two members from the task force.

At Harbor Point, as at King's Lynne, there were rumors at first that management was using evictions to throw out the old low-income residents and bring in their own low-income families—or worse, to eliminate low-income tenants altogether. However, the communities soon learned that that was not the case. In Lynn, for example, of the 169 original families that were guaranteed relocation in the new community, 90 are still living there twenty-five years later. Of the others, some were evicted, some died, and some moved out for a host of other personal reasons. Of the 350 Columbia Point families that stayed and were rehoused at Harbor Point more than ten years ago, 220 still remain—a remarkably low attrition rate of 3.88 percent per year, as compared with a national rate of 16 percent for residents of public housing. In fact, management is reluctant to initiate any eviction. According to Wendell Yee, eviction is the last recourse after every other measure has failed:

> I think it's appropriate when you've given every opportunity to a family or a person to turn their problems around. If it's housekeeping—you go in there and you find a complete disaster—you get HOU to go to the family or the person and say, look, let us assign a caseworker. We'll work with you. We'll get some outside agency help for you. But management will be inspecting this unit every month for the next six months.
>
> If you see no appreciable improvement or a lack of caring, then I think it becomes appropriate to make a move. Because you've got other people living next door that you've got to be concerned about— the infestation of roaches, the bad smells that emanate from those units. Or some people continually are late paying their rent. If after intervention by HOU and several private conferences with management to try to straighten this out, you cannot get this person to pay their rent on time, [eviction] becomes appropriate.

Dan Murray describes one such recent eviction case: "[The family] literally ruined the unit. The judge said, 'Fix the unit, give her a chance.' We fixed the unit. They ruined it again. We fixed it again. Told the judge. We went to court five times. The judge said to her, 'Next time you're going to go.' . . . She had a drinking and drug problem. She wasn't taking care of the kids. Then they bring in the friends—the boyfriends, the buddies—usually they're not a great class of individuals that enhances the property."

According to Murray, eviction is never something management wants to do; it is a long, messy, painful, expensive process. In fact, Wendell Yee, a tough-minded manager who has worked for years in CMJ's mixed-income communities, and who oversaw some of the most dangerous phases of restoring the enforcement of rules at Columbia Point, finds some evictions the most difficult part of his job: "The toughest thing, on a personal level, is to have to evict a family with a whole bunch of small children. Because they refused the help. They refused to make an attempt to turn their lives around. That's a very tough situation, to see a moving company come in and take people's personal belongings with five, six, seven small children. Where are they going to go? People say management has to have a cold heart. We don't all have cold hearts. It's a very difficult and very traumatic thing to see that happen. But it has to be done." The consolation, Yee says, is that these evictions may serve as a warning to others in the community: "The end result is that usually the message gets out and people who were hesitant on starting to turn their lives around, maybe that will wake them up. Not to say we use that as an example, but it becomes an example."

The issue of eviction can raise tensions not only between the task force and the community but also between the members of the tenant-developer partnership. At Harbor Point, for example, when CMJ's interim management was working to prepare the remaining Columbia Point families for the new community, one of the major efforts was evicting residents who were known to be involved with drugs and other criminal and violent activity.

Management's attempt to evict one such individual involved in drugs and violence led to a serious test of the tenant-developer relationship. The lawyer for a tenant taken to court for eviction approached Wendell Yee, manager of Harbor Point at the time, saying that the tenant would be willing to move out and drop the case if he received three thousand dollars in "moving expenses." CMJ, aware of the multiple costs, social as well as financial, of having him in the community—from the criminal activity and ongoing nonpayment of rent to the accumulating legal fees and the impact of the protracted eviction proceedings on marketing—felt that three thousand dollars was a small price to pay for ridding the community of the individual.

Yee paid the "moving expenses," but did so without first securing the agreement of the task force. When the task force members dis-

Harbor Point residents gather in the future site of Old Harbor Park, 1988.

Left to right: Metropolitan District Commissioner Ilyas Bhatti, former governor Michael Dukakis, and Kitty Dukakis at the formal dedication of Old Harbor Park, 1992.

Left to right: Joe Corcoran, Etta Johnson, and Father George Carrigg of St. Christopher's Church at the formal dedication of Old Harbor Park, 1992.

Photos courtesy of Corcoran, Mullins, Jennison.

covered what had happened, they were furious. From their point of view, the payment amounted to rewarding one of their residents for his own bad behavior—unacceptable no matter what the extenuating reasons. Moreover, the payment had been made by the developer without the tenants' say-so—in the task force's opinion, a serious violation of the tenant-developer partnership.

The task force demanded that Wendell Yee be removed as manager of Harbor Point. "I thought Wendell did the right thing from his point of view," Joe Corcoran explains, "but he had a partner. He ignored the partner, so I couldn't defend him, and as a consequence he was taken off the site." However sensible from the developer's point of view the three-thousand-dollar investment to get a bad apple out of the barrel, to the tenants it was intolerable. In the interests of the partnership, Yee had to leave Harbor Point, even though he was, in Corcoran's words, "an ace manager." The incident demonstrated the importance and the power of the tenant task force. "Two years earlier," Corcoran says, "they never would have had the guts to [demand that he be fired]—because they weren't empowered at that point in time. But now they saw the process, and they knew they were a 50 percent partner." As it turned out, Yee was too effective in his job to be cut off completely. CMJ had to reinstate him in a new position and promise he would no longer be on-site, though the new manager of Harbor Point would still report to him—an arrangement to which the task force agreed.

The partnership has weathered disagreements—some of them minor, a few major—over the years. Jaundoo explains that the partnership between CMJ and the task force hasn't been "all peaches and cream." "We have our amount of disagreements," she says, "but I think we all come to an understanding of what's best for the community":

> It's not "this is what we think is best" and "this is what they think is best." Our partners are business people. We understand that. And I think they understand that we're residents. And we've got a better view of what we think is needed here. They can look at it from a business perspective, but we don't want to put them in a place, either, where they're going to go down the drain financially because of something that we do. So we have to look at the whole picture and say, "How beneficial is this to the community at large," and then come to some sort of compromise.

A recent example of "coming to a compromise" was over the issue of carpets. In effect, as Jaundoo saw it, a double standard had devel-

Old Harbor Park

Old Harbor Park, a six-and-a-half-acre stretch of Metropolitan District Commission (MDC) park land that runs along the edge of Dorchester Bay at Harbor Point, was dedicated in 1992. The park is used by community residents as well as joggers, cyclists, and walkers—all those drawn to the water's edge for recreation or simply to sit on one of many benches along the park's perimeter and stare at the sea.

Julia O'Brien, the MDC's chief planner, explains that a small park built with federal funds had once stood at the far edge of Columbia Point. Federal regulations governing existing parks, coupled with state waterfront licensing regulations, mandated construction of the new park as a condition for the redevelopment of the former public housing project. To facilitate this, the Boston Housing Authority transferred the land to the MDC, which supervised the park's design and construction. Harbor Point's management company is responsible for maintaining the park's landscaping and keeping it clean. O'Brien says the park is important to Harbor Point and the larger community as well: "It's a critical link in terms of our continuing waterfront, especially the eight miles of unparalleled urban waterfront from Castle Island in South Boston to the Neponset River. It reconnects Dorchester with the shoreline, from which it had been badly cut off by the Southeast Expressway."

CMJ's Wendell Yee in a
1997 photo. *Courtesy of
Corcoran, Mullins,
Jennison.*

oped for market-rate and subsidized residents. Each year, some three hundred units turn over at Harbor Point, most of them market-rate, and worn or damaged rugs are replaced before these units are re-rented. Meanwhile, the people who have been living in the subsidized units, some for as many as ten years, still have their original carpets. When the Massachusetts Housing Finance Agency refused to approve the expense of new rugs for the subsidized units because it had not been budgeted, Jaundoo called them on the carpet: "One of the things that really annoyed me about that is that families have a yearly inspection, and a lot of times they were marked poorly because of their rugs. I mean, come on. You have kids. Rugs are not going to last forever. You're not getting the best grade of rugs in the first place, let's face it. In the last two years you just had to yell and scream and say, hey, listen. People are going to have to have new rugs. Because I was on the verge of telling folks, hold your rent."

"Ruby understands the injustice," says Harbor Point manager Miles Byrne. "She knows that it's been ten years that none of her low-income residents have had their rugs replaced." After months of wrangling with the MHFA to approve spending the $285,000 it would cost to replace 171 rugs, suddenly approval came through. "Within a week," Byrne continues, "I got a call from Dan Murray saying we're going to start the rug replacement. Bang, the money shows up. That's power. And Ruby doesn't even know it; she's the worst in recognizing what her contribution is. She was this gift that we all got. Where do you get people like this?"

Over the many years Dave Connelly has worked at Columbia Point and Harbor Point, he has developed close relationships with many residents. When Connelly sees Harbor Point today, he—like everyone who lived or worked in both the old and the new community—is struck by memories of the old days. "They're vivid memories for me," Connelly says. He remembers taking Columbia Point residents home after going out for a beer at the end of the day and being struck by the differences between them: "Once in a while, I used to walk Ruby home when she was right over by [where the Bayside Exposition Center is today]—when it was a place that, you know, you'd try to walk her home. I always waited until she got in the front door, and in the beginning, I used to wait until she waved. They just risked a lot."

Dave Connelly knows that there is an unspoken dividing line between him and the people who lived at Columbia Point and live at

Harbor Point today. Although the friendships he has formed with these residents are close, he says, he is often reminded of the differences between them. The residents of Columbia Point who stayed and fought for the new community took a risk that no one else can really understand. Dave Connelly still drives away at the end of the day, but he feels very different leaving his Harbor Point friends behind: "When they walk down to their new place, it also strikes me that it's terrific now when I'm leaving them at night that they're walking to a great apartment that they're happy about. Years ago when I left them they were going into that crap of having to walk around the people who were sitting and drinking on their front steps and the hallways. It's changed so much and they really deserve it and they feel good about it."

Ten years after the opening of Harbor Point, the task force members do feel good about it. But their work isn't done. "Some folks haven't got their rugs changed yet," Jaundoo says. "I'm trying to tell them to be patient."

28 Lessons from Harbor Point

In the very beginning, after Harbor Point was up and after all the construction was done and the trees were planted, I would come outside and, honest to God, I would have to close my eyes and shake my head and look around and say, "Is this really for real?" Sort of like night and day.

—*Ruby Jaundoo*

The community that was christened on a cold January day in 1987 is now more than ten years old. People who used to live in Columbia Point still walk around in their new community with a strong sense of the past. Harbor Point is completely different from Columbia Point—"like night and day"—yet this strikingly different community is in exactly the same place, with many of the same buildings and many of the same people. Harbor Point residents who used to live in Columbia Point will sometimes give one another directions by saying, "Well, you know where 40 Montpelier used to be?" The physical and personal memory of the project is literally right beneath the surface.

The promise of a new community came true. Today Harbor Point is virtually 100 percent occupied. So, too, the promise of mixing residents of different incomes, even though the mix is difficult to categorize. Although approximately two-thirds of the units are market-rate and one-third are subsidized, the actual number of residents is more evenly distributed because the subsidized households

tend to be larger; 57 percent of the twenty-nine hundred residents at Harbor Point are market-rate, and 43 percent of the residents are subsidized. The overall racial mix of market-rate tenants is also more evenly distributed than would be found in similar apartment complexes in Boston. At Harbor Point, 54 percent of the market-rate tenants are white and 46 percent are minority. But the majority of residents (63 percent) as well as the majority of subsidized residents (85 percent) are minority. This in a city whose population is 63 percent white and 37 percent minority.

In addition, subsidized residents tend to stay at Harbor Point far longer than market-rate residents. In 1993, for example, the rate of turnover for low-income residents was just 7 percent, while the turnover rate for market-rate residents was 47 percent. In 1998, the most recent year figures were available, there was still a difference: the turnover rate was 8 percent for low-income residents and 43 percent for market-rate residents.

"Your market renters, they come and they go," Ruby Jaundoo observes. "Subsidized families are here for the long haul." Yet Harbor Point's turnover rate for market-rate residents, while far higher than that of its low-income residents, is not any higher than the average turnover rate for market renters in the Boston metropolitan area. And some market-rate residents have lived at Harbor Point for as long as nine years.

After ten years, the developers and the task force are fundamentally pleased with the new community. It is beautiful, well managed, and on firm financial footing. Joe Corcoran says it took about five years for King's Lynne to develop into a mature community. "Harbor Point might take another five," he says, because it's three times as large and has some social issues that will take longer to work out. "I really like Harbor Point," Ruby Jaundoo says. "And I think it works well. . . . What makes any community work is good management. Even if we had 1,283 subsidized units, the only thing that's going to make that work is good management."

The issues that come up in the community these days are mostly minor. A meeting of the task force in June 1998 offers a snapshot. The representative of security was not at the meeting to give his report because the security force was playing baseball at the time. Issues raised under "new business" included teenagers using bad language at a sports event; a broken spotlight still waiting to be fixed; security officers staying in their cars instead of walking through the community; an elderly woman claiming that a neighbor was practicing voodoo on her; twelve kittens found on the property; a trash chute backed up; central air conditioning not working in several units.

One task force member suggested that the practice of making visits to inspect the apartments of prospective low-income residents was unfair, since such visits were not made to prospective market-rate residents as well. (Under HUD guidelines, such inspections of

Ruby Jaundoo, 1998. *Roger Farrington.*

prospective low-income units are advised. Prospective market-rate tenants are subject to screening in the form of a credit check. If a market-rate tenant has no credit history, the lease must be co-signed by someone who does.) Another member reported that a rumor, completely unfounded, was circulating that CMJ had invested thousands of dollars in the newly opened sub shop and, as a result, everyone's rents would be going up.

The issue that received most discussion had to do with the security of the buildings. A member noted that some residents discovered that their individual keys could also open the building's emergency exit doors. Ruby Jaundoo, quiet throughout most of the meeting, suddenly drew herself up and said, "That's not right." She declared flatly that the building's security had been compromised and the entire building needed to be rekeyed.

After ten years, Harbor Point is still a work in progress. While the people who have been most closely involved in Harbor Point from the planning stages right through to the present day are pleased with their community, they are not complacent. "I'm not trying to say that everything's all milk and honey now," Jaundoo cautions.

SUPPORTING HARBOR POINT'S CHILDREN

At the top of Joe Corcoran's wish list for Harbor Point is a stronger program of activities for children and teenagers. He feels that there are too many kids and not enough services. He would like to see the Harbor Point kids do better in school, noting that they had the lowest reading scores in the state when CMJ first took over Columbia Point. The legacy of court-ordered busing, which ripped into the Columbia Point community in the 1970s, remains at Harbor Point: only 25 percent of the children are able to attend the schools that are right across the street—the Dever elementary school and the McCormack middle school. Some attend the Harbor School, a "pilot" public school that opened at Harbor Point in 1998, based on "expeditionary learning" and using the harbor islands as its laboratory. The rest of them are bused to schools across the city.

Like Joe Corcoran, Ruby Jaundoo's number one concern is the children. Although Harbor Point "is a great place for kids to grow up," she claims, "you've got teenagers here just like anyplace else. They got fresh mouths, they get into mischief, and they can be intimidating to some folk." There are still remnants of a gang at Harbor Point—the CPD gang, short for "Columbia Point Dogs"—named, interestingly, after the public housing project. The gang is nothing like the Columbia Point gangs of the late 1970s and early 1980s; when gang graffiti appears on Harbor Point buildings, management sees to it that it is cleaned off immediately.

"The main problem I find for younger kids is that there aren't enough recreation programs," Jaundoo says. "We've got the courtyards with the green space and that's it." Miles Byrne concurs: "We don't have enough things for all our kids." Although the programs the community provides look good on paper, Byrne argues, they don't reach enough of Harbor Point's children: "We've got twenty kids at the health center, we've got another ten who filter into the computer center, we've got fifty going to the youth center. What about the other kids? They're just wandering this property or they're shut into the home. And they're not fulfilling the full promise of Harbor Point." To begin to address this, Harbor Point recently asked the Boston YMCA to oversee an exercise program and to organize a basketball league for girls and boys. The league will depend on adult volunteers from Harbor Point to work as coaches and counselors, just as the teams of an earlier generation of residents did.

THE NEXT GENERATION OF LEADERS

Harbor Point is built on the extraordinary determination of the developers and a core group of Columbia Point tenants. Both sides were driven by a mission that bordered on obsession: to make Columbia Point a decent place to live. The faces around the table at a task force meeting today—Etta Johnson, Esther Santos, Betty Quarles, Ruby Jaundoo—are the same people who have been working in some cases for more than thirty years. They knew Columbia Point, they know how much has changed, and they know how hardwon the new community is. What will happen when the next generation of leadership comes along—people who never knew what Columbia Point was like?

"It's one of my biggest fears," Jaundoo says, "if the board was run by someone that didn't know the history. Will the interest still be the same? Will the focus be on the children? Every bit of money that we can generate and get our hands on through a grant, donations, or whatever goes into youth activities. Because I say that the youth of Harbor Point are either going to make it or they're going to break it."

Myles Byrnes, 1998.
Roger Farrington.

Ruby Jaundoo, Esther Santos, Betty Quarles, and Etta Johnson were all young mothers when they joined the task force back in the days of Columbia Point, trying to raise good families and make their community a decent place for their children to grow up. It has been difficult to get a new generation of young mothers involved in the task force. "You can always get people together in a crisis," Jaundoo says, "but as long as things are going fine, people don't want to be bothered."

Ironically, it is the task force's gift to the residents of Harbor Point that the new people take their community for granted. The new residents didn't have to fight tooth and nail for it; those who went before did it for them. But Harbor Point also has to be protected. "It took a lot of people a lot of years to make Harbor Point a reality," Jaundoo says, "and some of those same people continue to do the same thing, every day." They're not fighting anymore, she explains, but they are still "monitoring":

> Management has to be sort of monitored, too, to make sure that they're doing things correctly. One of the biggest things I say to management is, you make your job much easier if you don't bend the rules for anyone and everybody's treated the same. You don't have to go back and think about what did I do for Miss Jones, and later I have to do it for Miss Brown. You don't do anything for either one of them. You just follow the rules and the regulations and your life will be much easier.

Jaundoo remembers what it took for her to decide to join the task force back in the days of Columbia Point: "I think it was kind of like I said, 'Hey, I've lived here x amount of years, and if I'm going to continue to live here, I've got to get up off of my butt and start working.' I remember looking out my window and seeing Miss Santos going to a meeting, and saying, 'Hey, I wonder where she's going?' You've got to become a part of the solution."

With that look out the window, Ruby Jaundoo took her place in a long line of people, mostly women, who have graced the community from 1954 to today: Pat McCluskey, Erline Shearer, Anna McDonald; Joanne Ross, Sandy Young, Miriam Manning, Ruth Morrison; Esther Santos, Roger Taylor, Terry Mair, Betty Quarles, Etta Johnson. These people were and are the backbone of the community—smart, resourceful, humane, determined. They insisted on their basic right to a decent place to live. Who will continue to protect the interests of the low-income residents—people whose interests are by nature always in jeopardy? The next generation of leaders has yet to come forward.

BUILDING COMMUNITY ON THE PENINSULA

Harbor Point still faces the challenge it has had ever since Columbia Point opened in 1954: isolation. Developing additional housing on the peninsula—an idea Ed Logue first talked about in the 1960s—would be a sure way to build more of a community, but there is little available land left for doing so. Because there is no residential neighborhood within two miles, Harbor Point has to create an entire community within its walls. Simple things make that difficult: for example, kids from the Colonel Marr Boys and Girls Club on Dorchester Avenue near Savin Hill come out for free swims with the Harbor Point kids, but these events are planned and structured, not natural and spontaneous. There are a small convenience store and a sandwich shop at Harbor Point, but they have a difficult time sustaining themselves in a community of only three thousand people, even moreso since a new Star Market opened near the UMass/JFK T stop.

Harbor Point's isolation is in some respects beneficial, especially when the community is basically strong, as it was in 1954 and is again. Today it is one of the safest places to live in the Boston area. However, as Hubert E. "Hubie" Jones, assistant to the chancellor for urban affairs at UMass Boston, points out, "Any peninsula is generally isolated from the mainstream, the mainstream of the city and of other neighborhoods. [The Columbia Point peninsula] is not really visible. We're not in the line of vision of most of the leadership in this town."

Gary Jennison and Joe Mullins, 1998. *Roger Farrington.*

It is not that Harbor Point's neighbors lack clout. In fact, some are among the most powerful institutions in the city. It is more that they lack cohesion and common cause. There have been ongoing discussions at Columbia Point Associates—an eight-year-old "neighborhood" group whose past and present members include UMass Boston, BankBoston, the John F. Kennedy Library, Boston College High School, the *Boston Globe*, St. Christopher's Church, Corcoran Jennison Companies, the Massachusetts Archives, the Star Market, and the Geiger-Gibson Health Center, among others—about building more sense of community on the peninsula. CPA's focus reflects a membership that is primarily corporate and institutional, and the group finds itself still grappling with questions of image, safety, and public perception that linger long after the demise of the public housing project.

Although Harbor Point and some of these neighbors have grown up side by side, each, in effect, bolstered by the other's presence, their perspectives are sometimes quite different. When the liquor store at the Star Market announced that it would be named Harbor Point Liquors, some members of the tenant task force worried about negative associations; some other CPA members marked the name change as a coming of age for the community that would put these associations to rest. When a proposal was put forward that individual CPA members use "Columbia Point" on letterhead to strengthen the community's image, there was healthy debate, with some longtime CPA members in opposition and some newer members favoring adoption as a way of restoring the peninsula's historic geographic designation to pre–housing project neutrality. Ultimately, the proposal failed for lack of support.

Brian Toomey, director of the Geiger-Gibson Health Center and current chair of Columbia Point Associates, told members at a recent meeting that he has had difficulty expanding the client base at the health center because of the facility's location on Mount Vernon Street between the Bayside Exposition Center and Harbor Point. "Some people are still wary about coming here. They worry about what's 'down there,'" he says, waving his arm in the direction of the street. He also expressed concern that individual CPA members, for the most part, remain isolated from one another, businesses and institutions unto themselves with little or no interaction. Toomey and other members of the group would like to promote more lively activity "down there" that would lead to more cross-fertilization and cohesion. CPA is hopeful that UMass Boston's eventual plans for the pumping station, which it acquired in 1999 from the Boston Water and Sewer Commission in exchange for scholarships for Boston students, will include venues such as a restaurant and community meeting space where people can meet and rub shoulders.

In addition, the College of Public and Community Service at UMass Boston conducted a study and made a series of recommendations to the Chancellor's Office that would strengthen relationships among the Columbia Point peninsula's neighbors. The proposals include a range of activities from promoting two annual events on the peninsula to designing an integrated community calendar and to

April Young and Dave Connelly, 1998. *Roger Farrington.*

Esther Santos and Joan Goody at Harbor Point's tenth anniversary celebration, 1998. *Roger Farrington.*

opening the university's library, athletic, and computer resources to Harbor Point residents with a simple card system.

Hubie Jones believes that Harbor Point's success as a mixed-income community has important implications for the broader community as well. He recalls the lack of what he calls "social viability" and the threat of violence that hung over Columbia Point the day that he campaigned there as a black man challenging Louise Day Hicks for her congressional seat more than twenty-five years ago. "The social isolation of classes and races has been America's Achilles' heel," he says, adding that Harbor Point demonstrates that people from different classes and of different races can live side by side, more or less harmoniously. "We need more examples to prove this can work, but that is the ultimate benefit of Harbor Point and of its transformation."

Father George Carrigg and April Young, 1998. *Roger Farrington.*

HOME OWNERSHIP AT HARBOR POINT

Joe Corcoran would eventually like to introduce home ownership at Harbor Point in the form of mixed-income cooperatives. He would like to see market renters stay longer and put down more roots in the community. "We've had some great market-rate people," he explains. "A couple of them have been elected president of the task force. Then all of a sudden, they're gone. They get married or they can buy a house and they're gone. . . . It's tough on continuity. The task force members almost get a little cynical now when they see a real hard-charging market-rate person come in." They know that, before long, he or she will most likely move on. "If they owned an equity piece," he says, "they might stay longer."

Corcoran would like to see the ownership option extended as well to the low-income residents, who could use their Section 8 certificates to pay their cooperative rent, own shares, and gradually build up equity. Models for such cooperative ownership are in place at the reconstruction of the Ellen Wilson project in Washington, D.C., where Corcoran Jennison is building, marketing, and managing a HOPE VI project for a neighborhood Community Development Corporation. The task force is supportive of the idea, but it will require the support of lenders and investors as well.

AFFORDABLE HOUSING IN AMERICA

Affordable housing costs money—a price we as a nation seem unwilling to pay—and the need for affordable housing is growing year by year. In June 1998 the Center on Budget and Policy Priorities in Washington, D.C., reported that, in 1995, 10.5 million families

Henry Cisneros, former
secretary of the U.S.
Department of Housing
and Urban Development,
touring Harbor Point with
Ruby Jaundoo (left) and
Betty Quarles (right), 1998.
*Courtesy of Corcoran,
Mullins, Jennison.*

needed affordable apartments, but only 6.1 million units were available—a shortage of 4.4 million units. Although the Department of Housing and Urban Development recommends that a family should not pay more than 30 percent of its income for housing, in April 1998 HUD reported that 5.3 million low-income households were paying more than 50 percent of their incomes for rent.

Rachel Bratt, a professor at Tufts University and chair of the Department of Urban and Environmental Policy, maintains that the problem has been exacerbated by welfare reform. As people leave the welfare rolls and move into jobs, many of them earning the minimum wage, housing costs are eating up 50 percent or more of their income. According to Bratt's July 2, 1998, article in the *Boston Globe*, the numbers simply don't add up: in 1998, at the minimum wage in Massachusetts of $5.25 an hour, a person working forty hours a week, fifty-two weeks a year, earns $10,920 a year. Under HUD's guideline that a family shouldn't pay more than 30 percent of its income for housing, this person should pay no more than $273 per month for rent—hardly a realistic figure in view of dramatically escalating rents and housing prices in the greater Boston area and throughout most of the state.

While the federal welfare policy is designed to end subsidies and move people into wage-earning jobs, Bratt argues that the housing policy doesn't provide them with housing they can afford. According to the basic logic of economics, there are three possible remedies to the problem: raise wages, reduce rents, or produce more affordable housing. A fourth course—not logical, but prevalent nonetheless—is doing nothing while the gap widens.

Most people manage to find places for their families to sleep at night, and they will continue to do so. In the long run, however, the price we as a society pay for ignoring the lack of decent, affordable housing will undoubtedly be far greater than the price of addressing the problem directly.

A MODEL FOR AFFORDABLE HOUSING

Harbor Point is a model for one way of meeting some of this need— by reclaiming public housing projects and converting them into private, mixed-income communities. CMJ includes a few, simple elements in its mixed-income developments:

- The residents are co–general partners with the developer, with shared decision-making authority.
- All residents at the time of the development are guaranteed the right to move into the new development.
- The design and amenities offered are comparable to those offered in conventional market-rate developments.
- All units are built to the same design and specification standards, and low-income residents are mixed equally throughout the site. There is no distinction between low-income and market-rate residents.
- The location of the development is solid enough to attract mixed-income renters or owners.
- The development has strong professional management.
- An on-site, private social service program is in place to help families make the transition from public to private housing and to provide ongoing support.

Marty Jones, president of Corcoran Jennison Companies, points out that, while Harbor Point is a replicable model for mixed-income housing, the financial basis for such developments is constantly shifting: "People say you can't replicate Harbor Point because you don't have this or that [financial] program. Well, when we were doing housing twenty years ago we had different financial programs. It's important to draw that distinction. You can't replicate the finan-

Tanja Delgado Figueiredo, her husband, John, and children, 1998. *Roger Farrington*

Left to right: Mattie Burton, Dave Hanifin, and Martha Little, 1998. *Roger Farrington.*

Awards for Harbor Point

Harbor Point has won several major awards, including the Urban Land Institute's Award for Excellence in 1992, the Rudy Bruner Award for Excellence in the Urban Environment in 1993, and the International Real Estate Federation's Award for the Best Overall Project in 1996.

The citation for the Urban Land Institute Award reads, in part:

> Harbor Point is an outstanding example of a public/private partnership formed to address and solve a major urban problem. Creative site planning, attention to aesthetic details and tenant involvement have contributed to the successful physical and social transformation of a crime-ridden and destitute inner-city neighborhood. . . .
>
> Once the largest federal public housing project in New England, Harbor Point today is one of the country's most successful models of an economically and racially integrated urban neighborhood. Its physical and social transformation shows what can be accomplished when the public and private sectors, together with tenant organizations, work cooperatively to solve pressing urban problems.

The selection committee for the Rudy Bruner Award, made biannually by the Bruner Foundation to honor projects that transform cities, cited the following reasons for naming Harbor Point a 1993 winner:

> The selection committee was greatly impressed by the ability of Harbor Point to create an attractive community for both subsidized and market rate tenants. They praised the provision of construction jobs for people from the original Columbia Point and social services for current tenants. Most impressive, however, was the partnership between the developer and the tenants' group. Harbor Point would not have been created had it not been for the efforts of Columbia Point tenants. "They did a marvelous job and showed great tenacity"—and they continue to have a real voice in decisions and to share ownership in the project.

cial model—but you can find a formula if everyone involved has the will to do so."

Some critics argue that, although Harbor Point is a success, it costs too much to be a model for affordable housing. That cost may have been justified in this particular case, they argue, because a solution had to be found to the disaster Columbia Point had become. However, it is too expensive to be a sensible model for replication elsewhere. Moreover, they argue, Harbor Point represents a loss of eleven hundred low-income units. While Columbia Point had fifteen hundred low-income units, Harbor Point has only four hundred—a significant loss, especially at a time when low-income units are sorely needed.

On the contrary, Marty Jones argues, four hundred high-quality, low-income units were *gained* at Harbor Point, with a long-term guarantee through the ground lease. "There will never be and there would never have been fifteen hundred low-income units put back on that site," she says. "Practically speaking, that would just never have happened":

> It's the academic argument versus the reality: If all the low-income people had said, "We're not going to do anything unless they get fifteen hundred low-income units on this site," it would still be sitting there as public housing. It probably would be abandoned. And once it was abandoned, then what would have happened?
>
> There were an awful lot of people during the process who said we should have sold it off and made it high-end condominiums and made more money. There was always that pressure. So then what would have happened? Then where would they have built four hundred units of low-income housing in Boston? Not on a site as good as this.

Joe Corcoran points out that Harbor Point was no more costly than other affordable housing developments being built at the same time. A comparative financial analysis of three such developments in Boston, undertaken by Harbor Point, found that the cost per unit at Harbor Point was, in fact, slightly less than at the other two. Harbor Point cost $144,523 per unit, while the Boston Housing Authority's West Broadway or D Street in South Boston cost $145,263 per unit and Tent City, developed by a nonprofit housing organization for a local community development corporation, cost $154,673 per unit.

Corcoran points out another difference between Harbor Point and the BHA's rehabilitated West Broadway project. Of West Broadway, he says, "It's still public housing; it still looks and acts like public housing." Unlike public housing, Harbor Point pays $890,000 a year in real estate taxes to the city, picks up its own trash, plows its

own streets, has its own security force, and generates more than $400 per year per low-income unit to provide on-site social services. Most important, Corcoran says, Harbor Point repays its loans in full:

> When we build a unit, we get a loan, just like a person who buys a house, and we start paying it off. We borrow the money, in this case, from the Massachusetts Housing Finance Agency, we pay 7¾ percent interest, we pay it back every month, and at the end of forty years, it will be completely paid. This costs the federal and state governments nothing, and the city has a net gain because we pay for all our own services.
>
> Some would argue that government should reclaim public housing's good market sites, reap the profits from sale of these properties, and build affordable housing for the poor in less desirable parts of the city. That's exactly what brought us Columbia Point in the first place. Don't segregate the poor; integrate them, and maybe the next generation will not be poor.

HOPE FOR THE FUTURE

At the time that Joe Corcoran, Joe Mullins, and Gary Jennison walked into Columbia Point in 1978, no one had found a way to take a major federal public housing project—one that over many years had deteriorated so thoroughly—and transform it into a livable

At Harbor Point there is no distinction between market-rate and low-income residents. The waterfront location is an amenity for all. *Courtesy of George J. Riley.*

Project Data for Harbor Point
Compiled by the Urban Land Institute

Land Use Information

Site area	1,952,047 square feet, or 44.8 acres
Gross building area before renovation	1,100,000 square feet
Gross building area after renovation	1,703,975 square feet
Residential	1,652,751 square feet
Retail	5,093 square feet
Health Center	12,000 square feet
Community Building and Clubhouse	34,131 square feet
Residential units before renovation	1,500
Residential units after renovation	1,283
New low-rise units	214
New mid-rise units	760
Residential rehabilitation	309
Gross density	28.6 units/acre

Land Use Plan

Buildings	10 acres, or 22 percent of the site
Driveways and parking	15 acres, or 33 percent of the site
Landscaped and recreational areas	20 acres, or 45 percent of the site

Development Costs

Demolition	$ 5,850,000
Building construction	106,850,000
Site work/landscaping	12,740,000
Earthwork/piles	7,900,000
General conditions/ bonds	9,535,000
Surveys, permits, testing	3,155,000
Architecture, engineering	5,350,000
Construction interest	29,655,000
Taxes/insurance	1,490,000
Financing fees	2,065,000
Legal/title	2,050,000
Relocation/social services	3,495,000
Marketing	2,340,000
Operating reserve account	57,525,000
Total	**$250,000,000**

Financing

MHFA co-insured loan	$121,000,000
MHFA supplemental loan	30,000,000
Urban Initiatives Loan	9,000,000
UDAG loan	12,000,000
State Chapter 884 grant	3,000,000
Investor equity	75,000,000
Total	**$250,000,000**

Left to right: April Young, Wendell Yee, Mattie Burton, Conrad Pineault, Betty Quarles, Don Willis, Ruby Jaundoo, and Dave Connelly, 1998. *Roger Farrington.*

community. In fact, some of the most reasonable voices were saying that wholesale demolition of failed public housing projects and relocation of tenants were the only recourse.

In 1992 public housing projects in major cities across the country were deteriorating just as Columbia Point had more than a decade earlier, and the federal government was stymied in its efforts to solve the worsening problem. The HOPE VI housing program, inspired in part by the success of Harbor Point, was created by legislation passed by Congress in October 1992. HOPE VI was "a last gasp for public housing," according to Henry Cisneros, who succeeded Jack Kemp as secretary of the Department of Housing and Urban Development in 1993. The public housing program "would otherwise probably be eliminated entirely and transitioned to some kind of home ownership strategy. All the signs pointed to the demise of public housing as we know it," Cisneros says.

The purpose of HOPE VI was not to expand the supply of affordable housing but to clean up the existing mess of deteriorated public housing projects, making them assets to rather than blights on the community. Cisneros explains the goals of HOPE VI:

> It was the first attempt ever to put the requisite amounts of money into major public housing developments—up to $50 million for each development that was selected—so that they could be completely refurbished. It required a great leap of faith, because it's very difficult to imagine from the hulks of buildings—vacant, deteriorated, crime-ridden—that they could be transformed into quality housing. But the purpose of HOPE VI was to provide enough money to make that transformation in public housing developments across the country. The intent of HOPE VI was to do twelve to fifteen projects a year, indefinitely into the future—and to do them right.

Congress made sure that HOPE VI wouldn't fail for lack of funding. If it failed, Cisneros explains, it would show the nation that even the best efforts to save public housing were futile: "The dominant mood [in Congress] was that this was the very last hope, the last moment, the last chance, for public housing. And frankly, HOPE

1999 *Columbia Point Peninsula Demographics*

Tens of thousands of people travel to and from the Columbia Point peninsula annually. More than 1.2 million attend events, trade shows, and exhibits at the Bayside Exposition Center, including 150,000 for the annual Flower Show. The number of students at UMass Boston exceeds 12,000, the number of visitors to the Massachusetts Archives exceeds 13,000, and the number of visitors to the Kennedy Library exceeds 250,000. The businesses, schools, and institutions on the Columbia Point peninsula include the following:

- BankBoston (until 1999)
- Bayside Exposition Center
- Boston College High School
- The Boston Globe
- The Boston Teachers' Union Health and Welfare Fund
- Club Hotel by Doubletree at Bayside
- Corcoran Jennison Companies (which includes CMJ)
- The Walter Denney Youth Center
- The Paul A. Dever School
- Geiger-Gibson Community Health Center
- Greater Media (WMJX, WROR, WKLB, WBOS, and WSJZ radio)
- Harbor Point Apartment Community
- The Harbor School
- John F. Kennedy Library and Museum
- Massachusetts Archives and Museum
- The John W. McCormack Middle School
- St. Christopher's Church
- Standard Uniform
- Star Market
- UMass Boston
- WB56

VI was passed by the Congress in 1992 as a last-gasp measure. If HOPE VI failed, I don't know where else we would go with public housing. There was no other strategy—other than to demolish it and disperse the people."

According to Cisneros, Harbor Point was the model for what he hoped to accomplish with the HOPE VI program. "When I took office in 1993," he says, "there was no better example in the country of what was possible, of literally going from worst to first, than Harbor Point." While the members of Congress—and the American people they represented—saw a public housing program that was an ever-worsening national disaster, and wholesale demolition of the projects and relocation of their tenants were contemplated as the only recourse, Cisneros looked to Harbor Point.

When Cisneros visited Harbor Point that year, walking around outside, visiting apartments, meeting with families, and talking with managers, he says, "It was everything that I had heard. I saw the pictures of what was there before and what was there after. It took tremendous vision to have been able to make the transformation."

"Harbor Point taught us," Cisneros says,

that these can be made livable places. Harbor Point proved that with intelligent, private-sector management, with expertise of the kind CMJ brought, with an architectural scheme and design plan that would utilize the land area wisely, and with a dramatic remake instead of just tinkering at the edges—including the social component of mixing incomes and supporting work and creating recreational opportunities and expecting the families to take care of the property and helping them understand how to do that—with that total mix, a truly dramatic and wholesale change, that subsidized housing could be made to serve its original purpose.

Harbor Point, Cisneros says, "was the pioneer, the trailblazer. It gave us confidence. The model that Harbor Point represents," Cisneros says, "is immensely hopeful. It shows the way. One just needs to look at Atlanta, St. Louis, New Orleans, Chicago, Washington, L.A., Pittsburgh, Dallas, Seattle, Baltimore, to see what HOPE VI has meant and what can be done. It is very profound: when you take an area that was once filled with mega-structures and abandonment and decline and crime, and convert that into viable, attractive places where people can live, it is a huge turnaround for a neighborhood and a city." Moreover, Cisneros says, improving housing has "almost immeasurable" benefits. Better housing gives new life to neighborhoods, even cities, on the brink of hopelessness. "Some of

Left to right: Esther
Santos, Martha Little,
Betty Quarles, Linda
Wade, Mattie Burton,
Terry Mair, Etta Johnson,
and Ruby Jaundoo, 1998.
Roger Farrington.

these areas were absorbers of community energy, destroyers of community energy," Cisneros says. "Now they've not only been brought to neutral, but actually converted into positive assets."

Since 1993 an average of $500 million a year has been appropriated for HOPE VI grants each year, including $550 million for 1998 and $625 million for 1999. The entire HUD budget for assisted housing is expected to grow from $28.8 billion in 1998 to $33.2 billion in 2002, according to the National Low Income Housing Coalition. In contrast, the tax expenditure for mortgage interest and property tax deductions—which is viewed as a form of housing subsidy for middle- and upper-income homeowners—is projected to be more than twice as great. In 1998 those tax expenditures—or revenue losses to the federal government due to provisions of the tax law—amounted to $51.2 billion for the mortgage interest deduction and $17.7 billion for the local property tax deduction. These tax expenditures are projected to be stable through 2002, with increases in the mortgage interest and property tax deductions expected to be offset by declines in capital gains exemptions.

If there is a strong argument for continuing the mortgage interest and property tax deductions because they encourage home ownership, there is an equally strong argument for assisted housing outlays that turn around desperate public housing projects, create stable, mixed-income communities, and improve conditions for low-income Americans. Even though the economy is strong, the need for affordable housing is acute and worsening, but housing is not high on the national agenda. "Housing has always been a hard issue to mobilize people for," Marty Jones observes, "because there are so many people in need. That was President Reagan's rationale for killing the [national housing] program: 'Since you can't serve everybody, you shouldn't serve anybody.'"

Moreover, balancing the promise of HOPE VI is the practical reality of implementing its vision. Joe Corcoran argues that for HOPE VI to succeed, the roles of housing authorities and developers must be clearly and separately defined. "The housing authorities should become asset managers," he says, "and do a good job of selecting developers. My fear is that many of the HOPE VI projects will end up being controlled by the housing authorities and end up being another version of public housing. . . . I have a very strong opinion that unless HUD forces the troubled housing authorities to let go, HOPE VI, in those cases, could end up like the public housing projects they are supposed to replace." Corcoran insists that property management, too, should be private. Housing authorities should get out of the business of day-to-day operation of housing projects—a job for which they have established a long track record of failure. Instead, their job should be selecting and monitoring the best private developers and managers in the housing industry while obtaining additional funds for meeting low-income needs in their communities.

This idea is subject to debate among housing advocates and policy makers, as is a 1998 law that would force housing authorities to open more than half of all public housing units to middle-income tenants in an effort to reduce concentrations of poverty and create more of an income mix among residents. In a sense, this new law brings public housing full circle, back to the time when public housing projects like Columbia Point provided housing for the working poor. But some contend that it will be difficult to attract middle-income families to public housing, while others argue that the new plan, by providing apartments to higher-income persons, will only exacerbate the housing shortage for those who are most in need.

Joe Corcoran sees no reason why housing for the poor should be poor housing. His position is simple but radical: more affordable housing should be built and maintained to exactly the same standards as market-rate housing. In fact, there should be absolutely no distinction between the two. Since the beginning of the public housing program, housing for the poor has been separate and inferior. Corcoran believes it should be mixed and equal. Does the country agree? Are we willing to pay the price?

Epilogue

In September 1998 Harbor Point celebrated its tenth birthday on a glorious, late-summer Saturday, with the sun gleaming on the bay, sailboats bobbing at anchor, and a mild offshore breeze carrying the fresh smell of sea. The event had the feel of a family reunion, with the people who built the community gathering in a small but festive celebration in the clubhouse. Architect Joan Goody arrived pushing her granddaughter in a stroller. Corcoran Jennison president Marty Jones presented a plaque—proudly held aloft by her young daughter—engraved with the names of Harbor Point residents who had been members of the task force for five years or more. Wendell Yee reminisced about the 140 junked and burned-out cars his team had hauled out of Columbia Point when CMJ first took over. April Young caught up with her old friends from the task force, Ruby Jaundoo, Esther Santos, Betty Quarles, and Etta Johnson. Dave Hanifin, sitting at a table with old friends from his building, said that although he loves his Victorian house, he feels "landlocked"—and has an attachment to Harbor Point unlike that for any other place he has lived. Joe Corcoran, in shirt sleeves, leaned against the wall, smiling.

After the clubhouse gathering, the celebration spilled out onto the mall. At three throws for a dollar, teenage boys lined up, eager to hit the bull's-eye and plunge manager Miles Byrne into the dunk tank. Ruby Jaundoo and Betty Quarles stood behind a long table, serving Chinese food to raise money for the youth center. Across the mall, Esther Santos sold raffle tickets and kids lined up to bounce in the Moonwalk. A group of older men played horseshoes at one end of the mall, while at the other end, a rock and roll band played music, and a group of women danced, long into the afternoon.

Chronology

1630 Puritan settlers land on Columbia Point, a site called "Mattaponnock" by native Americans. The peninsula is used as a calf pasture for the town of Dorchester until 1869, a year before Dorchester is annexed by the city of Boston.

1878 Mount Vernon Street, also known as the "Mile Road," is built.

1884 The pumping station opens at the end of the Mile Road.

1928 Old Colony Boulevard opens; it will be renamed Morrissey Boulevard in the 1950s.

1934 The National Housing Act creates the Federal Housing Administration.

1937 The United States Housing Act creates the United States Housing Authority for low-rent housing and slum clearance projects; the Boston Housing Authority is established.

1942 Camp McKay is built as a prisoner-of-war camp for Italian prisoners.

1946 Camp McKay is converted to public housing known as Columbia Village.

1950 Boston College High School moves from the South End to the Columbia Point peninsula.

1951 Mayor John B. Hynes presides over the groundbreaking ceremony for the 1,504-unit Columbia Point public housing project.

1954 The Columbia Point public housing project opens and the first families move in.

1957 The Paul E. Dever Elementary School and St. Christopher's Church are built on the Columbia Point peninsula.

1958 The *Boston Globe* moves from downtown Boston to Morrissey Boulevard, directly across the street from Boston College High School.

1959 The Southeast Expressway opens.

1959 John F. Collins is elected mayor in Boston, beating Senate President John E. Powers in the general election.

1962 Six-year-old Laura Ann Ewing is killed by a dump truck on Mount Vernon Street; Columbia Point residents mobilize. The city is finally forced to close its dump.

1962 Edward F. Logue is named administrator of the Boston Redevelopment Authority.

1963 President Lyndon B. Johnson declares "War on Poverty" on November 24, two days after the assassination of John F. Kennedy.

1965 The John W. McCormack Middle School is built.

1966 The Columbia Point Health Center opens; it is the first community health center in the country.

1966 Construction begins on the Bayside Mall.

1967 Kevin H. White is elected mayor, beating Louise Day Hicks in the general election.

1968 The trustees of the University of Massachusetts decide to locate its new Boston campus on the Columbia Point peninsula.

1968 The Massachusetts Housing Finance Agency (MHFA) is created to spur the development of low-income housing throughout the state.

1971 Construction of the University of Massachusetts at Boston begins on the peninsula.

1974 UMass Boston opens its new campus in January.

1974 Court-ordered busing—the school desegregation plan ordered by Federal District Court Judge W. Arthur Garrity—begins in September.

1975 Tenants in several public housing projects file suit against the Boston Housing Authority.

1976 The trustees of the John F. Kennedy Library announce that the presidential library, to be designed by architect I. M. Pei, will be located on the Columbia Point peninsula.

1976 Public housing tenants file a motion in Judge Paul F. Garrity's court to put the Boston Housing Authority into receivership.

1977 Judge Paul F. Garrity issues a consent decree specifying actions to be taken by the BHA to fulfill its statutory obligations to residents of the city's public housing projects.

1978 The Columbia Point Community Task Force (CPCTF) is formally incorporated to work with the Boston Housing Authority and the Boston Redevelopment Authority to decide how to spend a $10 million federal grant for improvements at the public housing project.

1979 The CPCTF, the BRA, and the BHA in February sign a redevelopment agreement calling for the complete overhaul of Columbia Point. The task force will participate as partners in the new development.

1979 Judge Garrity orders the BHA into receivership in July.

1979 The Kennedy Library is formally dedicated in October. President Jimmy Carter and a host of dignitaries join the Kennedy family on the Columbia Point peninsula for the ceremony.

1980 Judge Garrity names Lewis H. Spence, former director of the Somerville and Cambridge housing authorities, as receiver for the Boston Housing Authority in February.

1982 The Columbia Point Community Task Force, the Boston Redevelopment Authority, and the Boston Housing Authority jointly issue a Request for Proposals for the redevelopment of Columbia Point.

1983 Three development teams submit proposals in February.

1983 Corcoran, Mullins, Jennison and Columbia Associates receive tentative designation as Peninsula Partners, the new development team for Columbia Point in October. CMJ is named the managing partner.

1983 Raymond L. Flynn is elected mayor in November, beating Melvin King in the general election.

1984 The receivership of the Boston Housing Authority ends.

1984 Corcoran, Mullins, Jennison takes over the management of Columbia Point, initiating a major cleanup and intensive maintenance improvements.

1985 Some Columbia Point residents are temporarily relocated and selective demolition begins in July.

1985 The Massachusetts Archives opens in November.

1986 The Tax Reform Act threatens the financing package for Harbor Point, but a last-minute compromise brokered by Senator Edward M. Kennedy is signed into law in October.

1986 Construction of Harbor Point begins in December.

1987 The dedication of Harbor Point in January brings dignitaries to the Columbia Point peninsula to mark the occasion with tenants and developers.

1988 Residents move into the first of the new units at Harbor Point. The no-pets policy stirs controversy across the city.

1990 Construction of Harbor Point is completed.

1992 Old Harbor Park, the Metropolitan District Commission's new six-and-a-half-acre waterfront park, is dedicated.

1992 The U.S. Department of Housing and Urban Development initiates the HOPE VI program—based on the mixed-income model pioneered at Harbor Point—to revitalize severely distressed public housing.

1993 After President Clinton names Boston Mayor Ray Flynn as the U.S. ambassador to the Vatican, city council president Tom Menino takes over as acting mayor in July; Menino defeats state representative Jim Brett in the general election in November.

1998 Harbor Point achieves 99 percent occupancy and celebrates its tenth anniversary as a mixed-income community.

Bibliography

ARTICLES IN THE *BOSTON GLOBE*

"Affordable Housing Crunch Getting Worse, Study Finds." June 17, 1998.

Anand, Geeta. "The City's Landlord." April 6, 1997.

Ball, Joanne. "Receivership of BHA Set to End Today." October 18, 1984.

———. "Smiles of Hope for New Housing." Public service magazine. December 15, 1985.

"B.C. High Sues to Shut Dump at Columbia Point." April 27, 1962.

"Boy Nearly Dies in 10-Ft. Puddle." October 21, 1956.

Bratt, Rachel G. "A Crash Course in Welfare Reform." Op-ed page, July 2, 1998.

Campbell, Robert, and Peter Vanderwarker. "Harbor Point: A Sea Change." October 21, 1990.

Canellos, Peter S. "Formula Eludes Harbor Point." July 2, 1990.

"City, B.C. High Officials Urge Housing Project." May 1, 1950.

"Columbia Point Fete Starts 34-Store Center." May 18, 1965.

"Columbia Point Housing to Be Ready June 30." January 27, 1954.

"Columbia Tenants Protest Cold Rooms." February 1, 1951.

"Court Orders Dump Reopened at Calf Pasture." July 26, 1962.

Cowen, Peter. "Columbia Point: Can It Be Saved?" March 11, 1973.

———. "Columbia Point: Physical and Spiritual Isolation for the Poor." January 23, 1972.

———. "UMass: Dorchester Sees More Threat Than Hope in Anticipated Demand for Student Housing." July 30, 1972.

Cullen, John F. "Harbor View Masks Night Warfare by Columbia Point Gangs vs. Firemen." July 5, 1971.

"Denies Project Is Gang Breeder." March 26, 1954.

Dietz, Jean. "Columbia Point . . . and a Bold Idea." January 9, 1965.

Dotton, Thomas. "Mall That Should Have Flourished Encountered Inhospitable Environment." March 11, 1973.

"5 Trucks Run Blockade before Mothers Line Up." April 25, 1962.

"500 Sign Demand for Buses." December 29, 1963.

Flint, Anthony. "Rebuilding the City." *Boston Globe Magazine*, September 28, 1997.

Friedman, Elliot. "Public Housing Tenants Sue to Hold Rent, Want Repairs." April 17, 1968.

Frisby, Michael K. "$5M in Linkage Funding Gives Project Fresh Hope." October 3, 1986.

"Gallagher Denies Columbia Point Will Lack Recreational Facilities." March 7, 1954.

"Gate Swings Shut on Dump." February 6, 1963.

"Globe Magazine Symposium." Public service magazine. December 15, 1985.

Gomez, Jim. "Mediation Time Is Up in Housing Bias Suit." July 18, 1987.

Griffin, Laura. "Priest Reflects on Columbia Point." June 20, 1975.

Grunwald, Michael. "A Fresh Path to Public Housing." January 25, 1998.

———. "Public Housing's New Era." September 9, 1997.

"The Harbor Point Experiment." Editorial. January 28, 1987.

Hartnett, Ken. "Tenants Find Hope at Columbia Point." June 23, 1972.

Haynes, Walter. "Soul and Sorrow in the Project." July 1, 1973.

"Help for Columbia Point." Editorial. December 22, 1962.

Hurt, Richard L. "Columbia Point I. 6000 Isolated on 'Island' — in Heart of Hub." September 9, 1962.

———. "Columbia Point II. City of Shame? Ridiculous, Says 3-Year Dweller." September 10, 1962.

———. "Columbia Point III. Neat Apartments Co-Exist with Others Hit by Vandals." September 11, 1962.

———. "Columbia Point IV. Does Unwritten Law Segregate Families?" September 12, 1962.

———. "Columbia Point V. $250,000 Area Unused as Kids Play in Street." September 13, 1962.

———. "Columbia Point VI. 1951 Prospects of Bright Future Mostly Unfulfilled." September 14, 1962.

———. "Columbia Point VII. Big Project Can Become Garden Spot: Here's How." September 16, 1962.

———. "Mothers Bully 10-Ton Trucks." April 25, 1962.

———. "Will Mothers' Wall Be Raised Again to Halt Columbia Point Dump Trucks?" May 6, 1962.

"Isolation on Wane." August 3, 1967.

Kenney, Charles. "The Poor Get Poorer." Public service magazine. December 15, 1985.

Kenney, Michael. "Columbia Point Plan: Scale Down, Develop." September 22, 1976.

Kirchheimer, Anne. "BHA Begins Relocating Columbia Point Tenants." January 1, 1976.

———. "Columbia Point: Tenants Flee from Constant Plague of Crime and Poor Living Conditions." June 27, 1975.

———. "Columbia Point Gets Aid, Maybe Too Late." October 23, 1975.

———. "Court Gives BHA Six Weeks to Make 2 Projects Livable." December 4, 1975.

———. "Long-Range Plan in the Works for Columbia Point." June 13, 1976.

———. "Vandals Undo BHA Effort to Improve Columbia Point." January 9, 1976.

Lewis, William J. "Boston Housing Plan Due for Vote Today." April 25, 1968.

Lovinger, Robert. "Can Harry Spence Fix Public Housing?" *Boston Globe Magazine*, August 23, 1981.

McCain, Nina. "Will UMass Have Campus by the Sea?" October 20, 1968.

McLean, Deckle. "An Edge of the Universe: Traveling a Hard Road at Columbia Point." January 10, 1971.

Meier, Mary. "Girl Scouts Go All Out to Form Units for Columbia Point Children." February 11, 1963.

"Mothers Dash out of Kitchens and Keep Closed Dump Closed." July 23, 1962.

"Mothers Halt March, City Vows New Relief." April 27, 1962.

"Mothers Plan Parties as Dumps Are Closed." June 21, 1962.

"Mothers to Pause Today When They Bury Little Girl." April 26, 1962.

Negri, Gloria. "Court Orders Closing of Columbia Point Dump." February 5, 1963.

———. "A Master Builder." May 11, 1997.

———. "The Women behind Harbor Point." October 4, 1998.

"New Dump Problems Brewing." February 6, 1963.

"No More Half Measures." Editorial. April 25, 1962.

Powers, John, and Joanne Ball. "Harbor Point Threatened by Financing Delay." October 9, 1985.

"Powers Will Act to Close Dumps." May 10, 1962.

Radin, Charles A. "City, UMass Eye Swap of Land, Scholar-

ships." March 13, 1999.

Richard, Ray. "And Still, Columbia Point Waits . . . for a Redevelopment Proposal That Will Work." February 23, 1982.

———. "A Better Day for Columbia Point." January 26, 1980.

———. "Hoping a Promise Is Kept." June 18, 1986.

Riddell, Janet. "Tenants Give BHA Roaches for Christmas." December 18, 1969.

———. "They Like Columbia Point, Not Rats." December 19, 1969.

Robb, Christina, "Searching for Security in a Sky-High Market." Public service magazine. December 15, 1985.

Scharfenberg, Kirk. "Rebuilding of Columbia Point Threatened by Dispute over Developer." August 13, 1983.

"Spence's Reflections on Leaving the BHA: Proud of the Past, Optimistic about the Future." August 12, 1984.

Stantor, Karen. "Columbia Point Project Closure Charge Denied." August 25, 1976.

Turner, Robert L. "Whatever Happened to the Days When Elected Officials—Not Judges—Decided Our Fates?" *Boston Globe Magazine*, November 8, 1981.

"U.S. Provides Cash to Study Columbia Point." June 11, 1963.

Von Hoffman, Alexander. "Whose 'Public' Gets Public Housing?" June 8, 1997.

Weinstein, Lewis H. "Ups and Downs of 50 Years of Public Housing." Op-ed page. October 30, 1987.

Wilson, David B. "An Explosive Solution for Columbia Point." March 14, 1971.

Wood, John. "Columbia Point: From Harangue to Harmony . . ." January 17, 1974.

———. "Doubts Exist on Making Columbia Point a Cinderella." January 21, 1974.

Yudis, Anthony J. "At Columbia Point: Developers Study Apartment Project." July 21, 1968.

———. "Columbia Point: Authority Cites Progress, Plans." December 13, 1962.

———. "Columbia Point's Needs Could Take Five Years." December 20, 1962.

———. "Community Development Sought for Columbia Point." July 2, 1967.

———. "Federal Loan May Link Columbia Point to Southie." February 24, 1963.

———. "1520 Housing Units and Two Schools Proposed for Columbia Point Project." June 28, 1964.

———. "Pledge to Improve Columbia Point." December 14, 1962.

———. "A Public Housing Transformation for Lynn." October 3, 1981.

———. "Top Consultant Called." November 28, 1963.

ARTICLES IN OTHER NEWSPAPERS

Alvarez, Lizette. "House Passes Bill to Replace System of Public Housing." *New York Times*, May 1, 1997.

Armerding, Taylor. "A Lynn Success Story." *North Shore: Sunday*, November 25, 1984.

Bass, Paul. "The Chairlady's Fall." *New Haven Advocate*, August 21–27, 1997.

"Boston Man Stoned to Death." *Boston Herald*, October 5, 1973.

"Boston War Zone Becomes Public Housing Dream." *New York Times*, November 23, 1991.

DeParle, Jason. "An Underground Railroad from Projects to Suburbs." *New York Times*, December 1, 1993.

——. "The Year That Housing Died." *New York Times*, October 20, 1996.

Diesenhouse, Susan. "Community Rises from Boston Slum." *New York Times*, November 15, 1987.

——. "Rundown Project Reborn." *New York Times*, March 13, 1988.

Droney, James F. "Project Families Very Cooperative." *Boston Herald*, August 18, 1963.

Farrell, David. "Garbage Dumps to Plague City Hospital, Housing Site." *Boston Herald Traveler*, January 22, 1953.

Forry, Bill. "Corcoran Recalls Local Successes, Looks." *Dorchester Reporter*, May 29, 1997.

Fuller, Chet. "Project Is What Public Housing Ought to Be." *Atlanta Journal*, July 17, 1993.

Gallese, Liz Roman. "Living Together: Massachusetts Tries Mixing Income Groups in Subsidized Housing." *Wall Street Journal*, June 25, 1974.

——. "Rx for Slums: Public-Housing Shift to Private Ownership Is Advanced to Cure Ills." *Wall Street Journal*, July 13, 1978.

Gelzinis, Peter. "Nuns' Faith Moves out of Harbor Point." *Boston Herald*, June 24, 1988.

——. "Point Is Life Worth Living." *Boston Herald*, January 25, 1987.

Georges, Christopher. "Work in Progress: As Welfare Rolls Drop, Changes Big and Small Hit a Housing Project." *Wall Street Journal*, December 19, 1997.

Hubner, John. "A Gem by the Ocean? Last Exit: The Fall and Rise of Columbia Point." *Boston Phoenix*, November 6, 1979.

Jencks, Christopher. "Half-Right on Public Housing." *New York Times*, May 20, 1997.

Kamin, Blair. "Good Intentions Didn't Prevent the High-Rise Fiasco." Series. *Chicago Tribune*, June 18, 19, 21, 22, 23, 1995.

Keller, Jon. "Financial Trouble Sharpens Point's Woes: Grand Design for Public-Housing Project Becomes Grand Illusion." *Boston Phoenix*, May 11, 1990.

——. "Upon Further Review . . . MHFA Calls for Closer Look at the Point." *Boston Phoenix*, June 1, 1990.

Kennedy, Randy. "In Turnabout, Housing Authority in New York to Favor Jobholders." *New York Times*, December 15, 1997.

Lewis, Roger K. "In Boston, a 'Point' for Public Housing." *Washington Post*, March 13, 1993.

Meyers, Susan. "Friends, Foes of Harbor Point Changes Clash over New Tenant Policies." *Dorchester Argus Citizen*, September 15, 1988.

Overbea, Luix. "Doris Bunte: Hub's Housing Director Knows Territory from the Ground Up." *Christian Science Monitor*, April 18, 1985.

——. "Modernization for Boston's Columbia Point." *Christian Science Monitor*, July 15, 1976.

Rezendes, Michael. "Failure by Design: Columbia Point and the 'Privatization' of Public Housing. *Boston Phoenix*, April 27, 1982.

Roberts, Eleanor. "UMass Plays Good Neighbor to Columbia Point." *Boston Herald*, October 14, 1973.

Rosenberg, Debra. "Harboring No Illusions: Cultures Clash in a Housing Experiment." *Boston Phoenix*, August 25, 1989.

"Two Teenagers Arrested in Stoning." *Boston Herald*, October 6, 1973.

"Woman Slain by Torch." *Boston Herald*, October 4, 1973.

MAGAZINE AND JOURNAL ARTICLES

Adler, Jerry, and Maggie Malone. "Toppling Towers." *Newsweek*, November 4, 1996, 70–72.

Berkeley, Ellen Perry. "Growth of a University." *Architecture Plus*, March/April 1974, 89–122.

Breitbart, Myrna Margulies, and Ellen-J. Pader. "Establishing Ground: Representing Gender and Race in a Mixed Housing Development." *Gender, Place, and Culture* 2:1 (1995): 5–20.

Cohen, Bernard. "Is Harry Spence God? Or Is He Just Damn Good?" *Boston Magazine*, December 1981, 168–96.

Dean, Andrea Oppenheimer. "New Hope for Failed Housing." *Preservation*, March/April 1998, 53–59.

Doyle, Brian. "Point Man." *Boston College Magazine*, summer 1989, 43–48.

Ford, Maurice. "A Field Trip to South Boston," *Nation*, October 26, 1974, 389–93.

Goody, Joan E. "From Project to Community: The Redesign of Columbia Point." *Places* 8:4 (1993): 20–33.

Lemann, Nicholas. "The Origins of the Underclass." *Atlantic Monthly*, June 1986, 31–55; July 1986, 54–68.

Mulroy, Elizabeth A. "Mixed-Income Housing in Action." *Urban Land*, May 1991, 2–7.

"On the Waterfront." *Architecture*, July 1990.

Pader, Ellen-J., and Myrna Margulies Breitbart. "Transforming Public Housing: Conflicting Visions for Harbor Point." *Places* 8:4 (1993): 34–41.

Sandler, Gregory. "Cuomo's New Vision for HUD." *Multifamily Executive*, June 1997, 60–65.

Schmandt, Henry J., and George D. Wendel. "The Pruitt-Igoe Public Housing Complex, 1954–1976." *Werk Archetese*, July 30, 1976.

Tunley, Roul. "Tragedy of a Vertical Slum." *Saturday Evening Post*, July 6, 1963, 89–93.

Whittlesey, Robert B. "Boston . . . BHA Case Is Explained." *Journal of Housing*, June 1980, 338–41.

BOOKS

Bratt, Rachel G. *Rebuilding a Low-Income Housing Policy.* Philadelphia: Temple University Press, 1989.

DiPasquale, Denise, and Langley C. Keyes, eds. *Building Foundations: Housing and Federal Policy.* Philadelphia: University of Pennsylvania Press, 1990.

Farbstein, Jay, and Richard Wener. *Rebuilding Communities: Recreating Urban Excellence.* New York: The Bruner Foundation, 1993.

Fisher, Sean M., and Carolyn Hughes, eds. *The Last Tenement: Confronting Community and Urban Renewal in Boston's West End.* Boston: The Bostonian Society, 1992.

Keyes, Langley Carleton, Jr. *The Rehabilitation Planning Game: A Study in the Diversity of Neighborhood.* Cambridge, Mass.: MIT Press, 1969.

Loftus, David J. *Boston College High School, 1863–1983.* Boston: Getchell, 1983.

O'Connor, Thomas. *Building a New Boston: Politics and Urban Renewal, 1950 to 1970.* Boston: Northeastern University Press, 1993.

Sammarco, Anthony Mitchell. *Images of America: Dorchester.* Dover, N.H.: Arcadia, 1997.

Whitehill, Walter Muir. *Boston: A Topographical History.* Cambridge, Mass.: Harvard University Press, 1968.

Wiseman, Carter. *I. M. Pei: A Profile in American Architecture.* New York: Abrams, 1990.

Wright, Gwendolyn. *Building the Dream: A Social History of Housing in America.* Cambridge, Mass.: MIT Press, 1988.

PUBLIC DOCUMENTS, THESES, AND ARCHIVAL SOURCES

Action for Boston Community Development, Inc. *Neighborhood Profile: Columbia Point.* September 1967.

Action for Boston Community Development et al. *A Struggle for Survival: Boston Housing Authority, 1969–1973.* 1974.

Action for Boston Community Development, Inc., in cooperation with United Community Services of Metropolitan Boston and the Boston Housing Authority. *Serving the People at Columbia Point Housing Development: A Report and Recommendations.* May 1964.

Armando Perez et al. v Boston Housing Authority. Order of Appointment of Receiver. Suffolk Superior Court, Civil Action no. 17222.

Boston City Planning Board. *General Plan for Boston: Preliminary Report.* 1950. Government Documents Department, Boston Public Library.

———. *Proposed Plan for Future Development of the Calf Pasture Area in the Dorchester District.* September 22, 1953. Government Documents Department, Boston Public Library.

Boston Housing Authority. *Annual Report, 1962–63.* Massachusetts Archives.

———. *Columbia Point Public Housing: Original Site Plan.* 1952.

Boston Redevelopment Authority. *Status Report on Columbia Point.* May 6, 1963.

———. Planning Department. District Planning Program. *Dorchester: Existing Characteristics.* Spring 1969. Government Documents Department, Boston Public Library.

Boston Society of Architects. Urban Design Committee. Columbia Point Focus Team. *Columbia Point: A New Vision.* 1992.

Broadman, Richard. *Down the Project: The Crisis in Public Housing.* Documentary film. 1983. Cine Research Associates, Cambridge, Mass.

City of Boston. Office of the Mayor, BHA, BRA, et al. *The Columbia Point Peninsula: A Program for Revitalization.* Joint report. January 1974. Government Documents Department, Boston Public Library.

Columbia Point Ground Lease. Landlord: Boston Housing Authority. Lessee: Harbor Point Apartments Company Limited Partnership. July 21, 1986.

Columbia Point Task Force, Inc. *Summary of Proposals.* June 1983.

Columbia Point Task Force, Inc., and Housing Opportunities Unlimited. 1993 *Brainstorm, Goal Setting, Making Harbor Point the Best Community in the World,* January 11, 1993.

Corcoran, Mullins, Jennison. *Point of Change*. Harbor Point video. 1992.

Corcoran, Mullins, Jennison, Inc., and Goody, Clancy & Associates, Inc. *Harbor Park: The Revitalization of Columbia Point*. February 22, 1983.

Corcoran, Mullins, Jennison, Inc., Quincy, Mass., and H. W. Moore Associates, Inc., Boston, for the City of Boston, Boston Redevelopment Authority. *Final Environmental Impact Report for Columbia Point Redevelopment in Boston, Massachusetts*. 1985.

———. *Harbor Point (Redevelopment of the Columbia Point Housing Project)*. *Final Environmental Impact Report*. EOEA #5076, 1985.

Garshick, Rachel R. "Mixed-Income Housing at Harbor Point: A 180-Degree Turnabout." Master's thesis. Tufts University, May 1993.

Glaser and Gray, Architects and City Planners, Boston and Washington, D.C., for the Boston Housing Authority. *Cow Pasture Development: Report #1*. October 31, 1950.

———. *Development of the Calf Pasture, Dorchester: Final Report*. December 28, 1950.

Harbor Point. Project reference file, vol. 22, no. 17, October–December 1992. The Urban Land Institute, Washington, D.C.

Harvard University. Graduate School of Design. Department of City and Regional Planning. Harvard–Columbia Point Planning Workshop. Professor Eduardo E. Lozano. *Columbia Point Development Study*. Fall–spring 1974–75. Government Documents Department, Boston Public Library.

Housing Opportunities Unlimited. *Permanent Relocation Plan*. Dorchester, Mass., July 19, 1985.

———. *Request for Proposals for Community Services to Residents at Harbor Point*. January 4, 1988.

Kennedy, Marie. "Mixed Messages: A Brief Story of Columbia Point and U.S. Public Housing." An essay to accompany *Columbia Point*, a video slide transfer by Linda Swartz. Center for Community Planning, University of Massachusetts at Boston, March 1989.

Kennedy, Marie, Charlotte Ryan, and Jeanne Winner. "The Best Laid Plans: The Early History of Boston's Columbia Point Public Housing." Unpublished manuscript. Columbia Point Oral History Project, Center for Community Planning, College of Public and Community Service, University of Massachusetts at Boston, 1987.

Kirchheimer, Anne, and Dexter Eure. "Columbia Point: A Potential Urban Laboratory." Unpublished report for the *Boston Globe*, 1971. Boston Globe Library.

Lee, Sharon Hsueh-Jen. "Redeveloping or Preserving Public Housing: The Future of Columbia Point." Master's thesis. Massachusetts Institute of Technology, 1981.

Loustau, Jeffrey J. *How Expensive Is Affordable Housing? A Comparative Analysis of Three Affordable Housing Developments in Boston*. Prepared for Harbor Point Apartments Co., 1992.

Loveluck, Juan Carlos. "The Redevelopment of Columbia Point: Financing a Political Imperative." Master's thesis. Massachusetts Institute of Technology, 1986.

National Commission on Severely Distressed Public Housing. *Final Report*. A Report to the Congress and the Secretary of Housing and Urban Development. Washington, D.C., August 1992.

Robert Gladstone and Associates. *Market and Economic Factors: Columbia Point Feasibility Study*. Washington, D.C., January 1964.

Swartz, Linda. *Columbia Point*. Video slide transfer. 1988. In author's possession.

University of Massachusetts, Boston. College of Public and Community Service. Harbor Point Collaborative. *Building Community: A Report to the Columbia Point Peninsula Community*. February 1999.

U.S. Department of the Interior. National Park Service. "Calf Pasture Pumping Station, Boston [Dorchester], Massachusetts." *National Register of Historic Places*, sections 7–8. Washington, D.C.: GPO, 1990.

Van Buren, Jane A. *History of Boston Harborpark Neighborhoods: A Profile*. Boston Redevelopment Authority Research Department, February 1985.

What Happened to Public Housing? A study guide for the film *Down the Project: The Crisis in Public Housing*, with commentaries by Rachel G. Bratt and Richard Broadman, 1983. Cine Research Associates, Cambridge, Mass.

White, Mayor Kevin H., Boston Housing Authority, and Boston Redevelopment Authority. *Developer's Selection Kit for Three Parcels at Columbia Point*. 1981.

White, Mayor Kevin H., Boston Housing Authority, and Boston Redevelopment Authority, in partnership with Columbia Point Community Task Force, Inc. *Columbia Point Peninsula: Request for Developer Proposals*. September 12, 1982. Government Documents Department, Boston Public Library.

INTERVIEWS CONDUCTED BY
THE AUTHOR

Aylward, Christopher, Columbia Point resident, February 1998.

Aylward, John, Columbia Point resident, May 1999.

Bailey, F. Lee, attorney for Columbia Point residents, February 1998.

Byrne, Miles, manager of Harbor Point, June 1998.

Cisneros, Henry, former secretary of the U.S. Department of Housing and Urban Development, July 1998.

Connelly, David, president, Housing Opportunities Unlimited, May 1998.

Corcoran, Joseph, chairman, Corcoran Jennison Companies, May 1997, September, 1997, June 1998.

DiMambro, Antonio, president, Antonio DiMambro & Associates, April 1998.

Duffy, James, Columbia Point resident, December 1997.

Geiger, Jack, founder, Columbia Point Neighborhood Health Center, March 1998.

Goody, Joan, principal, Goody Clancy & Associates, May 1998.

Haley, James, former commissioner of public works for the City of Boston, December 1997.

Hanifin, David, Harbor Point resident and member of the Harbor Point Community Task Force, June 1998.

Hernandez, April Mercedes, vice president, Corcoran Jennison Companies, and former director of leasing at Harbor Point, June 1998.

Jaundoo, Ruby, Columbia Point resident and member of the Harbor Point Community Task Force, June 1997, June 1998.

Jennison, Gary, vice chairman, Corcoran Jennison Companies, June 1997.

Johnson, Etta, Columbia Point resident and member of the Harbor Point Community Task Force, May 1997, June 1998.

Jones, Marty, president, Corcoran Jennison Companies, June 1998.

Kennedy, Senator Edward M., July 1998.

McCluskey, Kevin, Columbia Point resident, January 1998.

McCluskey, Patricia, Columbia Point resident, December 1997.

McDonald, Anna, Columbia Point resident, December 1997.

McHallam, Jean, former HUD official, March 1998.

McLeod, Peggy, Columbia Point resident, February 1998.

Mullins, Joe, chairman, Joseph R. Mullins Co., May 1998.

Quarles, Betty, Columbia Point resident and member of the Harbor Point Community Task Force, May 1997, March 1998.

Santos, Esther, Columbia Point resident and member of the Harbor Point Community Task Force, May 1997, May 1998.

Shearer, Deborah, Columbia Point resident, December 1997.

Shearer, Erline, Columbia Point resident, December 1997, January 1998.

Spence, Harry, former receiver for the Boston Housing Authority, April 1998.

Strong, Don, former director of Action for Boston Community Development, February 1998.

Taylor, Roger, Columbia Point resident, March 1998.

Werby, Elaine, former staff member of the Boston Housing Authority, February 1998.

Wessell, Eleanor, president, King's Lynne Resident Council, May 1998.

Wetterholm, Father Larry, former priest, St. Christopher's Church, February 1998.

White, Eleanor, former official at the Massachusetts Housing Finance Agency, June 1997.

Yee, Wendell, president, Beacon/CJ Management, June 1998.

Young, April, former Harbor Point resident, June 1998.

INTERVIEWS CONDUCTED BY OTILE MCMANUS

Connelly, David, president, Housing Opportunities Unlimited, January 1997.

Corcoran, Joseph, chairman, Corcoran Jennison Companies, September 1996.

Dukakis, Michael, former governor and government professor, Northeastern University, May 1998.

Garrity, Paul, former Massachusetts Superior Court judge and partner, ADR Solutions, May 1998.

Garver, Dick, deputy director, Boston Redevelopment Authority, June 1999.

Jones, Hubert E., assistant to the chancellor for urban affairs, University of Massachusetts at Boston, August 1998.

Jones, Marty, president, Corcoran Jennison Companies, October 1997.

Keyes, Langley, professor of urban planning, Massachusetts Institute of Technology, May 1998.

Kuehn, Bob, president, Keen Development, June 1998.

Logue, Edward, former director of the Boston Redevelopment Authority, April 1998.

Martin, Ed, former regional director of the U.S. Department of Housing and Urban Development, July 1999.

McCain, Nina, former reporter for the Boston Globe, February 1998.

Mintz, Sy, principal, Sy Mintz Associates, June 1998.

Murray, Dan, president, Corcoran Jennison Management Co., May 1998.

O'Brien, Julia, director of planning, Metropolitan District Commission, July 1999.

Quinn, Bob, former Massachusetts attorney general and attorney at Quinn and Morris, March 1998.

Ross, Stephan, former youth worker at Columbia Point, June 1999.

Ryan, Bob, former director of the Boston Redevelopment Authority and vice president, ML Strategies, December 1998.

Stainton, John, former staff member of the Boston Redevelopment Authority, May 1998.

Titus, Charles, athletic director, University of Massachusetts at Boston, July 1998.

Wampler, Jan, architect, March 1998.

White, Kevin, former mayor of Boston and professor, Boston University, May 1998.

Whittlesey, Bob, former court-appointed master for the Boston Housing Authority, July 1999.

Winn, Arthur, chairman, Winn Development Co., May 1998.

Wood, Robert, former president, University of Massachusetts at Boston and professor at Wesleyan University, February 1998.

INTERVIEWS CONDUCTED BY MARIE KENNEDY AND OTHER MEMBERS OF THE COLUMBIA POINT ORAL HISTORY PROJECT, COLLEGE OF PUBLIC AND COMMUNITY SERVICE, UNIVERSITY OF MASSACHUSETTS AT BOSTON, 1985–86

Heath, Marie, former Columbia Point resident.

Hines, Angie, former Columbia Point resident.

Katz, Carole, former Columbia Point resident.

Powell, Joshua, former Columbia Point resident.

Slavet, Joseph, former executive director, Action for Boston Community Development.

Titus, Charles, former Columbia Point resident and athletic director, University of Massachusetts at Boston.

Young, Alexzandrina, former Columbia Point resident.

Index

CPSIA information can be obtained
at www.ICGtesting.com
Printed in the USA
LVHW061819070221
678626LV00010B/777